The MBA's Guide to Career Planning

The MBA's Guide to Career Planning

Ed Holton

Director, MBA Program
Northern Virginia Graduate Center
Virginia Polytechnic Institute and State University

Peterson's Guides

Princeton, New Jersey

The College Placement Council's "Principles for Professional Conduct" and the tables adapted from CPC's salary surveys are copyright and may not be reprinted or utilized in any other way without the express written permission of CPC.

The ACCRA Cost of Living Indexes are copyright by American Chamber of Commerce Researchers Association and are reprinted by permission.

The business letter by Malcolm Forbes is reprinted by permission of International Paper.

"It Couldn't Be Done" and "Results and Roses" are quoted from *Collected Verse* by Edgar A. Guest. Copyright © 1934 by Contemporary Books, Inc. Reprinted by permission of Contemporary Books, Inc.

"On Work" is reprinted from *The Prophet*, by Kahlil Gibran, by permission of Alfred A. Knopf, Inc. Copyright 1923 by Kahlil Gibran and renewed 1951 by Administrators C.T.A. of Kahlil Gibran Estate and Mary G. Gibran.

"Rating the M.B.A." is reprinted by permission of *Harvard Business Review*. An exhibit from "Probing Opinions: Report Cards on the MBA" by Roger L. Jenkins, Richard C. Reizenstein, and F. G. Rodgers (September-October 1984). Copyright © 1984 by the President and Fellows of Harvard College; all rights reserved.

The passage by Richard Bolles is from *What Color Is Your Parachute?* © 1989 by Richard Bolles. Published by Ten Speed Press, Berkeley, CA.

Library of Congress Cataloging-in-Publication Data

Holton, Ed, 1957–
    The MBA's guide to career planning.

    Bibliography : p.
    1. Business—Vocational guidance. 2. Master of business administration degree. 3. Job hunting. I. Title.
HF5381.H573   1989   650.14   89-8726
ISBN 0-87866-845-4

Composition and design by Peterson's Guides

Printed in the United States of America

10   9   8   7   6   5   4   3   2   1

Contents

11 The Interview: Process and Principles

The Myths of Interviewing • The Key to Interviewing • The Purpose of an Interview • The Interview Process • Screening Interviews • Hiring Interviews • Getting Ready for Your Interview • Presenting Yourself • The Nuts and Bolts of the Interview • Answering Interview Questions • Interview Problems • Other Types of Interviews • New Trends • Your Rejection Action Plan

THE FINAL STRETCH

SPECIAL INFORMATION

Preface

This book has been a long labor of love and sweat. It grew out of years of frustration at not being able to find a career book that made sense for MBAs. Nothing seemed to hit the critical issues facing MBAs in the job market today. So many books are targeted at undergraduates, and often freshmen and sophomores. Authors haven't seemed to understand that you can't teach graduate students the same way you teach college sophomores.

"Wouldn't it be nice," I thought, "if we had a book that talked specifically to MBAs, written by someone who speaks their language and talks to them like the mature adults they are"? Well now we do. The system in this book has been tested for three years before publication with MBA students at The R. B. Pamplin College of Business at Virginia Tech. Many employers who hire Pamplin MBAs cheered me on to continue to tell it "like it really is." I know the system works. The most rewarding part of writing a book like this is knowing that it can make a real difference in people's lives. I feel great joy and gratification whenever I see the smile on the face of a student who has just landed his or her dream job. What's even better is to talk to such students years later and hear that their careers are continuing to enrich their life and happiness. I sincerely believe that such happiness and satisfaction are within the reach of every MBA in this country who really wants them and is willing to work to attain them.

As an MBA who has spent time in "typical" MBA jobs in industry, I know firsthand what it's like to compete in the MBA job market. Unfortunately, nobody was around to tell me the things you will learn from this book, and I screwed up and landed in a career path that was completely wrong for me. I now know that I need not have suffered so much and that you don't need to make the mistakes I made. I hope I can teach you what I didn't know and can use my personal journey to help you to a better career and life.

One thing you will quickly notice is that this book is not a cookbook. My main gripe with many career books is that they are more like a collection of "recipes" that purport to tell you how to transform yourself into a success. This book is different. Number one, I don't want to transform you into anything: I just want to open you up to everything you can be and help you get whatever you want. And there *is* no recipe; you have to quit trying to force yourself into other people's molds and make your own. And that includes career planning systems. To do that, I try to teach you the "why" as well as the "what." I assume that MBAs are mature enough not to need leading by the hand.

This book will teach you the concepts, theories, and techniques and show you how to make them work in your own personal way. So many people have told me that after reading preliminary versions of the book they at long last understand *why* they've been doing certain things recommended in their job searches. I think it's time you understood too.

Now I want to thank those who helped me with my labors. First, the employers I work with so much, who taught me what students really need to know. Then, my students, who taught me how to teach them what they really need to know. Next, my loving wife: Karen, I couldn't have done it without your love, support, and encouragement (not to mention typing and editing); thanks for believing in me. Then, my good friend and mentor Dave Hutchins, who taught me much of what I know about counseling and human development: thanks for always pushing me to reach for the next rung on my career ladder (including this book). Then, Ann Heidbreder-Eastman, our university publishing officer (retired) and now friend, without whose encouragement and confidence you would never be reading this today. Next, my many colleagues who have patiently listened to my ideas, reviewed the manuscript, and endorsed it: thanks for donating your time and interest. And, finally, my editor, Jim Gish, and the Peterson's staff for pulling it all together.

Introduction

Job search, career planning, resume, interviewing—if you are like most people, these words spark a rush of anxiety. Jobs and careers are such a critical part of our lives, of our well-being and self-esteem; yet we are never taught many of the skills we need to set and achieve our work and life goals. Most curriculums in schools and universities include not a single course on career and life planning. Most of us finish our formal education well prepared in the functional areas we have chosen but ill prepared to find a rewarding career.

For MBAs, the process is even more challenging and anxiety producing. The MBA job market is unique and highly competitive, one that demands special job search skills and a thorough understanding of the job market's idiosyncracies. Employers expect so much more of MBA candidates because of their more extensive training and their demands for challenging positions and higher salaries. The students often put added pressure on themselves because of the great sacrifices they've made to get the degree. In addition, they face pressures from peers and the job market itself that attempt to force them into specific career paths that may not be right.

To top it off, there are the negative MBA stereotypes fostered by the popular press. All of these pressures—and more—combine to make the job search especially tough for MBAs. As a result, thorough career planning is a must for high-quality candidates. In the chapters that follow, you'll learn about all the special elements of an MBA job search and how to deal with them effectively to get the job you want.

The book is all about building a successful and rewarding career. It is about a positive, creative process that will help you discover the unique combination of organization, task, and environment that will lead to a satisfying work life as well as the skills you need to find the job you want to begin your career. It will help you market yourself in a manner that clearly identifies you as a high-caliber MBA business professional.

Note that I emphasize achieving what *you* want. This book is dedicated to helping you overcome the anxiety involved in career planning and realize your full potential as a professional—on your terms.

It's doing your job the best you can
And being just to your fellow man;
It's making money—but holding friends
And true to your aims and ends;
It's figuring how and learning why
And looking forward and thinking high
And dreaming a little and doing much.
It's keeping always in closest touch
With what is finest in word and deed;
It's being thorough, yet making speed;
It's daring blithely the field of chance
While making labor a brave romance;
It's going onward despite defeat
And fighting stanchly, but keeping sweet;
It's being clean and it's playing fair;
It's laughing lightly at Dame Despair;
It's looking up at the stars above
And drinking deeply of life and love.
It's struggling on with the will to win
But taking loss with a cheerful grin;
It's sharing sorrow and work and mirth
And making better this good old earth;
It's serving, striving through strain and stress;
It's doing your noblest—that's Success!

—Berton Braley
"That's Success"

From *Poems That Touch the Heart,* a Doubleday anthology compiled by A. L. Alexander.

WHAT IS SUCCESS?

My objective in writing this book is really quite simple. I want you to find a job and a career in which you will be happy and successful. Throughout this book you will read about a process that can help you succeed. Before you begin, perhaps I should define what I mean by "success."

The fact is, I can't—only you can. There are many people eager to try to tell you how you should define your career and its measures of success. But counselors, friends, faculty, and family can only facilitate your own growth and discovery process. A recurring theme of this book is that you—and you alone—set the standards of success against which you will measure yourself.

I have become increasingly disenchanted with the accepted notion of success today. Usually it involves some combination of money, power, and material wealth. I have no quarrel with those who choose this route. What bothers me is that I see little room for other, equally valid definitions of success. What I look for and encourage is not a particular definition of success. Rather, it is the ability of a person to set his or her own personal definition of success and then find the courage to pursue it and the skills to achieve it.

For MBAs, this presents a problem. The stereotypical MBA career is fast-track, high-paying, and demanding, with the opportunity for big bucks and lots of power and responsibility; often it is in a large corporation. I have talked to too many MBA students who feel guilty because they don't want this. My advice is: Don't! It's okay to seek whatever you want in your career. It's okay to not want a fast-track job, to not set your sights solely on salary, to want to run the family farm rather than go to Wall Street. It's also okay to want to be a CEO, to want to make a million dollars a year, to want to manage lots of people.

The point is there are no rules in this game. You don't need anyone's permission, except your own, to plan your career. What matters is that you live the way you want and according to what makes you happy. If you will open yourself to this new definition of success, you'll find this to be an exciting process that can lead you to a satisfying and rewarding career.

CAREER PLANNING AND PLACEMENT MYTHS

So what do most people do? They try their best, usually with very mixed results. Many people spend several years attempting to discover what it is they want to do and finding a place to do it. Out of this process have arisen a number of myths about career planning and the job search:

- *It's a shot in the dark.* It's like playing pin the tail on the donkey. You have a general sense of where you should be going, but the best you can do is hope you come close. Of course, if you try enough times, sooner or later you'll find the right spot.
- *All you have to do is write a resume and mail it out.* You can pull a resume together in a few days, and, if you just mail it out to enough firms, you'll find a job.

- *Work is work and it's just a necessary evil.* Work pays the bills and puts a roof over your head, but it's really a pain. Therefore, there is no need to worry about what you want—and perhaps no point in doing it.
- *Salary is the most important thing.* Go for the bucks; the money is where it's at.
- *The employer calls all the shots.* There's not much you can do to affect the process; take what you can get and hope you get lucky.
- *It's trial and error.* Finding a rewarding career is a matter of chance and luck.

A NEW APPROACH

Sound familiar? In this book, I propose a new approach, one that gives you control of your own life and career. It is a *positive* approach that says:

- *Work is something to enjoy.* It is an important part of your life and your personal growth. Life is too short to spend it doing something you don't enjoy. You owe it to yourself to discover what work you enjoy doing and to find a way to do it.
- *Trial and error is not the way to plan a career.* There is another way that allows you to maximize your chances of achieving your goals. There is never any guarantee, and people do change, but you are not subject to the whims of employers or to the "luck of the draw." You can analyze the direction in which you should go and plan how to get there.
- *There is no one "right" career.* You are an individual with unique values and goals. There are many, many types of careers with many different rewards. Several of them may be right for you.
- *You can find a great job fresh out of school.* Achieving all your goals as soon as you leave school is not possible. However, if you work at it, you can find a very satisfying job in which you will be happy and have growth potential.
- *You have control.* Peers, family, friends, social mores, and convention do not have to dictate what type of career you have—you decide.

Does that sound a little more inviting? It should; but as with everything in this world, it has its price. It takes time and effort to use this approach. It demands starting early, planning ahead, committing time and resources, and cultivating patience. Frankly, it can be a full-time job in itself. Since most people continue to go to school or work while seeking a new job, this effort can be a significant drain on your time and energy. But it's worth it. At stake is your career. The payoff from the time invested up front can bring a lifetime of rewards, positive challenges, and happiness.

It is a very exciting process—exciting because it allows you to take control of your own destiny. It allows you to develop your own values and goals and to develop a plan for your career that will make your life rewarding to *you*. Your success depends on your own personal initiative and hard work; you have both the opportunity and the responsibility for your success or failure. I hope that you are challenged by this and will seize the opportunity.

HOW TO USE THIS BOOK

This book is intended to be a comprehensive guide to your career-planning and job-hunting journey. It contains a tremendous amount of information that cannot possibly be absorbed at one sitting. I hope you will not be intimidated by its length or depth.

The book is designed as a reference that will be read in parts as you progress through the process. I suggest that you first read Chapters 1–5 for an overview of the process. Then you should evaluate your own development in relation to the model presented in Chapter 5. After you decide which steps of the process you need and develop your action plan, you should read the rest of the book. But I suggest that you read only those sections that pertain to your particular stage. It will do little good to read about on-site inter-views while you are involved in self-assessment. Similarly, self-assessment will hold little interest if you already know what you want to do. Use the book as your companion throughout the process. It is the type of book that lends itself to reading to get some ideas, carrying out these ideas by taking action, then reading some more to get more ideas.

Finally, this book is not a substitute for an experienced career counselor. I encourage you to use this book in consultation with a knowledgeable career counselor, preferably one who knows the MBA job market. Career counselors are one of your most impor-tant resources; use them.

BASIC CONCEPTS

Chapter 1

State of the MBA Job Market

The MBA job market has undergone significant changes in recent years, and it still remains quite volatile. The media continue to report on the problems of MBAs and of those who employ MBAs, especially charting the decline in the demand for these professionals trained at the graduate level. Conflicting tales of oversupply and astronomical salaries for a few superstars continue to create uncertainty. It is difficult to sift through all this information to get a balanced view of the situation.

There is no question that the MBA job market has become much tighter due to the large cutbacks made in corporate staffs during the last recession, the increased number of students graduating from MBA programs, the reclassifying of jobs (from those requiring the skills of an MBA to those needing training at the undergraduate level), and economic uncertainty for the future. But the fact is that the MBA degree remains the premium business degree and commands significant respect and money in the business world. I still recommend it to students wanting the maximum advantage, flexibility, and opportunity in their business careers.

Why then do the press reports seem so negative? What is sometimes reported as a demise in the popularity of the MBA actually represents a very natural shakeout. In the seventies and early eighties, the MBA was proclaimed to be the "end-all" degree. Corporate leaders assumed extraordinary performance from MBAs, expecting them to vault to the top of corporations, make a major impact in a very short time, and generally perform as superstars. Students recognized the tremendous advantage of having an MBA and lined up for the degree; schools rushed to provide them.

The result was overblown expectations on the part of employers and students. Companies were required to pay higher and higher salaries to the MBAs they employed; MBAs became disgruntled with slower-than-expected promotions and fewer challenges. Employers assumed Harvard Business School performance from small-school MBAs, while the students from smaller schools expected salaries commensurate with those offered Harvard-trained MBAs. Employers, criticizing MBAs for wanting too much and job hopping, began to hire fewer of them. The job market became tougher, more competitive.

Although there are fewer jobs for MBAs available today, in many ways it is actually a better job market. Earlier, many of the jobs created for MBAs really didn't require a businessperson trained at the graduate level. Today, the jobs that exist are for the most part truly MBA-level jobs. Both employers and MBAs have recognized their previous unrealistic expectations. Furthermore, the recent reductions in the size of corporate staffs have resulted in companies' giving MBAs greater responsibility and more challenging assignments earlier in their career rather than insisting that they spend time in less important positions. Thus, the job market that remains is smaller but of a higher quality.

This chapter is devoted to examining the MBA job market in depth. At this point, you probably realize that the picture it presents is not all rosy. As you read the chapter, you may be surprised by the sharpness of some of my criticisms of MBAs, particularly since I am an MBA and am in the business of training MBAs. Make no mistake that I believe in the value of the MBA. It is outstanding preparation for an excellent business career, and the MBA job market is very healthy (although frequently misrepresented). However, there are some very real danger signs in the job market today, and some alarms should be sounded. I am issuing a call for some fundamental changes in the way MBAs approach their career. Unless MBAs begin to realize what is happening in the marketplace, get their attitudes and expectations in line, and develop the proper perspective on their value, today's healthy marketplace could disappear quickly.

A VERSATILE DEGREE

The MBA is a wonderful degree that can do many things for you. Its real strength (and sometimes its liability) is that it is marvelously versatile, useful in an enormous variety of occupations and organizations. The following tables give you some idea of the tremendous breadth and depth of the MBA job market. MBAs are found in just about every conceivable business function and in almost every type of organization.

It would be impossible to list all the career opportunities available to MBAs. As these tables show, there are clearly some industries and functions with a greater concentration of MBAs than other industries and functions. But the fact is that all organizations need to be managed, and an MBA is a potential candidate for any management position. Government, education, and nonprofit and for-profit organizations all need managers. In addition, all companies employ workers for basic business functions, such as accounting, budgeting, marketing, and personnel. If a need exists for the best-trained management professional available, then an MBA has to be a strong candidate.

Where MBAs Work by Function

(Top 10 Business Areas for MBAs)

Marketing/Sales	20.3%
Accounting/Control/Auditing	12.7%
Finance	12.4%
Consulting/Project management	9.7%
General management	7.9%
Operations and production management	7.0%
Information systems	6.4%
Commercial lending	4.9%
Planning/Corporate staff	3.7%
Human resources	1.8%

Source: Association of MBA Executives Inc., *The 1984–1985 MBA Career and Salary Census.* (Sample size: 5,477.) Data are for 1983. © Copyright 1985, Association of MBA Executives Inc.

The tremendous dispersion of MBAs in the work force is also a result of the MBA degrees earned by students who have an undergraduate degree in a nonbusiness area. A common misconception about the MBA degree is that it is only for students with an undergraduate degree in business. Nothing could be further from the truth. Over half the students enrolled in most MBA programs *do not* have an undergraduate degree in business. These students often have degrees in such areas as engineering, science, agriculture, liberal arts, humanities, and education. Some business school professionals would even suggest that graduate study in business is more valuable when combined with an undergraduate major other than business.

Professionals from all disciplines have found an MBA degree invaluable as they have advanced into management. Every day, managers discover new ways to use the skills of MBAs. The appropriate question concerning this degree is not "Where can I use an MBA?" but rather "Where *can't* I use it?" The answer: Not many places.

Where MBAs Work by Industry

(Top 15 Industries Employing MBAs)

Accounting	9.7%
Commercial banking	9.6%
Office machines/Computers	7.3%
Electronics	6.6%
Management consulting	5.3%
Investment banking	5.2%
Consumer products	5.1%
Health-care/Pharmaceuticals	4.3%
Aerospace	4.2%
Telecommunications	3.4%
Oil	2.3%
Manufacturing	2.3%
Insurance	2.3%
Government	2.2%
Chemicals	1.8%

Source: Association of MBA Executives Inc., *The 1984–1985 MBA Career and Salary Census.* (Sample size: 5,477.) Data are for 1983. © Copyright 1985, Association of MBA Executives Inc.

WHAT AN MBA CAN (AND CAN'T) DO FOR YOU

For all its value, the MBA does have limits. The continuing misunderstanding of just what an MBA can and can't do is a very real problem in corporate America and U.S. business schools today. Employers constantly complain that MBAs have an inflated view of their value (most college graduates do, but MBAs are usually worse offenders in this regard than undergraduates). It is critical that today's MBAs clearly understand their true value in the marketplace and exactly what their degree and training can and can't do for them.

Completing an MBA program and earning the degree will do certain things for you. Your training and degree can:

broaden your horizons—Since the MBA is an interdisciplinary degree, you will go to school with professionals from a variety of backgrounds, from different career areas, and from different age groups. You will receive a comprehensive education and gain new perspectives. This exposure will make you a more valuable employee.

encourage maturity and growth—Everyone seems to grow from the challenges and rigors of an MBA program. But this is especially true of younger students. They have the advantage of spending an additional year or two in school at a critical time in their development. They enter the job market more mature as a result of having stretched themselves to succeed in graduate school.

give you personal satisfaction—You will feel proud of having completed a rigorous course of study in graduate management. The training will provide many opportunities to build your confidence and self-esteem.

earn you professional respect—The MBA will give you the skills and credentials that can help you earn the professional respect you seek. The degree is widely recognized in many industries. The designation "MBA" is now as familiar as "MD" and "JD."

enhance an employer's perception of you—The MBA degree demonstrates to employers that you have the traits they are looking for: the discipline to work hard, the ability to learn, and the intelligence to succeed. They know that only highly qualified, ambitious, and motivated individuals would undertake the challenge of an MBA program.

open the doors to management—Although an MBA is no longer a prerequisite for a management position, the degree does provide the holder with a greater range of opportunities. The training provides students with advanced management skills and enables them to enter high-visibility positions, giving them a headstart in the race up the business ladder.

facilitate a career change—The MBA can be a vital tool for the career changer. Many people use the degree to jump into the business world from a nonbusiness area. For example, the MBA is a very valuable complement to a technical degree in today's job market. The MBA can provide any person from any background access to a business career.

give you an above-average starting salary—The MBA usually leads to a higher salary than could be obtained with an undergraduate business degree only. In addition, the management career paths that it opens offer much higher career earnings potential than many other career paths.

help you develop a successful attitude—An MBA program will teach you how to work with others to achieve goals, how to work hard, and how to succeed. MBA graduates tend to have a much better attitude and more ambition, which prepare them for success. Employers know that toughness and dedication are worth pursuing.

However, an MBA degree will *not:*

guarantee you a job—The MBA will only open doors for you. If you are not a fully prepared, high-caliber candidate, the MBA will be of little value. The degree is an *indication* of competence and intelligence, but you must still prove that you possess the qualities that the employer is seeking.

provide job security and earn you promotions—Too many MBAs believe that their degrees will ensure job security. Others think that they deserve titles and promotions simply because they hold the degree. Only proven performance will enable you to keep your job and advance in the company.

replace experience—Businesspeople need a certain street savvy and toughness to survive and prosper in the business world. You cannot learn these qualities from the textbooks. Realize that years of experience are necessary before you will be ready for top-level positions.

guarantee you a fat salary—The big salaries go only to those students who have the potential to be top performers for the employer. Remember that in the long run the employer will never pay you more than you can earn for the company.

be your last learning experience—When you complete your MBA, you will know a lot, but not enough. Your studies have given you a great foundation, a solid start. Most important, you have learned how to learn. But you have only just begun the learning process. Expect to be humbled by what you don't know.

What I want to see is a balanced attitude. MBAs can be very valuable to business. They are the best-trained businesspeople in the world and should command premium salaries to compensate for the extra years of rigorous training. They are capable of truly outstanding performance. However, realize that corporate America can well do without them. America's industrial strength was built without MBAs, and American business will survive without them if it has to.

Employers are sick and tired of inflated egos and prima donna attitudes. While there are certain sectors of the business world where such attitudes are tolerated (perhaps even encouraged), in most organizations they are despised. Many firms have stopped hiring MBAs because their cocky attitudes and incredibly elevated salaries are destructive to the organization. If MBAs do not keep their sense of self-worth under control, there is a real danger employers will simply look elsewhere.

The MBA in the Press: Mixed Reviews

"Critics argue that B-schools turn out greedy, overambitious people with little more than basic financial skills. Once in the business world, they focus their time and energy on financial activities—not on effectively leading people, making better products, or assuring manufacturing quality."

"Where the Schools Aren't Doing Their Homework," *Business Week*, **November 28, 1988**

"What has changed most in the after-crash era is that the MBA no longer is a near automatic entree to the executive ranks. The degree is now considered a minimum credential—one that must be accompanied by relevant work experience and a track record of job accomplishments."

U.S. News & World Report, **April 25, 1988**

"Not surprisingly, an M.B.A. no longer carries the cachet it once had."

"The Battle of the B-Schools Is Getting Bloodier," *Business Week*, **March 24, 1986**

"Executives of major corporations are increasingly worried about the men and women coming out of U.S. Business Schools. 'Something has happened. Those young people seem intent on destroying each other to get to the top.'"

"How to Humanize MBAs," *Fortune*, **March 31, 1986**

"A master's degree in business administration—the MBA—has become the degree of choice in graduate education for thousands of people. Many view the MBA as the starting gate on the fast track to rapid promotions, greater responsibilities, and paychecks to match. . . . Many employers believe that MBA graduates have these skills and are willing to pay top dollar to get them."

Occupational Outlook Quarterly, **Winter 1985**

"The ugly truth is, many [part-time MBA students] would fare better by going for a drink with the boss after work or putting in more time at the office. The MBA is, without question, the most oversold degree in the history of education."

"The M.B.A. Mills," *Forbes*, **November 19, 1984**

The only reason MBAs command a premium in the marketplace is that employers expect them to be outstanding producers. If you cannot demonstrate the level of performance expected, your degree will be worthless. The most sought-after MBAs in today's job market are those who are well trained, smart, and ambitious and who realize their potential but balance that with a solid work ethic and an appreciation for what they don't know. If you are that kind of MBA, you have a promising career ahead of you.

THE FACTS ABOUT MBA SALARIES

The most often reported item about MBAs is their salary. Newspapers and magazines quote the spectacular salaries of a few superstar graduates who can command $50,000–$100,000+ "starting" salaries. While this makes for a good story, these reports tend to distort the true picture. People read these articles without understanding all of the facts. Their mistaken notions have led to considerable negative public opinion and an image that is worse than it needs to be. These reports have also led students to expect salary offers that are unrealistic, expectations that are damaging to them in their job search. It is very important that you know the facts about MBA salaries. Let me try to set the record straight.

You cannot look at a few dramatic salary reports and draw any conclusions about MBA salaries. Yes, there are graduates of top schools who command extremely high salaries upon graduation. Usually, though, these students are offered those salaries because they have extraordinary qualifications in terms of job experience and degrees and are going to work in metropolitan areas with high living costs. One of my students took a job on Wall Street at the relatively modest (for Wall Street) salary of $75,000 and freely admitted that it probably was not much better than $35,000 or $40,000 in Richmond, Virginia. Even broad averages don't mean very much since MBA graduates make up such a heterogeneous group. Basically, there is no such thing as "an MBA" and no such thing as "an MBA salary."

This doesn't mean that salaries are not high—they are excellent. But to really understand MBA salaries, you have to consider the individual combination of student and employer. Salaries vary widely depending on:

- the age and maturity of the student
- the student's previous work experience
- the relevance of prior work experience
- the student's undergraduate degree
- the future employer's industry

Average Monthly Salary Offers

	80-81	81-82	82-83	83-84	84-85	85-86	86-87	87-88	88-89
M.B.A. with a nontechnical undergraduate major EXPERIENCE									
Less than 1 yr.	24,000	25,620	26,580	28,500	28,584	30,348	31,884	33,492	33,903
1 to 2 years	26,736	28,176	29,808	32,328	32,280	33,936	35,784	39,780	42,419
2 to 4 years	27,396	30,036	31,584	33,216	34,080	36,384	39,816	41,508	43,883
Over 4 years	27,648	29,316	32,064	33,816	34,140	37,740	38,712	41,700	44,549
M.B.A. with a technical undergraduate major EXPERIENCE									
Less than 1 yr.	26,268	27,768	30,288	30,492	30,444	32,388	34,248	38,304	38,847
1 to 2 years	28,368	29,544	32,664	33,336	33,744	34,656	37,536	43,560	44,590
2 to 4 years	29,820	31,152	33,360	34,752	35,208	37,932	41,904	44,352	47,967
Over 4 years	30,384	31,620	33,600	36,048	34,956	38,436	42,888	45,780	49,024
M.S. in Accounting	19,764	22,164	22,692	23,196	24,660	25,584	25,956	27,480	28,874
M.S. in Business	23,808	25,188	25,464	27,348	29,448	28,044	28,608	31,296	32,979
M.S. in Industrial Management	24,636	23,856	26,352	26,676	28,860	24,444	32,820	34,128	31,883

Source: College Placement Council Annual Salary Survey 1989.

- the future employer's size
- the future employer's geographic location

Only after you consider these variables can you arrive at a reasonable comparison of salaries.

A more accurate picture of MBA salaries is shown in the following two tables. These salary data are reported by the College Placement Council (CPC), which is the leading national organization for the representatives of college placement and employer recruitment offices. These tables include data collected from 164 placement offices at 418 colleges and universities around the nation. They contain salary information from most of the leading business schools in the country, including, for example, New York University, Stanford, Northwestern, Carnegie Mellon, UCLA, Duke, and Columbia. Together, they present enough across-the-board information to enable you to form an idea of the marketplace and the salaries offered in it. While certain top-ranked schools may offer higher average salaries, these figures give you a more realistic picture of what the broader MBA market offers.

Using the information presented in these tables, we can begin to understand the salary issue. The most recent data show that in 1987–88 MBAs, on the average, received starting salary offers ranging from $33,903 to $49,024 per year. MBAs with a nontechnical undergraduate degree and no experience saw their average salary grow by 41.3 percent between the years 1980 and 1988 versus a growth of 47.9 percent for candidates with technical backgrounds and no experience. MBAs with more than four years of experience also witnessed drastic salary increases over the same period of time. For those with nontechnical backgrounds, the growth was 61.1 percent, and, for those with technical backgrounds, it was 61.4 percent. When you look at the salaries by industry, the range was even greater. For MBAs with a nontechnical background, the average 1988–89 salary ranged from $21,920 a year in the federal government to $43,461 a year in investment banking. For MBAs with a technical background, the range was $25,332 (1988) in nonprofit organizations and education to $52,600 in investment banking. These first stages of our analysis show that salary offers have been strong but not as fantastically high as often reported.

Now let's try to put MBA salary information in a larger perspective. In 1987–88, CPC data showed that candidates with a bachelor's degree in business administration and management were offered an average starting salary of $22,274 a year. At the same time, an average starting salary of $33,903 a year was offered to candidates with no previous experience who held an MBA and an

Average M.B.A. Annual Salary Offers by Selected Industry Groups (for Inexperienced MBAs)

	nontechnical under-graduate major		technical under-graduate major	
	88–89	87–88	88–89	87–88
Accounting, public	30,579	30,384	30,918	32,064
Banking	34,677	37,356	43,375	37,608
Consulting	35,214	35,016	42,119	49,680
Merchandising (retail and wholesale) and services	28,697	30,744	NA	39,996
Automotive and mechanical equipment	38,066	34,548	40,066	44,400
Chemicals, drugs, and allied production	37,537	36,732	40,679	39,240
Computers and business machines	36,205	36,252	39,386	39,780
Electrical and electronic machines and equipment	36,187	32,268	36,267	35,676
Food and beverage processing	34,877	38,892	NA	41,844
Petroleum and allied products	35,018	30,336	38,627	37,740
Real Estate	38,769	NA	NA	NA
Utilities, public (includes transportation)	34,030	33,612	NM	36,684
Federal government	21,920	25,632	NA	NA
Local/state government	26,833	27,588	NA	NA
Nonprofit organizations and education	NM	27,672	NA	25,332
Investment banking	43,461	NA	52,600	NA
Health services	30,768	35,488	NA	38,076

Source: College Placement Council Annual Salary Survey, 1989. NA = not available. NM = not meaningful.

undergraduate degree in a nontechnical area. A comparison of salaries offered to those with an undergraduate degree and a technical background and salaries offered to MBAs with a technical background is more difficult to draw since there are so many disciplines lumped under the heading "technical background." However, a single example will give you an idea of the salary difference. The occupation of electrical engineer will serve to demonstrate the ranges. Among bachelor's degree recipients in the sciences and engineering, electrical engineers were the fourth-highest-paid professionals and the largest group of science and engineering graduates in 1988–89. Graduating engineers would have been offered an average salary of $30,661 a year in 1988–89, while MBAs with an undergraduate engineering background and no experience would have been offered an average salary of $38,847 a year, a difference of $8,186 per year. Other disciplines show a much wider difference in salary offers. (In the area of computer science, the difference of the two salary averages was $10,290 a year.) In addition, the MBA degree helps technically trained undergraduates to circumvent the salary compression that occurs at the top of professional career ladders in those occupations.

Clearly, significantly larger starting salaries are offered to those men and women who hold an MBA, although increased earnings potential throughout a career is often the only way to justify the expense of an MBA. (Expenses would include program costs and, if the degree were pursued full-time, the income lost while in school.)

Further insight into MBA salaries can be gained from comparing them with the median income of workers with five or more years of college.

Median Income of Workers with Five or More Years of College

	Men	Women
All ages 25 and over	32,891	16,755
25–34 years old	24,001	15,518
35–44 years old	36,036	17,920
45–54 years old	39,981	20,300
55–64 years old	39,580	18,515
65 years old and older	21,543	14,336

Source: U.S. Department of Labor, Bureau of Labor Statistics, 1984.

It is also quite interesting to look at the salary progression of MBAs after they leave school. Unfortunately, the data for MBAs alone are not easy to obtain. The last comprehensive survey of MBA salaries after graduation was done by the Association of MBA Executives in 1984. Even though the figures are a bit dated, they are the best available and, while the numbers may have changed since then, the conclusions most likely have not. In 1984, inexperienced MBAs fresh out of school were earning $28,500 (nontechnical) to $30,492 (technical) on the average. In that same year, MBAs who had been out of school for fourteen years were averaging almost $62,000 a year. MBAs out of school for five years (1979–80 graduates) were earning an average salary almost equal to the average salary of men between the ages of 55 and 64 who could have had thirty or forty years of experience!

Clearly, MBA salaries are at a premium level, providing graduates with a very high standard of living. It is also clear that $30,000 to $45,000 a year is a long way off from the reported salaries of $70,000 and $100,000. New MBA graduates would be well advised to focus on the salary data offered in this chapter, ignoring the exceptional salaries reported in the press.

Average Salaries After Graduation, 1984–85

Graduation Year	Average Salary
Up to 1970	$61,961
1971–72	53,148
1973–74	52,045
1975–76	48,542
1977–78	42,723
1979–80	39,056
1981–82	34,220
1983–84	31,172

- Average of three to four years of work experience.
- 27.8 percent have technical undergraduate degrees; 72.2 percent do not.
- Overall average: nontechnical undergraduate, $36,442; technical undergraduate, $41,629.

Source: Association of MBA Executives Inc., *The 1984–1985 MBA Career and Salary Census.* (Sample size: 5,477.) © Copyright 1985 Association of MBA Executives Inc.

SUPPLY AND DEMAND

MBA programs offer their graduates an opportunity to enter the ranks of the best-paid businesspeople. But the high salaries have put a lot of pressure on the market, enormously increasing competitiveness among job seekers. Fewer jobs are sought by more and more MBAs.

MBA programs have enjoyed phenomenal growth, showing twenty-five years of increased enrollments. According to the U.S. Department of Education Center for Education Statistics, only 4,814 MBA degrees were awarded in 1959–60 compared to 67,137 in 1985–86 (the most recent figures available). The number of MBA degrees conferred increased by more than 400 percent in the sixties, more than 250 percent in the seventies, and more than 20 percent in the first half of the eighties. The rate of conferral of

MBA degrees has grown faster than that of the total master's degree population. In addition, the number of MBA degrees conferred increased between the years 1977 and 1984, when the total number of master's degrees awarded actually declined annually. It was not until 1985–86 that the number of MBAs awarded leveled off. Today master's degrees in business make up 18.5 percent of all master's and first professional (law, medicine, dentistry, etc.) degrees awarded in the United States.

The U.S. Department of Education Center for Education Statistics also provides information on graduate enrollments nationwide. The most recent survey of this information was conducted in 1984, at which time there were over 200,000 students enrolled in graduate programs in business, more than were enrolled in graduate programs in engineering, medicine, law, the sciences, or dentistry. (Most of the students enrolled in graduate programs in business were seeking the MBA degree.) And this trend shows no signs of reversing. In 1987–88, approximately 210,000 prospective MBAs sat for the first time for the GMAT (a standardized test required for entrance into most MBA programs). The successful students among them enrolled in one of over 700 MBA programs throughout the country. At this point, you probably don't need any more statistics to convince you that there are a lot of MBAs in the job market and more coming each year.

The demand for MBAs is much more difficult to quantify. According to the 1986 edition of *Occupational Projections and Training Data* (a publication of the U.S. Department of Labor Bureau of Labor Statistics, most recent edition), most of the fields that MBAs enter after school are expected to enjoy healthy and higher-than-average growth through 2000. The jobs are expected to be available, but will MBAs fill them? Therein lies a key point about the MBA job market. There is no such thing as a job that *requires* of the employee an MBA degree. There are jobs that require MDs and JDs. For example, when you need to hire a doctor, you have to hire an MD—there is no substitute. The same is true for a lawyer, nurse, CPA, dentist, etc. But for the majority of business positions, an MBA is not an absolute must. While many companies may prefer to hire an MBA, in most of these jobs, a top-quality undergraduate with additional training can perform just as well as an MBA. Some very competitive companies choose to hire and train the brightest undergraduates they can find, largely ignoring the MBA population. Because the MBA is replaceable, it is extremely difficult to determine what the demand will be for MBAs. Furthermore, there are no good data available on the number of MBAs who are unemployed or, equally important, underemployed.

Current hiring patterns are a function of today's salary levels and perceived value of the MBA relative to that of the undergraduate. What I see is a definite change in attitude from ten or fifteen years ago, when MBAs were very highly touted as "saviors" of business. Today, the degree is still very highly regarded, but many employers also see viable alternatives to hiring MBAs. Companies continue to hire MBAs *only* because they remain a competitive purchase in the marketplace. There is a very real danger that the demand for MBAs *could* (not will) decline.

There is evidence of unrest in the MBA job market. Surveys of employer attitudes taken in the mid-eighties have shown that many employers are dissatisfied with the performance of MBAs. A recent *Northwestern-Endicott Report,* a highly respected annual survey of leading U.S. employers (262 respondents), included a special section questioning employers' opinions of MBAs. Results to note:

- 75 percent of the respondents thought that too many MBAs were entering the market.
- 51 percent thought that MBAs were too expensive; 36 percent were neutral.
- 67 percent of the respondents thought that MBAs have unrealistic expectations, which could lead to job dissatisfaction.
- 66 percent thought that hard work and intelligence would compensate for not having an MBA degree.

In a *Business Week*/Harris Poll, 488 senior executives responded to questions about MBAs. Their answers supported the opinions uncovered in the *Northwestern-Endicott Report:*

- 45 percent of the executives believed that MBAs were paid too much.
- 78 percent thought that employees with a graduate degree from business school tended to have unrealistic expectations about career advancement.
- 64 percent of the executives thought that it didn't make sense for people with MBAs to get higher salaries than people with the same work experience but no degree.
- 63 percent said that the younger employees with MBAs tended to have less company loyalty and tended to job hop a lot more than employees without the degree.

Furthermore, a survey of presidents and personnel directors of Fortune 500 companies showed relatively little satisfaction with the skills of MBAs in many of the areas for which they are actually hired (see table on page 24).

Clearly, there are problems in the MBA job market. It is easy to see that there are a lot of dissatisfied customers and that the job market has become much tighter in recent years. I know from conversations I have had with employers that many wonder whether they should hire MBAs anymore. They know that MBA training is sound and that MBAs are capable of outstanding accomplishments, yet many of the MBAs they hire don't perform to their expected potential. Employers feel that they are not getting their money's worth. Think about what you do in your own purchasing of goods and services. What would you do if the cost of buying a dinner at your usual restaurant continued to get more expensive but you were less and less satisfied with the quality of your meal, and there were plenty more restaurants available? You would probably begin eating out at another restaurant. You might even decide to cook your own supper at home. Now, you tell me: What do you think that MBA employers will do if the salaries and the level of dissatisfaction continue to rise?

The boom days of the seventies and early eighties, when the "plain vanilla" MBA with little or no professional work experience

Rating the M.B.A.: Satisfaction of Fortune 500 Companies with M.B.A.'s

% satisfied with	Presidents	Personnel Directors
Bad News		
Administrative skills	32%	35%
Oral communication skills	48%	56%
Written communication skills	47%	40%
Interpersonal skills	28%	37%
Managerial skills	43%	21%
Work ethic	65%	45%
Leadership skills	36%	47%
Short-term operational decision-making skills	41%	45%
Strategic planning skills	46%	48%
Good News		
Poise and maturity	67%	58%
Ability to conceptualize	68%	67%
Analytical ability	87%	85%
Level of initiative	75%	74%
Specific functional knowledge	76%	85%

Note: Response rate was 42%.

Source: *Harvard Business Review,* September–October 1984.

and only average qualifications was almost guaranteed a fat salary and a fast-track job, are all but gone. Employer concerns have resulted in an increasing emphasis on quality. Employers are simply demanding high-quality preparation before they will pay the price for an MBA. The messages they are sending the MBAs of today are loud and clear:

- High-quality academic training is a must.
- Professional work experience (preferably business-related experience) is highly desirable, whether it be a permanent job or a co-op/internship experience.
- MBAs must learn how to work with people, not just numbers. They should develop a good attitude that makes them part of the team.
- Job candidates must show strength in most, if not all, job requirements.
- Thorough career planning and preparation for resumes, interviews, etc., are a must.
- Premium salaries must be justified by skills, competence, and a realistic attitude.
- MBAs must understand their real worth in the marketplace.

There's a world of difference between a strong ego, which is essential, and a large ego—which can be destructive. The guy with a strong ego knows his own strengths. He's confident. He has a realistic idea of what he can accomplish, and he moves purposefully toward his goal.

But the guy with a large ego is always looking for recognition. He constantly needs to be patted on the back. He thinks he's a cut above everybody else. And he talks down to the people who work for him.

—Lee Iacocca

From *Iacocca* by Lee Iacocca with William Novak. Bantam Books. © 1984 by Lee Iacocca.

You can look at the market as troubled, but I prefer to see it as full of opportunity. While many employers may cast a doubting eye toward an MBA, they are usually ecstatic to discover a *high-quality* MBA candidate. Most say that there is a shortage of good, well-trained MBAs. In today's economic environment, employers simply aren't willing to pay premium salaries unless they get premium quality and performance. If you are looking for an easy ticket, forget it. But if you are willing to work hard to become a top-quality candidate, you will not find the competition that severe.

It's up to you to decide what type of candidate you'll be. I challenge you to make up your mind to do what it takes to be the type of MBA who can take advantage of the wonderful opportunities available. If you are levelheaded, ambitious, and hardworking, your future is bright. If you develop unrealistic expectations, adopt a cocky attitude like many of your peers, and aren't well prepared, you're going to have trouble. The decision is yours.

THE FUTURE

Nobody really knows what will happen in the future, but I am going to make the best predictions I can (some general and others specific) given the information I have.

I believe that the MBA has been firmly established as a worthwhile degree program. The number of international students enrolling in MBA programs in the United States and the number of companies that send their fast-track executives to get an MBA are convincing evidence of its value. As in any discipline, there will be a continuing dialogue about the best curriculums, and programs will evolve. Despite the calls for changes to curriculums, I think that American business will continue to actively recruit good MBAs.

Many have talked of a shakeout in the MBA market, and I tend to agree. It is possible that there are too many MBAs and too many MBA programs. It is hard to imagine that American business needs over 67,000 new MBAs each year. These students are graduating from more than 700 MBA programs, many of which cannot meet the standards for a strong accreditation (for example, only 200 have AACSB accreditation). A program of high quality is expensive to build and operate. Many of these programs are newcomers to the MBA business. Some lower-quality programs must be considered in jeopardy. I'm not predicting any massive closing of programs, but I don't think they can all survive.

The more important shakeout that I see happening (and continuing in the future) will affect MBAs from every business school. American business is clearly growing tired of the prima donna elitist and selfish attitudes that have characterized many MBAs. The emphasis of business is appropriately placed on quality and productivity. Tomorrow's successful MBAs will be those who can prove their worth to employers. More and more employers will view the MBA as an option, not a necessity. If they can hire outstanding MBAs, they will. If they don't see quality, they won't pay the price.

On the average, MBA salaries will not continue to grow much faster than inflation except in certain well-defined segments of the market. They are already at premium levels, and I don't think that the economic climate will support greater increases. With the growing sentiment among at least some of the business world that an MBA isn't enough "bang for the buck," a period of leveling off of MBA salaries is a real possibility. I don't think that dissatisfaction in the marketplace will result in a lowering of salaries. Rather, it could lead to fewer MBAs hired and salaries holding steady.

Business is always hungry for leaders. There is always a supply of managers and analysts, but MBAs who can present themselves as leaders for the future will be in an excellent position. That means MBAs will be expected to demonstrate stronger preparations in the "soft" skills such as people management and communication. Business needs more MBAs who can motivate employees to reach their highest levels of productivity and potential. Leadership also means the ability to rise above the traditional MBA analytical, numbers-oriented perspective to develop a strategic vision for business success. A strong international orientation will be a must. Students need to understand that tomorrow's high-paid MBA will have to demonstrate true leadership potential, not just strong technical and administrative skills.

There will be growth in the demand for MBAs in particular job functions. While some executives have been cutting back on the hiring of MBAs with business backgrounds, they have discovered the value of employees who combine an MBA with a technical or scientific undergraduate degree. These students are uniquely qualified to fill integrating and liaison roles in high-tech firms. In essence, they know how to speak two languages and understand several often very different cultures. I see no slowdown in the technological advances in our economy, so these MBAs should become more valuable.

MBAs can expect to find fewer glamour positions available in the future and will face more pressure to work their way up organizations from the field and plant. There has been a significant trend in the eighties to run companies "lean and mean," away from large corporate staffs. Jobs have been pushed down the organization closer to the customers and products. Put another way, employers are creating positions in their profit centers where money can be made and eliminating them in cost centers, such as corporate staffs where MBAs often work. This means that MBAs who are willing to give up some of the "three-piece-suit" glamour and get their hands dirty in manufacturing and operations or go into marketing and sales, where they are close to the customer, will be in high demand. MBAs in these positions can make a real impact very quickly on the bottom-line earnings of an employer. High-quality manufacturing-oriented MBAs are particularly tough to find and will be in a good position in the job market.

One of the mainstays in the MBA job market has been a career in corporate finance. Finance jobs will still be strong in the future; I don't see that changing. Finance is especially well suited for MBAs since the jobs are usually very analytical, often employ sophisticated techniques, and allow MBAs to put their creativity to work. However, I do see a trend toward requiring them to have stronger accounting backgrounds for corporate finance positions (this is not generally popular with MBAs). Having worked as a financial analyst, I understand why employers need their finance people to have a better grasp of accounting concepts. Many are requiring MBAs to rotate through accounting positions; tomorrow's MBAs had better get used to it.

Another mainstay for MBAs has been consulting. I don't see that changing. Consulting organizations need lots of highly skilled and highly trained people to provide sophisticated services for their clients. MBAs are ideal candidates because of their business skills and their people skills. For MBAs, many consulting firms offer lucrative salaries with rapid advancement and are therefore ideal employers. In fact, since the stock market crash of 1987, management consulting has been more popular than ever.

Financial services (investment and commercial banking and finance products) will continue to be a strong field for MBAs. Many of the jobs are entrepreneurial in nature, and this industry tolerates ambitious, hard-driving MBAs much easier than the corporate world does. The investment banking industry has not lost its hunger for top MBAs but is still suffering the effects of the stock market crash of 1987. Many MBA jobs on Wall Street were eliminated, and hiring has continued to be soft. One certainty (maybe the only one) about the financial markets is that they always run in cycles. The investment banking industry will return to strength, and so will its MBA hiring. Money will always need to be loaned and invested, so opportunities will always exist for MBAs in this industry.

MBAs with a strong computer orientation and an understanding of how information and computer systems can meet business needs will also be in a strong position in tomorrow's marketplace. The world is full of technical types who can build great computer systems but is short on managers who can make money with them.

As business becomes increasingly dependent on computer technology, more and more jobs will be created in this area.

Our world is fast becoming a global marketplace. "Internationalization" and "globalization" are key words for American business and business schools today. MBAs who can learn to deal with the often monumental complexities of our changing marketplace will be particularly well poised for career success in the future. Many of our traditional ways of thinking simply won't work in a global marketplace. One need only look at our trade deficit, the impact of Japan and other Asian countries, the changes forthcoming in the European Common Market, the Soviet perestroika, and the impact Third World debt has had on our economy to appreciate the significance of this trend. MBA graduates are in a unique position to capitalize on this trend, if they can adapt.

Another important trend that should continue has been the broadening of the MBA job market. No longer confined to the corporate, for-profit sector, education, government, and non-profit organizations have learned that the MBA is just as valuable to them. More and more MBAs are using their degree to launch careers in these organizations since the skills transfer very nicely. While these careers are often not as profitable financially, they offer many other rewards. These organizations will grow in their desire for professionally trained managers, and I think more MBAs will realize the satisfying life-styles they provide.

One criticism of MBAs has been that they lack an entrepreneurial spirit. However, there are indications that more MBAs are considering careers in small business, either their own or somebody else's. While it is difficult to start your own business without any work experience, MBAs with experience are finding this to be a more satisfying path. More and more express the desire to "run their own show" rather than fit into a larger organization. Since most *new* jobs in this country are now being created by small businesses, not large ones, more MBAs will need to consider career paths in small to medium-sized organizations in the future. While often not as glamorous as the big companies, they usually offer outstanding experience and growth potential.

A final caution: there is a real danger that MBAs can price themselves right out of the market, both by pushing salaries higher and by ignoring calls for higher value for the salaries being paid. The market is sensitive to salary levels and could shrink dramatically. An economic slowdown or recession in particular would add pressure. The solution is fairly simple: keep salary expectations in line with quality and contribution to the firm.

Good, well-qualified MBAs will always be in demand. The message I hear from employers is usually "We always have room for good people." It is your challenge as a prospective MBA to be sure that employers perceive you as a high-quality candidate. Good career maturity and preparation, as presented in the following chapters, compose an essential part of a quality image.

Chapter 2

Career Advice

Careers. What place will a career hold in your life? What type of a job do you expect to find when you graduate? Will salary and benefits be the most important factors for you in choosing a job? How do you know whether you have the proper perspective on your career? To whom should you turn for good advice? If you are like most MBA students, you are probably thinking about some of these issues. This chapter will guide you in developing answers to these and other career-related questions.

WHO KNOWS BEST?

Everybody you talk with seems to have a different idea about your career. Well-meaning people tell you that "this job is the best" or "that career choice is best." They bombard you with advice, trying to help you make career decisions. And it is very difficult not to be swayed by the opinions of others, particularly when you are in your twenties. However, remember that although many people may think they know what's "best," what's best for them may not be best for you.

Despite the good intentions of family and friends, their advice may be misdirected because it usually reflects their values and not your own. Finding your own path is the key to a successful career— and, probably, to a happy life. Your challenge throughout the career planning process is to define what success and happiness in a career mean to you and you alone. I strongly encourage you to dedicate your energies to discovering what your own personal goals are and how *you* define success and happiness.

There are no right or wrong careers or work styles. Yes, some career paths involve fewer risks than others, and some increase your chances of advancing in the company, attaining power, and earning a top salary. The career moves you make will lead you in different directions. Therefore, you must pay attention to the ramifications of any decision you make about your career. But—and this is critical—you have the freedom to choose what course you want to take, regardless of whether it fits the values and expectations of your peers and family. To those people who seem to know a "right way," say, "Thank you," and politely turn away. To those who offer you the benefit of their experience while acknowledging that what is right for them may not be right for you, listen closely.

When you get what you want in your struggle for self
And the world makes you king for a day;
Just go to a mirror and look at yourself
And see what THAT man has to say.

For it isn't your father or mother or wife
Who judgment upon you must pass;
The fellow whose verdict counts most in your life
Is the one staring back from the glass.

. . . .

He's the fellow to please, never mind all the rest,
For he's with you clear up to the end.
And you've passed your most dangerous, difficult test
If the man in the glass is your friend.

—Anonymous
From "The Man in the Glass"

Your job will occupy a huge portion of thirty-five to forty-five years of your life. What it doesn't consume in actual working hours it consumes in preparation time, commuting time, and emotional energy. As you move into the professional ranks and perhaps become a manager, your responsibilities and commitments make it difficult to leave the job behind when you go home. You will likely find yourself thinking about the job in off hours, dreaming up new ideas and new ways to contribute to the organization. In short, a career is a *major* commitment in your life.

You owe it to yourself to maximize the chances that you will be happy in your chosen career. It is easy to think that it's no big deal if you get into a job in which you're not happy. In reality, spending 50 to 70 hours a week at something you don't like is misery (ask anyone who has done it). Your job can be a wonderful, happy, and rewarding part of your life, helping you grow personally and professionally. It can be something you look forward to that you seek out and love doing. It can do and be all this and more—if it is a good match for you. You owe it to yourself to find a career that contributes significantly to a happy life—and only you can define that type of career.

Many people spend years and years trying one job and then another, hoping to stumble into the one that is right. By following a more systematic career planning process, you will save yourself some of the pain of trial and error. Experience shows that your chances of being happy in a career increase dramatically if you'll take the time to discover and define your individual goals. The stakes are high; the choice is yours.

THE ROLE OF WORK IN YOUR LIFE

When you are planning for your life and career, you want to ask yourself a crucial question: What role will work play in my life? Richard Bolles, in his book *The Three Boxes of Life*, suggests that there are three major boxes, or components, that make up our lives: work, learning, and play. Each of us must decide in our own way how we want to integrate these three boxes.

Most of us are familiar with the traditional cycle of learning from birth to the mid-20s, working from the mid-20s to retirement, and playing from retirement to death. This approach, based on the Puritan work ethic, suggests that the priority should be on work during much of life. I (and Bolles) challenge that. You have the freedom to choose the proper balance for your life. The goal is achieving satisfaction and happiness as defined by your own personal values structure. For some, the balance may mean a huge commitment to career and work. For others, it may mean a lesser commitment to work to allow for more learning and leisure. You must discover in what proportions you want to mix work, play, and learning to maximize your own satisfaction.

MBAs are typically a hard-driving, ambitious group of people who place a high value on a successful career. They seem particularly subject to the "all work, no play" trap. That's fine—if that's what you want. However, it is nowhere prescribed that you *must* make work your top priority if you have an MBA. MBAs should give themselves permission to find the balance that works best for them and not feel pressured or pushed in the one direction just because they have an MBA.

Extensive evidence shows that a more balanced life may be

more desirable for many people. The growing number of cases of failed marriages, burnouts, depression, alcohol abuse, and drug abuse among busy, fast-track professionals suggests that a 100 percent devotion to work is not healthy. Few people seem to be able to maintain peak performance over long periods without time away from their careers on a regular basis. The evidence also suggests that the incidence of heart attacks, strokes, cancer, and many other ailments increases dramatically in those with an extreme focus on work.

Genius, that power which dazzles mortal eyes,
Is oft but perseverance in disguise.
Continuous effort of itself implies,
In spite of countless falls, the power to rise.
'Twixt failure and success the print's so fine,
Men sometimes know not when they touch the line;

. . . .

A little more persistence, courage, vim,
Success will dawn o'er failure's cloudy rim.

Then take this honey for the bitterest cup;
There is no failure, save in giving up.
No real fall, so long as one still tries,
For seeming set-backs make the strong man wise.
There's no defeat, in truth, save from within;
Unless you're beaten there, you're bound to win.

—C. C. Cameron
From "Success"

So what should you do? Moderation seems to be the key. It seems clear that the extremes, "all work, no play" and "all play, no work," are unhealthy. Over the long term, the healthiest individuals are those who recognize that they need to nourish all parts of themselves. They need to work, they need to play, and they need to continue to learn and grow. Those people with a singular devotion to work are quite often discovered to be secretly frustrated with their lack of attention to other areas of their lives. Of course, we must recognize the right of an individual to choose his or her own balance. Some people do find work to be the most rewarding part of their lives. The ideal situation is that you find work you enjoy doing so much that it becomes your hobby. That's achievable with careful career and life planning and the courage to follow your own convictions.

Each of these elements of our lives is vital to our long-term psychological and physical well-being. In the short term, all of us make sacrifices in some areas to achieve goals in other areas. But, in the long run, learn to pay attention to your body and mind so that you know you are getting what you need to sustain your life. Depression, listlessness, anger, and decreased productivity are just a few of the symptoms that something is out of balance. Find the balance that keeps you at your peak level of energy, enthusiasm, satisfaction, and happiness.

THE REWARDS OF WORK

The rewards of work are many and varied. Recognition, money, accomplishments, power, prestige, and perks are just some of the many benefits that we can get from work. Different careers and different companies yield varying proportions of these and other rewards. As individuals, we seek different rewards, depending on our background and our needs at our particular stage of life. I encourage you to discover all of the rewards that you can receive and make the critical decision about which are truly important to you.

All too often, job seekers, particularly those coming directly out of college, focus on money. At a time when you don't have much money, getting some seems like the most important thing that a job can give you. Unfortunately once you have that money, it doesn't seem nearly as exciting as it did when you didn't have it. It is perfectly OK to make salary a top priority, as there is nothing inherently right or wrong with wanting a lot of money. But it is wrong to assume that money will make you happy, passively accepting a large salary as your primary goal and selection criterion. Again, you have to identify your personal priorities.

Let's be honest, none of us wants to be poor. However, most people who have been in a job that made them unhappy will tell you that the money doesn't mean as much as being satisfied with your work. Look past the money. Remember that your paycheck only comes once a month or once every two weeks. Don't believe that the dollars will give you day-to-day satisfaction.

You will discover that jobs provide many types of rewards besides money. It is important that you focus on the total compensation package, not just the salary. By compensation, I mean all rewards, tangible and intangible, that you receive for your efforts on behalf of an organization. These may include:

salary	social contacts
bonuses	training
benefits	challenges
perks	experience
self-esteem	career advancement
prestige	potential
a desirable life-style	power

As you evaluate career options and job offers, be careful to review the entire compensation package, being honest with yourself about the rewards that are most valuable to you. You may find that salary is not at the top of the list. In fact, training, opportunity for advancement, and experience are often more important to a person just beginning a career.

BE REALISTIC

All too often we idealize jobs that we are considering. We expect big things, usually based on little or no information, and, when they don't materialize, we are disappointed and become disgruntled. It is particularly important that MBAs develop realistic expectations about work. The following list contains some of the most common myths about work:

Work can fill all of your needs and make you happy. People usually find that work can fill only some of their needs. They need friends and activities outside of the office to feel happy and fulfilled.

You will enjoy all aspects of your job. Every job has its distasteful and boring parts; you must learn to accept those along with the fun parts.

Work will always be challenging. Work can be very mundane. Recent graduates, who were used to being mentally challenged on a daily basis, are surprised when the level of learning and mental stimulation on the job differs from that in the classroom. Don't expect to be challenged each day.

Promotions will come quickly. Competition is tough in most major firms. Promotions will be hard earned and often will come only after a certain amount of time has passed. The fast track does exist but only for a select few.

A good company won't have any problems. Every company has its shortcomings. Learn to recognize them before you take the job and to accept them after you get there.

In short, don't expect a near-perfect job in a near-perfect organization, particularly early in your career. Try to understand what the world of work is all about before you go into it. Develop realistic expectations about what a career can do for you and your life. When it comes to the actual job search, a mature career perspective sells.

DANGER SIGNALS

There are certain mental traps in the career planning process. Learn to recognize the danger signals. If you catch yourself thinking, feeling, or acting upon any of the following, reread this section and rethink your priorities and approach to the job search. Stop yourself before you make a mistake:

You are doing what others think you should. Do you hear yourself using the words "should" or "ought to" frequently? If so, are you really doing what *you* want to do or are you living up to others' expectations?

You are doing what MBAs "should." There exists a fairly well defined stereotype of what an MBA ought to be doing. Are you following the crowd? Are you seeking a certain type of job just because that's what an MBA should do or because that is what your peers are doing? Be careful that you do not fall into the MBA mold unless it fits your individual needs.

Your only decision criterion is making money. Do you find yourself making job decisions based on a few thousand dollars? Do you know anything about companies other than their salary and benefits? When you compare companies, do you compare them on other criteria as well? Ask yourself what other rewards you will receive on the job.

You are ignoring "nonglamour" companies and positions. Have you ignored certain jobs and certain employers because some person, some stereotype, or the rumor mill says that they aren't right? Have you investigated every possible opportunity, or have you eliminated some because they're not what you "should" do? Are you looking only at companies and jobs with flashy reputations? Remember, you never know where you'll find the right match.

You are paying too much attention to perks and frills. Do fancy offices, three-piece suits, impressive lobbies, and paneled conference rooms put stars in your eyes? Companies know that these things will impress you; beware that you are not sucked in by them. I will assure you that the luster of these perks and frills wears off when you are faced with the reality of the day-to-day job.

You are feeling guilty about a job you want. Why should you feel guilty about taking a job that you want, one that you think will make you happy and will satisfy you? If you have done a careful job of analyzing a company and a career choice and are fully aware of the risks and ramifications of that choice, there's no reason to feel guilty about doing something *you* want to do.

It is important that you penetrate these myths and come to terms early on with the other obstacles that may sidetrack you and prevent you from laying out a career plan that above all is true to you.

Chapter 3

Getting Started

The toughest part of any project is getting started: discovering the type of career you want and finding a job are two of the most demanding steps you will have to take in your career. But even though these stages are difficult, you can prepare yourself for them—and for success—by developing the right attitudes and skills and by building a strong understanding of effective career planning and job search strategies. This chapter will acquaint you with what is expected of candidates for MBA-level jobs and help you master the fundamentals needed to begin this process with confidence.

BUILDING YOUR PORTFOLIO

During the course of an MBA program, most students are exposed to at least a small measure of portfolio theory. When you build an investment portfolio, you look for investments that, when combined, yield consistently good returns to the investor. Each investment has strengths and weaknesses. By itself, an investment may not be as desirable as it is when considered part of a portfolio. The emphasis in portfolio theory is on the performance of the package, knowing that, if properly assembled, one investment's strengths will compensate for another's weaknesses.

You, too, are a portfolio. You are a collection of skills, abilities, knowledge, and experience. You are very good at some things and not so good at others. An employer wants to see a package—a portfolio—that as a whole will yield an effective employee. Each skill, piece of knowledge, ability, or experience is not as important as how the package functions as a unit.

Each person has a unique portfolio that derives from his or her interests, personality, and development. There is no one "right way" to prepare yourself—no one best combination of courses or best type of experience. Every decision you make about courses, internships, and projects must be evaluated in the context of its impact on the total portfolio. For example, if you have a well-diversified portfolio of blue chip stocks, including Ford and GM, should you buy Chrysler? Probably not. You already have good exposure in the auto industry. Chrysler might be an excellent stock to own, but it won't add anything to your portfolio and can hurt it by overexposing you to auto industry cycles. Similarly, if you already have four finance electives and two years of finance experience, do you need more? Maybe not (depending, of course, on your objective). You already have good exposure to finance, but you may be short in management and people skills.

You see, everything you do in school and in your professional life is an investment in your portfolio. Just as a business needs to earn a good return on the assets it owns, so must you. Unless you are doing something just for fun, the only reason to invest your time, energy, and money in it (e.g., taking a course or volunteering to help on a consulting project) is to derive a good return on your effort in the form of increased employability. Each advance in professional development is another asset in your portfolio. Employers are looking to invest in (hire) a strong portfolio (employee) to provide them with a good financial return on their capital (salary and benefits) when they invest in you.

A portfolio perspective may sound impersonal and a little harsh, but let's examine some of its advantages. This perspective operates on these principles:

- You are a unique blend of strengths and weaknesses.
- You can transform your weaknesses into strengths if you wish.
- You may freely add to your portfolio or subtract from it at any time.
- Each portfolio can be tailored to meet individual objectives.
- A portfolio is dynamic, changing as you grow and change.

Critical to a successful career planning program is a candid assessment of your portfolio. Evaluate your professional portfolio just as an investor would look at a stock portfolio. It is very important that you do this well *before* you start your job search. You need to realize that you are investing a lot of time, money, and effort in developing a marketable portfolio. If you begin to assess your portfolio at an early stage in the career planning process, you will have the opportunity to take an active role in developing the kind of assets employers like to see. Your portfolio is extremely valuable, and it takes years to build. Let's make sure it works for you.

Job requirements differ, as do job seekers. But there is a core group of characteristics that most MBA recruiters look for in candidates they hire. A list of these qualities and skills follows. Use this list to judge your professional portfolio as you would use stock market indices to judge the performance of a stock portfolio. A note of caution: Don't let this list intimidate you! Career planning should be a freeing experience, helping you to find your niche. This list is not intended to restrict or mold you. No one person can have all these strengths (and no one should be limited to just these). However, MBA recruiters will look for candidates who have

---

The key to success is not information. It's people. And the kind of people I look for to fill top management spots are the eager beavers. These are the guys who try to do more than they're expected to. They're always reaching. And reaching out to the people they work with, trying to help them do their jobs better. That's the way they're built.

—Lee Iacocca

From *Iacocca* by Lee Iacocca with William Novak. Bantam Books. © 1984 Lee Iacocca.

---

the majority of these assets, preferring the candidate who has the greatest number of them. Use the list to identify weaknesses and to develop directions for professional growth. Don't panic if you aren't a "10" in everything.

Employers like to hire candidates who have the following qualities and skills. Show them:

You are competent. Show that you are qualified to do what the job requires. No matter how much employers may like you, they are making a business investment. It is particularly critical that, as an MBA, you demonstrate to employers that you are worth the premium salary they are paying.

You have a lot of energy. High-paid MBAs lead a fairly busy, active life. It takes a lot of energy to keep up the pace on the fast track. Employers expect MBAs to move at a heightened pace.

You are enthusiastic. Companies prefer to hire people who appear enthusiastic. Employers know that if they can find the right job for you then you have the potential to become enthusiastic about their organization.

You have a strong work ethic. MBAs have been criticized for not wanting to work hard. Business needs MBAs who know what it means to work their way up an organization, expect to earn what they get, and don't run from demanding assignments.

You have a positive attitude. Having an optimistic, upbeat attitude toward life and your career will go a long way toward helping you succeed in business. No organization wants someone with a chip on his or her shoulder.

You are creative. Managers and leaders are expected to generate new ideas and new approaches to doing things. Show that you can take initiative and develop original thoughts.

You are able to learn. Bright, intelligent people do great things for companies. You must show employers that you have a quick mind and can learn easily.

You are results oriented. Doers, not thinkers, get the jobs. Companies need people who can accomplish things; they look for individuals with a "can-do" attitude, not naysayers.

You are a self-starter. Business wants MBAs who don't need close supervision, can think for themselves, show good judgment, and make things happen without being asked.

You have strong communication skills. On the job, you will be required to inform and persuade people with your thoughts and ideas. Employers hire people who can articulate and convey ideas in a clear and concise manner.

You are assertive. Show your ability to present your opinions forcefully but tactfully. Employers like people who are frank and persuasive.

You have a pleasant personality. Organizations are simply groups of people doing their jobs. Employers hire people, not machines. Show that people will like working with you.

You are well-rounded. Well-rounded people are a real plus in a company; book smarts are not enough. Employers want MBAs who have a variety of interests and facets to their personality because these employees typically can handle a variety of positions and work well with their colleagues and customers.

You are flexible. Show that you are flexible and adaptable, because companies will ask you to take on a variety of functions. Employers want people who can change as the company itself changes and grows.

You have good social skills. MBAs must have the interpersonal skills to be comfortable working and dealing with people day in, day out.

You have respect for fellow workers. Employers need managers who have an overriding interest in the well-being of their staff.

You are compassionate and humble. Although tales abound of bosses who are tough and autocratic, those who exhibit warmth and humility are more the rule. Be confident but not pompous.

You behave ethically. The majority of businesses are looking for students who are principled and know how to do business cleanly and honestly.

You have leadership ability. MBAs are usually expected to move into management. Show that you have the charisma and intelligence to lead people and are willing to take on responsibility.

You are self-confident. For an employer to have confidence in you, you must have confidence in yourself. Believe in yourself and your ability to learn and perform. It's contagious, and it sells.

You have determination. Let the employer know that you have the persistence and fortitude not to stop until you reach your goals.

You are a winner. Everybody loves a winner. Show through your past successes and accomplishments that you have the competitive edge to make yourself a winner in the company and the company a winner in the marketplace.

There is likewise a core group of characteristics that most MBA recruiters avoid like the plague. Besides a lack of any of the already mentioned positive qualities, employers do not like:

Candidates who are shy. Shy people have considerable difficulty communicating their thoughts and ideas. Since business involves people working with people, shyness is a significant impediment at the managerial level.

Candidates who are narrowly prepared. Although bookworms may be knowledgeable in their area of specialty, they lack the perspective and flexibility to be effective. Your book learning will sell, but it is not sufficient.

Candidates who are arrogant. Employers do not want arrogant, pompous MBAs that will not be well liked within the organization. Employees who are disliked are ineffective.

Candidates who are bitter. Bitter, angry people also do not function well in an organization. Their vindictiveness gets them nowhere.

Candidates who have unrealistic expectations. Job hunters should be realistic about how far and how fast they will move up in a company. Employers are not always looking for the next chief executive officer.

Now that you know what recruiters are and are not looking for, you should sit down and evaluate your portfolio. I invite every one of my students to meet with me to go through this stage of the process. A brief case history will give you some idea of the portfolio perspective in action.

> Brian was a first-year MBA student who had worked for twelve months as an insurance adjuster. He received an undergraduate degree in business administration from a small liberal arts school. He was neat and well groomed and a little on the shy side. Our first subject of discussion was his background. Brian had done very well in school but spent little time in extracurricular activities. He enjoyed his job as an insurance adjuster but decided he wanted more of a challenge and opportunity for advancement as well as a higher salary. After some discussion of career opportunities, it became obvious that finance was really his first love, and he had thought that he would like to pursue this field. We talked for a while about his strengths and weaknesses relative to a finance career. His undergraduate degree was heavy with "soft" skills but short on analytical skills; he would have to add these to his portfolio. Furthermore, his undergraduate school was too small to have much in the way of computer equipment, so that improving his computer skills would be a priority for him. Without these skills, prospective employers would not perceive him as well prepared.
>
> Brian had clearly demonstrated that he was bright and capable of learning, but his portfolio was severely lacking in leadership skills. I urged him to look for a chance to take charge of a part of the MBA Association (a student club). His participation would show initiative and help him to develop management skills. He needed to broaden his activities so that he would not be perceived as a bookworm.
>
> One of Brian's real strengths was his personality. He was a friendly person to whom people warmed very quickly. He would be able to establish a rapport with recruiters and colleagues easily. However, he lacked some confidence in his abilities. I advised him to look for opportunities to get some hands-on experience so he would feel more confident. This would also strengthen his qualifications by showing more accomplishments.

While Brian talked easily with people, he seemed reluctant to assert himself and show much enthusiasm. This would hurt him in an interview. I told Brian he needed to learn how to project himself better and suggested joining the local Toastmaster's Club as an excellent way to do that.

Finally, we discussed his ideas about an appropriate career plan. Brian had a very good handle on what type of career would suit him best; this was a real asset. However, his expectations for how far and how fast an MBA would take him were out of line. I warned him that unrealistic expectations would destroy his chances in the MBA job market. I advised him to do some extensive research so that he would better understand what an MBA career path would really be like. With this information, Brian would give a good interview and be perceived as a mature, well-directed candidate.

This type of candid appraisal of your strengths and weaknesses early on in an MBA program will give you a chance to strengthen your portfolio before you try to sell yourself. Your work will be much the same as that of a financial planner reviewing a stock portfolio, selling off weak, poor-performing stocks and adding new strong ones. You now know the elements of an ideal portfolio. Where are you weak? What things can you improve on? What strategies can you use to turn weaknesses into strengths?

MBAs, THE GREAT COMMUNICATORS

I want to highlight and expand on one of the key traits of successful MBAs—strong communication skills. It is almost impossible to find a job at the MBA level that does not require strong oral and written communication skills. Most entry-level management-track positions require extensive work with a client, either inside or outside the firm. Just a few examples will demonstrate this. Commercial lenders have to build close working relationships with clients. Financial analysts consult with departments within the company in the course of their analysis work. People who work in marketing are almost always interacting closely with customers. Investment bankers work with clients to structure deals. Real estate developers have to coordinate the activities of contractors, financial institutions, and tenants. Personnel people recruit, hire, fire, and counsel employees all the time. Quite simply, there just aren't many positions that require the MBA to be secluded in a back room or otherwise detached from other people.

MBAs usually find themselves joined with colleagues in a team effort, since no organization advances very far without a total team effort. The tasks and projects facing modern business today are just too complex and multifaceted for one person to tackle alone. This means that you as an MBA will have to know how to communicate effectively and how to get along with others, earning their respect and trust. Most of the business world will not tolerate an MBA who can't be a team player. Part of being a team player is attitude, but a very large part is learning good interpersonal communication skills.

MBAs are usually hired to become managers. They are not generally considered career specialists but rather are evaluated before being hired on their potential for growth into management (a key justification for your premium salary!). Once you become a manager, a large part of your job becomes people, both inside and outside the organization. Your job is to direct, control, motivate, reward, and reprimand the employees you supervise. You will be charged with the responsibility of directing those people toward organizational goals, seeing that their productivity is maximized, and helping them grow professionally. You will also be required to keep morale up in the organization. In addition, when you become a manager, you will likely have greater responsibility for maintaining relations with a company's outside constituencies. You will probably have more meetings with financiers, customers, suppliers, and representatives of regulatory agencies, for example. All of these tasks require that you attain a very high level of skill in interpersonal communications and relations.

A very important part of your career as an MBA will be selling. Many MBAs don't like to think of themselves as salespeople, but they are. You might be required to sell a product to consumers, your ideas to your boss, a budget to a vice president, or yourself to a recruiter. Selling is just a fundamental part of the business world. And, you guessed it, selling requires strong interpersonal skills.

I haven't even begun to talk about writing yet. The business world is full of writing tasks, such as letters, memos, reports, proposals, and prospectuses. You will be required to communicate on paper as effectively as you would in person. You need to be able to put your thoughts and ideas on paper concisely, precisely, and flawlessly. It is quite embarrassing to be called on the carpet by a senior executive because your grammar or spelling is wrong. More important, money can be lost if agreements are not written precisely. And, heaven knows, you can't survive if you can't write a memo.

Have I made my point? Both oral and written skills are equally important to businesspeople, and executives complain about the inadequate training offered in business schools in both these areas. However, employers seem concerned most about oral communication skills when evaluating a candidate. They have discovered that good writing skills can be taught in a relatively short time but that it can take years to teach good interpersonal skills (and, in some cases, these skills are never acquired, even after years of instruction).

The bottom line then is that you must have good oral communication and interpersonal skills as an MBA. It is not an optional item or one that will just help you get a better job. It is a prerequisite for a good MBA-level job and for success in that job. Employers will be closely evaluating these skills every time they meet or interview you. Communication skills are almost a "blackball" item in that if employers can't see at least a reasonable level of proficiency, they will not even consider you. I strongly suggest that you candidly appraise your capabilities. If your skills are not strong, you must take action *now* to improve them. Not only is the ability to communicate well necessary for your future success but without it you will not be able to sell yourself to the employer during an interview.

CHARACTERISTICS OF A GOOD JOB HUNTER

After observing students for some years, I found myself wondering why some students seem to be successful at their job search while others struggle so much. My surprising conclusion is that in most cases success in the job search process has little to do with business training and qualifications. Just about every MBA has the native intelligence to do a good job for a company if his or her degree is from a decent school. But successful job hunters seem to have a set of skills and attitudes that helps them negotiate this journey more effectively than others. The difficulties of the struggling students frustrate me to no end because I know that a successful, rewarding career is within reach of almost every student who enters a good-quality MBA program. All that these students lack is the right attitude to attack the job search. What makes up that attitude?

First of all, it takes *commitment.* A job search can be very demanding, requiring a great deal of time. In fact, finding a job is almost a full-time job in itself. Successful students seem to have decided before they begin an MBA program that they are going to find a good job when they graduate, and they will do anything it takes to accomplish this objective. They have that "set-jaw, steely-eyed" determination that just dares anybody to stop them from finding a good job. Their only questions are, "How much do I do?" and "When should I do it?" What chance do students who always seem to be looking for an easy way out have against this competition?

In addition to having commitment, good job hunters always *start early.* You have two years to complete your job search (if you are attending a program full-time). When you first enter an MBA program, you might think that two years is a long time, but it's not. I tell the students gathered for orientation, "Today is the first day of your job search." These new students may not even know where the restrooms are yet, but it's time for them to start looking for a job. In the MBA job market, the early bird really does get the worm. Part of commitment is making your job search a top priority and beginning to work on it the day you start your MBA program, if not sooner.

Luck happens when preparation meets opportunity.

—Anonymous

You must start early because a job search takes a lot of *planning* and *preparation.* Good job hunting requires you to learn a whole different set of skills and concepts. You have to prepare your career goals, research prospects and career options, and learn how to network, write a resume, and interview, among other tasks. If you don't, you are going to be left behind. There is very little in business that you can accomplish without thorough planning and preparation. Your job search will be your first lesson in implementing these skills.

Furthermore, it takes a certain *aggressiveness* and *hustle* to win in the MBA job market. MBAs are by nature an ambitious and aggressive bunch, which is one of the reasons employers like to hire them. Since MBAs are usually recruited for managerial careers, employers want to see a candidate who is confident, motivated, competitive, and aggressive. Managers who beat the competition, bring a new project to market, and turn around an ailing division have these same traits. The MBA job market is no place for the meek, complacent candidate. Good old-fashioned hustle plays a major role in creating opportunities.

MBAs are often criticized for being too aggressive. A call for aggressiveness doesn't mean you have carte blanche to be brash, cocky, offensive, and inconsiderate. The right kind of aggressiveness means taking initiative, following up, being first in line, not always taking no for an answer, and generally working as hard as you can to get a job and keep it. The art is learning how to be aggressive in strategy without developing an offensive, pushy style in interpersonal situations.

The winning kind of aggressiveness comes from a certain *hunger* to succeed. Students from less-advantaged backgrounds are often some of the best job hunters. They have such a voracious appetite for success and financial security that they just won't be denied. If a good career really means something to you and you are determined to succeed, you can.

The most successful job hunters are noted for their *perseverance.* A job search can be a long, tedious process. It is very easy to get tired and discouraged, but you just have to keep at it. Usually, you aren't going to find a job overnight. You have to keep making calls, mailing resumes, and knocking on doors. You can't give up or quit early. You will encounter some adversity along the way, but you have to be tough enough to keep on trying.

Let's not forget *boldness* and *creativity.* I am constantly amazed at the ways hungry, aggressive students invent to find jobs. I can never predict how the good students will get their leads, make their contacts, and sell themselves to win at job hunting. The best job hunters have a sense of boldness that is almost a reckless disregard for risk. They seem not to fear rejection and aren't afraid to be told no. Their hunger for a good career seems to override any fear they may have of the process. This attitude enables them to say "Why not?" instead of "Why?" and to invent new, creative ways to land a job. They will always try a new approach as long as it is within the bounds of honest, ethical behavior. They embody the entrepreneurial spirit that is so necessary in business today. Everybody uses the traditional job search strategies; be bold and creative enough to stand out from the crowd.

It is a very tough and competitive job market these days for MBAs. You can succeed in it, but you must realize that there are many MBAs with the characteristics I have just described who will beat you to the best jobs if you let them. Although I've told you that you *can* have a successful career, I'm not saying that you *will.* Your success depends almost entirely on how much effort you choose to expend and on how soon you start.

CHARTING YOUR COURSE

A fellow author said it best when he titled his book *If You Don't Know Where You're Going You'll Probably End Up Somewhere Else.* Too many MBAs approach their job search like a rudderless ship, wandering aimlessly among the many choices and opportunities. Simply stated, you must have a direction for your professional life before you embark on a job search. Why? Because a sense of direction will help ensure that you compete effectively in the job market and that the job you take will provide you with personal and professional satisfaction.

Having a direction in your professional life greatly increases the likelihood of your finding a rewarding and fulfilling career. It pains me to see people taking the rudderless ship approach to their professional lives. They run through a cycle of hopes and expectations followed by disappointments: another great new job just doesn't work out. The stress this cycle can cause often results in such unhappiness as marital and family problems, health problems, and substance abuse. These people are constantly searching for happiness, but they have no plan or direction in their search. Some lucky ones stumble into it through trial and error, but most stay frustrated.

The worst aspect of such stumbling is that it's unnecessary. With only a moderate amount of effort, you can discover a direction for your professional life that gives you satisfaction. The older I get the more I realize that life is too short to waste it in unsatisfying careers. It is particularly wasteful for you as an MBA to wander among choices and opportunities since you have the training and credentials that qualify you for so many satisfying and rewarding careers. Because you have put a lot of hard work into your education, you don't have to make the same compromises in your career that many people with less education do. All you need is to head in the right direction.

A career direction, then, is necessary; it is one of your most immediate needs. Without one you have little chance of succeeding in a business interview. Just about every employer wants to see that you have a direction charted for your career and that that direction fits in with the company's career opportunities. Businesspeople, in particular, are very goal oriented. They are trained to plan and organize, to set goals, and, of course, to accomplish them. They usually live in an environment of one-, three-, and five-year plans (some of even greater duration), each with profit, sales, and cost objectives. At the end of certain time periods, businesspeople measure their progress against these goals and are held accountable to them. Planning and goal setting are considered fundamental skills.

Think, then, how it will appear to an employer if you have not taken the time to develop any plans or directions for your career. You are in an interview, and sitting across the table is an employer who is shopping for a person with those skills fundamental to business success—planning and goal setting. Imagine his or her reaction if you haven't bothered to develop a plan for what should be one of your highest priorities—your career. An undergraduate might be able to get away with not having a career direction, but an MBA cannot. No self-respecting employer would consider hiring you; it's that simple. The employer will extend the inattention and carelessness you have shown in regard to your career to your expected performance on the job.

Furthermore, employers have learned that MBAs without well-developed career directions often leave in their early years with a company. This is a particularly troublesome problem for MBA employers, since high MBA salaries make MBAs expensive to train and therefore costly to lose. Employers are particularly alert to undirected MBAs and avoid them like the plague.

Notice that I stress formulating *directions* instead of goals. I am concerned about the way that goal setting is usually taught and implemented. Now, I am a strong believer in the motivating power of goals. Goals give us something to strive for and help us feel good about ourselves when we reach them. Life on a job without goals could quickly become empty and frustrating. However, being goal oriented by nature, businesspeople have a tendency to go too far with their goals. The attainment of goals can become an obsessive, driving force, marking a person as a success or failure. Goals are often rigid and inflexible, blinding the goal setter to new opportunities and directions. Too often, they are unrealistic and unattainable. In fact, many "success" books (particularly those in sales training) teach this single-minded pursuit of goals. People can become addicted to their goals, losing perspective on what these goals really represent. And MBAs are particularly susceptible to this addiction since goal setting is such a large part of their training.

While this approach to goal setting may work well in some business situations, it is a rather poor strategy for career and life planning. A more balanced and flexible approach is required. As already stated, people need direction. But a direction is just that—a broad plan, not a narrow path. It is not important for you to know *precisely* what job you want, but it *is* important for you to know what type of job you want. You need to move your career in a fairly well defined direction, but it is counterproductive and unreasonable to focus too narrowly. Your career direction should be sufficiently defined to enable you to focus on jobs that stand a strong chance of satisfying you, to easily develop job search strategies, and to demonstrate career maturity. At the same time, your direction needs to be broad enough to enable you to explore a variety of jobs and keep you open to opportunities that may present themselves. The approach taken in this book will help you define your interests, skills, values, and aptitudes in generic terms so you can identify the many different careers and different environments in which you could be happy—not just one "right" job.

Your career is a journey. The objectives you set for yourself are really just milestones of that journey as you see them at a given point in time with the often-limited information available to you. The problem is that this journey is not one you can plan very precisely. Your priorities and values will change as you age. Society and the world will continue to evolve, and the world of work will continue to change, probably more rapidly than ever. The days of linear, well-planned career paths are fast fading. Today, individuals are being challenged to develop skills that can be transferred to different environments. You need only to look at the upheaval caused by corporate mergers, restructuring, and takeovers in the eighties to appreciate the significance of being able to adapt to changing circumstances.

Most people who have worked for many years will tell you that they never expected to end up where they did in their career. For a variety of reasons (sometimes good and sometimes not so good), life moves in unexpected directions. That's why I suggest having objectives instead of goals. Objectives connote something to aim at and strive for. They seem to allow for the possibility that we may not reach them, and we tend not to feel too bad if we don't. Goals imply the end of a process, and not reaching them seems to make a person feel like a failure.

As you progress through your career, you need constantly to reevaluate your objectives. If you don't keep yourself open to redefining your objectives, you may miss out on a great opportunity. For example, should you pass up a promotion to manager of software marketing just because your goal is to become manager of customer service? Should you decide not to talk to Hewlett-Packard just because your goal has been to work for IBM? Of course not.

Your career journey never ends. Achievements and goals just mark your progress along whatever course you set. You will probably fail to reach certain objectives, exceed some, and discard others as no longer important. Chart your course, but be ready to change it when it makes sense. Aim as high as you want and set objectives, but be kind to yourself. Don't let your self-esteem get too closely tied to attaining your professional objectives.

BELIEVE IN YOURSELF

Start your job search with one fundamental premise—*you are good.* You must believe that you are the best person you know to hire and that you can perform well. All you need to prove that you are good is to find the right match for your skills and interests.

Let me try to persuade you that believing in yourself is crucial to your job search. Ask yourself these three questions: If I don't believe that I am the best person to hire, why should the employer choose me? If I don't think I can do outstanding work, why should the employer? If I don't believe I am good, how will I ever convince an interviewer I am? Get my point? If you don't believe in yourself, then nobody else will believe in you either. Since employers only want to hire good people, you'll be out of a job. I'm not asking you to deceive yourself, but there is no way that you could make it through an MBA program if you didn't have intelligence, motivation, and ambition. You may not be good at everything or good for every job, but you *are* good!

You have to have a positive attitude and confidence in your qualities as a professional and as a person. When you believe that you will succeed, the chances are greatly increased that you will. Of course, a positive attitude will not overcome substantial weaknesses. But once you have worked to qualify yourself, believe in yourself. Confidence works, and it's contagious. It will help you project the right attitude and insulate you from some of the ups and downs of the job search.

You also need to stop sending yourself negative messages. How many times have you told yourself that you are not experienced enough or not ambitious enough, your grades aren't good enough, or you're not whatever enough? You've probably done that many times. But how often have you told yourself that you are good, that you've done well at certain courses, or that you did a good job for your boss? How many times have you told yourself that you are very good at certain types of work? Probably not many.

You need to build your self-esteem. Tell yourself right now: "I am good." Say it louder. Say it as if you really mean it: "I am good." Say it more assertively. Think about all of your accomplishments and your awards. Now say it again: "I am good." Look in the mirror and tell yourself: "You can be a great employee and do a great job." Say these things over and over until you really believe them and feel it inside.

Okay, so you don't have much experience, or your grades could be a little better. You are never going to be perfect. Identify your weaknesses and work to overcome them, but don't dwell on them. Just because you have a few weaknesses doesn't mean that you aren't good. Quit being a perfectionist; nobody is perfect. Even the most successful people have weaknesses. In fact, successful people are usually far from perfect, but they have learned to have confidence in their strengths and to find a place where their strengths let them succeed.

Quit comparing yourself with others. Sure you need to know your competition and work to prepare yourself to meet it. But you shouldn't become convinced that you aren't good every time you see someone who is "better" than you are (whatever that means). Being good is not an either-or game. There will always be people who are better than you and worse than you in this world. Just because you are not "the best" or perfect does not mean that you aren't "good." Even the most successful person can find someone who is more successful by some measure than he or she is.

You have to believe in who and what you are as a job candidate. Believe in yourself. Be proud of what you have to offer. But don't get a swelled head, and don't get pompous. Be humble enough to know where you can improve. The odds are heavily stacked in your favor that there is a good spot for you in the working world if you are realistic enough to know where you fit best. The job search can be tough on your ego, and you wouldn't be human if your confidence never wavered or you never had doubts. What I'm talking about is not the day-to-day ups and downs but rather a foundation, a core belief that you really are good at what you do. With that, you can bounce back from rejection letters, survive cold calls to employers, endure endless hours of worry. If your foundation is solid, you'll press on.

MAKE SOMETHING HAPPEN

Of course, it is not enough just to believe in yourself. Just because you have an MBA doesn't mean you won't have to work hard to get a job. An MBA is a wonderful degree that will help to open many doors in your job search. But opportunity will not seek you out. While an MBA may help open the door when you knock, you have to be there knocking. Far too many MBAs become complacent in their job search. It's as if they believe that now that they have the degree they have joined the elite ranks of the business world and don't have to work at finding a job.

Let me state some cold, cruel facts: a large part of the business world isn't convinced that the MBA is worth something and, unless persuaded otherwise, will not even think about seeking you out. Other employers want to hire MBAs, but they will quickly pass by pompous, elitist job candidates. In addition, the MBA job market is as tough and competitive as any in this country. It is full of ambitious, hardworking people (like you) who will do anything it takes to get a good job. If you don't want to work to get a job, there are plenty of hungry MBAs out there who will. Being good doesn't change that.

I see it all the time in my own students. Each year some very smart people don't get jobs because they just don't work at it. Many MBA employers hire only a few candidates from each school. Each year the go-getters line up early in the year and walk away with the best jobs. Then, later in the year, others come to me complaining because they don't have any. Most of the time the simple fact is they got beaten by someone who hustled more than they did. Or they got beaten by students who worked harder to prepare themselves. They wonder why their friend was chosen for a site interview over them. Often it's because that student worked harder by taking more classes, volunteering for special projects, doing extra research, or spending more time on career planning.

The point is, folks, the MBA job market is very competitive. Not everybody has to be as hard-charging as a Wall Streeter or become cutthroat and ruthless, but you have to hustle and work to get what you want. Good jobs won't just fall into your lap. You have to take charge of your own fate and make something happen. The number one reason I see people fail in their job search is that they don't work hard enough at it. Maybe they don't believe in themselves enough to try, or perhaps they are just scared. But it doesn't matter. If you want a job bad enough, then you have to make something happen. If you don't get moving, who do you think is going to get you a job? Your teachers? Your placement director? Your parents? Your spouse? Your fairy godmother? You must commit yourself to taking charge of your own destiny if you want to succeed at the job search.

You have to make your own opportunities. So often I hear people talking about being "lucky" or "in the right place at the right time." People to whom good things happen usually have set themselves up to succeed. A student walks into my office and says, "I got lucky. I called this company and found out that a job is available right away. The employer says that I'm perfect for the position." Luck you say? I doubt it. Invariably, if I question the student, I find out that he or she did extensive research to find high-potential companies, made dozens and dozens of calls, and networked to get the contact. That student hustled and found an opportunity. It is rare to find anyone who got a "lucky break" without hard work playing a major role. You can make your own opportunities.

How? First, you must develop marketable skills and capabilities. The best step you can take to ensure a long and successful career for yourself and to open up opportunities is to arm yourself as well as you can with strong skills and capabilities. That means going beyond what the average MBA does. Business is starving for good people, and opportunity flows to talented people, even in bad job markets.

Unfortunately, being competent is not sufficient. All the skills in the world aren't much good unless you can find a place to use them. Some of these places will be obvious, but many will not be readily apparent. To make something happen, you have to open yourself up to all the possibilities. Those who find the most opportunities have the ability to keep an open mind as to jobs and companies that fit them and to the strategies that could be used in the job search process. Too many students seem to have blinders on. Too many students make gross assumptions about employers based on rumors on the "grapevine" and stereotypes. One student assumed that the largest Big Eight accounting firm did only accounting work. When told that it was also the largest consulting firm in the world, he went to work there. Another student assumed marketing was not a good choice until she attended a career program and learned what it really was about. Still another couldn't believe an alumni contact could lead to a job, but it did. Get rid of those blinders and open your eyes if you want to make something happen.

Should ye see afar off that worth winning,
Set out on the journey with trust;
And ne'er heed if your path at beginning
Should be among brambles and dust.
Though it is but by footsteps ye do it.
And hardships may hinder and stay,
Walk with faith, and be sure you'll get through it;
For "Where there's a will there's a way."

—Eliza Cook
From "Where There's a Will
There's a Way"

In *The Best-Loved Poems of the American People*, a Doubleday anthology compiled by Hazel Felleman.

You have to be where opportunity is. Rarely does opportunity come seek you out, particularly early in your career. If you aren't aggressive enough to get yourself into all the right places, then you can't possibly see an opportunity when the right time comes along. Successful people create their own luck with a hustling, aggressive attitude that leaves no stone unturned in the job search. They make every contact they can, use every strategy, and see all the companies they can. They know that an opportunity could be anywhere. Their approach creates a "right place at the right time" situation. I can't guarantee that your hustle and aggressiveness will create an opportunity (although they do about 90 percent of the time), but I can almost guarantee that there is little chance of your finding an opportunity if you aren't aggressive enough to go after it.

Let me translate this advice into some practical guidelines for making something happen:

- Get all the training you can while you are in school. You never know what particular skill will make you stand out from the crowd. Constantly look for chances, in and out of the classroom, to learn something marketable.
- Never miss a career program at your university. Nine times out of ten, an employer will talk about career options that you haven't thought of. One of them may fit you.
- Tell your family, friends, colleagues, and acquaintances that you are looking for a job. Everyone you know is a possible source of information that might lead to a job. The person you least suspect may give you your best lead.
- Use several job search strategies to maximize your reach. In particular, don't just depend on your college placement office.
- Never miss a chance to make contact with an employer, no matter how brief. If you can even just introduce yourself, it may pay off.
- Never rule out any employer until you have specifically been told no and told not to contact the company again.
- Never rule out a specific job until you have read the job description; job titles can be very misleading.
- Don't be afraid to ask for a job; people can't read your mind.
- Never give up.

I guess it all boils down to how much you want a job. Your success in job hunting will be proportional to your effort. Take control of your life; do something for yourself. Make something happen; don't wait for things to happen to you. I have seen many MBAs fail by not trying, but very, very few fail when they have tried their hardest. Into which category will you fall?

ETHICS AND HONESTY IN MBA PLACEMENT

The career planning and placement process is extremely important to the colleges and universities, employers, and students involved. All you have to do is to sit in the counselor's chair and help an MBA decide what to do with his or her life one time to realize the tremendous responsibility thrust upon all parties. Although, as discussed in a later chapter, the system can be easily abused, I have found that only a minute percentage of the employers I have dealt with have acted in an illegal or unethical fashion. The vast majority of the people in this business are highly competent professionals who conduct themselves in a strictly professional manner.

Most of the business world will not tolerate MBA job candidates who use unethical or illegal practices. I suggest that you decide from the beginning that you are going to conduct yourself in a manner that is above doubt or questioning. Employers generally have seen all the tricks, and you have very little chance of getting away with anything. If you plan your career and job search properly, you won't have any need to be deceitful. Such actions will only stand to hurt your chances of getting a job. In short, honesty truly is the best policy.

The College Placement Council, the professional organization for college placement officials and corporate recruiters, has issued the following statement of ethics for its members. Most graduate schools of business subscribe to these policies and expect their students and recruiting employers to do the same. This statement tries to establish standards of behavior that will ensure a fair and honest process for all parties. Read this statement carefully. I suggest that you adopt as your guiding principles the standards outlined in the section for job candidates. You should also familiarize yourself with the codes that apply to the college placement office and prospective employers.

PRINCIPLES FOR PROFESSIONAL CONDUCT FOR COLLEGE CAREER PLANNING, PLACEMENT, AND RECRUITMENT

The following principles are intended to provide a framework for the professional relationships among the colleges and the universities, employing organizations, and candidates involved in the recruitment of college graduates.

Colleges and Universities

Career planning and placement practitioners are responsible for establishing and monitoring practices which ensure the fair and accurate representation of students and the institution in the recruitment process.

Career planning and placement practitioners should promote and follow nondiscriminatory practices.

The professional services of a career planning and placement office, including all counseling and information aspects, facilities, and support services, should be available to students and organizations without charge when utilized for recruiting purposes.

The candidate's freedom of choice in the selection of a career or a position should be protected from undue influence by faculty, placement staff, and recruiters.

Career planning and placement practitioners should inform students of obligations, both financial and otherwise, when utilizing the services of agencies or other organizations performing recruiting services for a fee.

Recruiting Organizations

Organizations are responsible for the ethical and legal conduct of their representatives throughout the recruiting process and must assume responsibility for all representations made by authorized representatives.

Recruiters should be qualified interviewers and informed representatives of their organization and should respect the legal obligations of career planning and placement offices and request only those services and information that legally can be provided.

Recruiters should honor the policies and procedures of individual institutions and should refrain from any practice that adversely affects the interviewing and decision-making processes.

Recruiters should make a full and accurate presentation of all relevant information during the recruiting process and should advise the career planning and placement office of all recruiting-related activities not conducted through that office.

An employment offer that is accepted is a contractual agreement that is expected to be honored.

Candidates

Candidates should honor the policies and procedures of their institutions and should adequately prepare for the interviewing process and accurately present their qualifications and interests.

Candidates should sign up for interviews only when seriously considering the position for which the organization is interviewing, and should notify the career planning and placement office if they must cancel an interview appointment and the employer if they must cancel a plant/office trip.

Candidates are responsible for notifying organizations of their acceptance or rejection of offers by the earliest possible time and no later than the time mutually agreed upon.

Reimbursements for visits at an organization's expense should be only for those reasonable expenditures pertinent to the trip. If other organizations are visited on the same trip, the candidate should inform the organizations and prorate the costs.

An accepted offer is a contractual agreement that is expected to be honored. After accepting an offer, candidates should withdraw from the interviewing process and notify the career planning and placement office and other organizations with offers pending.

Remember that all parties involved are expecting you to behave ethically during the job search process. Employers will interpret your behavior as a job candidate as an indicator of your behavior as an employee.

CAREER PLANNING AND PLACEMENT OFFICES

If you are still in school, your greatest ally throughout this whole process will be your MBA career planning and placement office. It will usually provide a wide variety of services such as personal counseling, career interest testing, personality testing, career workshops and seminars, resume and interview training, and on-campus interview programs. It will also maintain a library of career resources and directories (including subject-specific, custom-designed resources), salary data, and job listings. In fact, never again in your job hunting lifetime will you find such a centralized wealth of assistance. To top it all off, it's free! You would be foolish to overlook it. All MBA candidates should visit these offices and become well acquainted with what they have to offer. Most provide some type of orientation program to familiarize you with their services.

Some universities have a single placement office to serve all academic divisions and all disciplines (a system known as centralized placement), while other universities have several placement offices serving the various divisions and student groups. The most desirable situation is for an MBA to have access to a placement office exclusively for MBAs. Less preferable but also desirable is a placement office for business students only. To provide specialized placement services for MBA students, some universities using a centralized placement office have a hybrid organization in which a member of that office is closely linked with the MBA program to provide specialized services. Whatever the form, you should take advantage of the placement services offered by your university.

The biggest advantage to having a specialized placement office or person devoted exclusively to MBAs is that placement services can be tailored to the particular needs of graduate business students. Every group of students trained in a particular discipline at a specific level is a little different from every other group of students when it comes to placement. And MBAs are no exception. Their job market is different, their career objectives are different, and their counseling needs are different. MBA-specific placement personnel often spend much of their time working with individual students, advising them on their job search, and with specific employers, helping them to fill particular job openings. This approach, called direct placement, differs from the more mass market approach often found in large undergraduate placement offices. In addition, specialized placement offices are more likely to have the special resources needed for the MBA job market.

If your school doesn't have a placement office just for MBAs, you should still plan to make maximum use of the services available. However, be aware that counselors who are unfamiliar with the MBA job market may give you some misleading advice (unintentionally, of course). For example, you may be told that you don't need a resume because the placement office uses a standard data sheet. For undergraduates, a data sheet is perfectly adequate. However, MBAs must have a resume. The job market requires it. Or, uninformed counselors may give you the wrong advice about what salary to request, salaries for MBAs being much higher than those for undergraduates. Also, be careful in your dealings with counselors who work mostly with students in technical fields; these counselors may overlook the importance of demonstrating good communication skills and selling yourself in an interview. To avoid the problems of being misadvised, you should seek out counselors who have some experience in the MBA job market.

If you are reentering the job market (even if you graduated several years ago), you should contact the placement office at your alma mater. Most placement offices provide alumni with access to their services in some fashion. In the MBA market, employers recruiting new graduates usually have openings for experienced hires as well and will often discuss non-entry-level MBA positions with university placement representatives. Many schools publish newsletters to which you can subscribe that contain periodically updated information on job openings. Some maintain a credential file of graduates through which employers can browse. Most graduate schools of business work very hard to maintain good relations with their alumni, and most are eager to assist a graduate reentering the job market.

Chapter 4

Marketing Yourself

First and foremost, you must understand that your job search is a form of marketing. Most job seekers fail to understand this principle. Their failure is a fundamental error that creates a barrier between them and their goal of finding a satisfying job. To be truly effective in the job search process, you must accept that you are setting out to market a product—you. Your task is to plan a marketing campaign that will successfully sell you to employers. Let's examine some of the fundamentals of a marketing program.

THE MARKETING CONCEPT

Suppose we use the example of a homeowner attempting to sell his house on his own. This homeowner needs to develop a marketing campaign. How would he do it? First, he would evaluate the house and property. What type of house is it, and what are its features? Based on his answers to these and other questions, he would set a price. Let's suppose that his house has a country-contemporary look and is fairly new. It is the kind of home that would appeal most to a young family (young professionals with one or two children). Reviewing its features, he decides to price the house at $125,000. Already he knows who is most likely to buy the property, so he needs to develop a plan to target the young-family market.

To attract prospective buyers to the house, he would write some advertising copy that identifies the house's strong points for young families. He would present this information in different forms, creating notices, classified advertisements, and probably some fliers and memos. The notices would be posted on bulletin boards, the ads would be placed in the classified section of local newspapers, and the memos and fliers would be distributed to friends, colleagues, and neighbors, among others. Of course, he would need "For Sale" signs for his lawn. In addition, he'd probably fix up the house a bit to make sure that it makes a good impression on prospective buyers. He might even plan an open house. Anticipating the arrival of potential customers, he'd want to have a sales pitch ready. And his sales pitch would change a little depending upon the person to whom he is talking. He would follow his marketing program, adjusting his strategies until he accomplished his objective: selling his house.

You're probably beginning to get the idea. Conceptually, your job search varies only slightly from the selling of a house, a car, soap, or any other product. The implementation of the strategies may differ, but the concepts are the same. Just as a homeowner must spend a substantial amount of time planning how to market his house or Procter & Gamble must devote lots of time to planning how to sell a particular laundry detergent, so must you plan your marketing campaign. It is not something you can approach with seat-of-the-pants tactics.

Your product is you. You too must determine your job objective and develop a target market based on that objective. You too need to identify likely prospects through your career research. You must decide on a price (your salary) at which you will sell your services. Next, you need to find appropriate channels through which to advertise. Your resume and cover letter are your primary advertisements. Their purpose differs little from that of a print or television ad. Interviews are your time to sell yourself, the time to persuade your customer (the employer) to buy (hire) you. Your marketing program needs to be very carefully orchestrated to bring you to the point of receiving a job offer.

Thus, you can see that your job search is just a series of basic marketing transactions. But you would be surprised at how few MBAs really seem to understand this—and even fewer implement it. The problem is not that MBAs don't go through the job search steps described but that they approach the process incorrectly. Competing in the MBA job market is not just a matter of listing your credentials on a resume and sending a copy of that resume to 150 names pulled from a directory, nor is it telling an interviewer why you dearly love finance. That's not marketing; that's wishful thinking. What this chapter presents is a new perspective. I urge you to read it closely so that you will learn how to market yourself more successfully.

FOCUSING ON THE EMPLOYER'S NEEDS

The modern marketing concept begins with the idea that you, the seller, must focus on the customer's needs. Consequently, the whole marketing process is cued by and revolves around the needs of the customer. Let's apply this concept to the job search process. The customer is the employer, since he or she is the one you want to purchase your services. At all times during this process, you must focus on the employer's needs. What are they? What qualifications

The heights by great men reached and kept
Were not attained by sudden flight,
But they, while their companions slept,
Were toiling upward in the night.

—Henry Wadsworth Longfellow
From "The Ladder of Saint Augustine"

is the employer looking for? What does the employer want new employees to do?

Generally, every employer will be trying to answer three basic questions about you:

- What are you like?
- What can you do for me now?
- What is your potential in my organization?

Each stage of the job search is designed to help the employer answer these questions about you. Before you will be hired, you must convince the employer that:

- You are the type of person who will fit into his or her organization.
- You can contribute significantly to that organization in the short run.
- You have the potential to take on greater responsibility and produce more for that organization in the future.

Notice that in this customer-oriented approach there is no mention of the employer's being concerned about your meeting your objectives. Although employers are concerned about the objectives you have for your career, they are interested primarily because you will be more productive for *them* if your objectives are met. Too many MBAs tell the prospective employer what they *want* rather than outline what they *can do* for that employer. You will never sell yourself to an employer by telling him or her how the company will meet *your* needs.

Let's use an example to underscore the dynamics between the buyer and the seller. A woman decides that she wants to buy a new car. She goes to her local car dealership. As the buyer or customer, she doesn't care how much money a sale would make for the car dealer or whether it would increase the dealership's volume. However, she does care whether the car performs well and is fun to own. She wants to know what the car is like, what it can do for her, and whether buying it would be a good investment. If she is concerned at all about the dealer's getting a fair price, it is only because she wants the dealership to stay in business to service the car. Of course, the dealer also has his or her own objectives to meet. The two of them come together in a marketing transaction. They negotiate a purchase, and, if the terms satisfy their respective needs, a sale is made. Even though the transaction must meet the objectives of both parties, the stages prior to the agreement are all customer oriented.

In this example, you are analogous to the dealer (both of you are doing the selling), and the employer is analogous to the customer (both of them are doing the buying). The car dealer knows that the woman must be persuaded that the car meets her needs before she will buy it. Similarly, you must show an employer that you can do what he or she needs. It is up to the dealer to make sure that the sale meets his or her needs just as it is up to you to make sure that a job meets your needs. But in neither case is the customer responsible for the seller's objectives. In order to encourage interest in the product or service, the seller must focus on the customer's needs.

Fortunately, hiring employees is not nearly as impersonal as buying a car. Employers do care about you as a person. However, their professional responsibility is to hire someone who can make money for the business and who will be able to produce for the company in the long run. Therefore, your focus has to be on showing employers how you can meet their needs.

SELLING YOURSELF

The job search process, especially the job interview, is a classic case of personal selling. In order to win a job, you must eventually come face to face with an employer and sell yourself. Whether you are offered a position ultimately depends on your ability to communicate with the employer and persuade him or her that what you have to offer is worth buying.

So how do you actually sell yourself? Let's look at some examples. When I teach workshops on this subject, I usually start by asking students to do some selling. First, I ask a student to stand up and sell the group his or her favorite record album. The student generally finds this relatively easy. A typical sales pitch goes something like this:

> This is a fantastic album. The title cut is one of the best songs I have ever heard. When I listen to the music, I feel excited and

happy. The album is great for getting a group of people dancing at a party. The lyrics are easy to understand, and I often sing along with the songs. The words are really meaningful to me. It's an album I just love to listen to, and I strongly recommend it.

Can you hear the student's enthusiasm for the album? This is clearly a product that is worth its price to this person, and, more important, you as the potential buyer know what it will do for you.

Next, I pick two people from the group, and I set the scene. There are two friends: one is a job hunter, and the other works for a company that has a job opening. I ask the friend of the job hunter to sell this person to the company's personnel director. Students usually find this task relatively easy as well. They generally say such things as:

> This person did a great job for her previous employer, and I think she would be really productive in our manufacturing area.

> Tom is really terrific with numbers. I would trust him to do any type of financial analysis for me.

> I really admire the way Sue works with people. In our home-owner's association, she is always able to smooth out differences and negotiate good compromises.

> His colleagues tell me that he is one of their highest-rated employees. It would be a real coup if we could get him.

> Karen is a great team player. She would fit in really well with our new marketing team.

> It would be a big mistake not to talk to this person. Trust me, she's good.

Notice the enthusiasm in these recommendations. The students can sell another person without difficulty.

Now comes the clincher. I ask a student to stand up and sell himself or herself to the group. At stake is that student's ideal job. Immediately, every student freezes and looks the other way, hoping I won't choose him or her. When I finally pick someone, that person usually protests and then, with a good deal of embarrassment, stuttering, and contemplation, says such things as:

> I did well in my last job.

> I have an MBA and a BS in finance, and I think I'm really well prepared.

> As you can see from my resume, I have some experience in marketing through my internship last summer.

> People tell me that I work really well with people.
>
> My class project last year was a research paper in the chemical industry, so I am familiar with your problems.

Notice how uninspired these statements are and how much less they sell than the previous statements. Students are usually terrified when asked to sell themselves. They can think of strong sales pitches for a record album and for their job-seeking peers, but they don't know how to begin to sell themselves. When they are asked to sell themselves, they lack enthusiasm and confidence and are unable to tell the prospective employer that they are good and how they can meet the employer's needs.

I think you can see by now that selling yourself for a job is really no different from selling a record album. Let me ask you a few questions:

- If you aren't enthusiastic about yourself, why should the employer be?
- If you don't have confidence in your abilities, why should anyone else?
- If you don't think you are good to hire, why should the employer?
- If you don't tell the employer how you can help meet the employer's needs, how will he or she know—by osmosis? mind reading?

Yes, I know that selling yourself is not easy. But I also know the top candidates do it. You will be called on to sell throughout your career in the business world. You will have to sell your ideas, your proposals, your products, your company, and yourself. You might as well start learning now. After all, what more important product do you have to sell than yourself?

My formula for successful selling is not very complicated, but implementing it does take work. To sell yourself effectively, you must:

- know your product—you
- know your customer—the employer
- focus on what you can do for the customer
- communicate with the customer in a clear and confident manner
- have courage

No salesperson can be effective if he or she doesn't know the product well. How can you begin to tell an employer why you would be a good employee if you don't know why yourself? That's one of the reasons self-assessment is the first step in this process. Think about that record album. Would you try to sell it if you hadn't listened to it often enough to know it well? The same is true for your friend. Would you walk into the personnel director's office at your company and recommend that person for a job if you didn't know him or her very well? Of course, you wouldn't. But you would be amazed at the number of students who walk into an interview without a clear idea of what career will suit them best and what their marketable strengths are. You *must* know yourself. Don't be fooled into believing that this type of knowledge comes naturally. It doesn't. I can guarantee you that it won't simply be there when you are faced with selling yourself.

Somebody said that it couldn't be done,
But he with a chuckle replied
That "maybe it couldn't," but he would be one
Who wouldn't say so till he'd tried.
So he buckled right in with the trace of a grin
On his face. If he worried he hid it.
He started to sing as he tackled the thing
That couldn't be done, and he did it.

. . . .

There are thousands to tell you it cannot be done,
There are thousands to prophesy failure;
There are thousands to point out to you, one by one,
The dangers that wait to assail you.
But just buckle in with a bit of a grin,
Just take off your coat and go to it;
Just start to sing as you tackle the thing
That "cannot be done," and you'll do it.

—Edgar A. Guest
From "It Couldn't Be Done"

You cannot be effective at selling yourself unless you know what your customer's needs are, since our whole marketing concept revolves around meeting those needs. Even if you took my advice and know yourself like a book, you will be lost unless you know how your strengths will help the employer. You might have tremendous skills in certain areas, but those skills must be needed by the employer for you to be hired. Or the employer may not realize how you could meet one of his or her needs. The whole process boils down to meeting employer needs—if you don't know them, you're lost.

Carefully researching every employer that arranges a screening interview may be impractical (although you probably should prepare thoroughly for this stage for your top choices). But you need to be generally familiar with the industry and the types of firms with which you are interviewing. Let's suppose your career objective is getting a job in the banking industry. You may not know Citicorp, NCNB, or Mellon very well before the screening interview. However, you should be aware of general trends in the banking field. You should realize that banking is undergoing many changes—for example, that because of deregulation, acquisitions have transformed the industry, that managing customer relationships is increasingly important, and that profit pressures are intense and escalating. That much you had better know before choosing banking as a career objective, just to be sure you will fit well and be happy there. But if you do know that much, you'll also know enough to be able to tell a bank how you can help it in today's banking environment. The good news is that the elements of the selling process I have outlined so far—knowing yourself and knowing your customer—are also the basic elements of career planning. As you will see, you should not choose a career objective unless you already know yourself and the industry well enough to know that you would be a good fit.

However, knowing yourself and knowing the company are not quite enough. Many MBAs simply recite their life history, review their courses and wonderful grades, and list their work experiences. They never so much as say to the employer, "I think I can do a great job *for you*." Sure, employers may be able to assume some things from your credentials, but that's not selling. In marketing, there's an old saying: "Sell the sizzle, not the steak." What this means is that you don't sell the fact that the steak is a half-pound, choice T-bone. You sell how delicious it's going to taste, its wonderful aroma, the pleasure the customer will derive from eating it, and how good that customer will feel after he or she eats it. You sell what it *can do* for the customer, not what it *is*. You sell the benefits of your product, showing the customer how it meets his or her needs. You should use the same strategy when you sell yourself. Sell yourself by using facts (for example, your courses, grades, and experience) as concrete, supporting evidence to back up your basic statement that *the employer* (not you) will benefit tremendously if you are hired.

It's your job to show employers why they should hire you, not theirs to discover it. It's your job to show them the ways in which you are superior to other candidates. And it's your job to persuade them that you will perform well in the position you are seeking. And I don't mean meekly or apologetically. I mean with direct, confident statements that say pointedly, "I am good, and these are my credentials." You need to follow this approach when you write your resume, cover letter, and follow-up letter and when you give your interview. Make sure that the employer knows unequivocally what you can do for the company.

Does the prospect of telling an employer that you are good and that you are the best person you know to hire put a lump in your throat? I understand that it is not always comfortable to sell yourself. You'll need courage to walk into an employer's office and tell him or her that you are good. But if you don't, somebody else will, and that person will get the job. You'll never totally get rid of the butterflies—you'll just have to push through them. But how do you get the courage? Experience and accomplishments are the surest confidence builders I know. Successful classwork, a class project, a successful internship, or a leadership experience in a student club can really help boost your confidence. All of us are unsure of our abilities until we test them and prove to ourselves that we can perform. Even with your experience and accomplishments, you probably will still be a little scared. Remember that courage comes mainly from facing fear and looking past it. What's the worst that can happen? You might feel a little embarrassed afterward, but is feeling a bit flustered really so bad? I think not. There aren't any magic answers for finding courage. You will just have to make up your mind to be confident, pushing yourself to forget your fear.

Finally, you must have the interpersonal communication skills needed to articulate the reasons you should be hired. You need to put it in words that are persuasive and enthusiastic. MBAs are expected to be strong communicators. Not only do good interpersonal skills help you articulate what you want to sell but they also demonstrate to the interviewer that you possess skills essential to career success. Fortunately, most MBAs seem to be pretty good communicators; it's the lack of knowledge that gets in the way.

Now let's look at how it might sound if you sell yourself properly. The following are revisions of the weak personal selling statements that appeared earlier in this section. Here we have selling statements that really do sell:

> In my last job, I was commended several times for my superior performance. I believe that I can accomplish the same thing with your firm.

My MBA and BS in finance demonstrate my extensive preparation in finance. I believe that that preparation will enable me to become a productive financial analyst with your company very quickly.

As you can see from my resume, I was a marketing intern last summer. In that position, I worked on a project similar to those you are describing. During this assignment, I developed some of the market research skills I need to work in product management.

My colleagues and friends have always commented on my people skills. I believe that my greatest strength is my ability to integrate quickly into a work team and to get along with a wide variety of people.

It's interesting to hear you talk about the productivity problems in the chemical industry. Last year, I did a research paper on that topic. Instead of being frightened away from the industry, I was actually drawn to it because I think my combination of engineering and business skills can help solve some of those problems.

Notice how effective these statements are. Each presents an enthusiastic, confident, and concrete assurance of something the job hunter can contribute to the employer. The candidate's meaning is very clear. He or she is saying, "I can do something for you," and, "I am good at something." That's how you sell yourself.

Now that I have you all fired up and ready to begin selling yourself, let me remind you that there is such a thing as overselling. MBAs, in particular, are criticized for being too aggressive. Good marketing is not obnoxious. There is a big difference in being aggressive in strategy and being aggressive in style. An aggressive marketing strategy works; an aggressive marketing style only turns people off. Be forthright, direct, honest, and self-promoting, not pompous, arrogant, or demanding. In a word, sell to employers with the same tact you'd expect from them if the roles were reversed.

TARGETING YOUR MARKET

The most effective job campaigns are those in which the job seeker devotes time to identifying high-quality prospects. Your individual portfolio will not appeal to every employer nor will you want it to. You need to take the time to locate the market "segment" to which you want to sell your services. This segment will comprise a group or groups of employers who are likely to have a need for an employee with your qualifications and with whom you stand a good chance of being happily employed. You will probably only waste your time, money, and effort with a shotgun approach. Contrary to what you may believe, narrowing your field of potential employers will actually increase your chances of success. (For a more detailed discussion of the steps involved in targeting your market, see Chapter 9, "Planning Your Job Search Campaign.")

Stories of job seekers who found employment using all sorts of untargeted methods abound. While these stories may be true, there is no doubt that the highest yields result from a carefully researched and targeted effort. I knew one student who landed a job with a few dozen letters, but those letters were developed after weeks of research. Each letter identified the particular company's problems and showed how the candidate's training had prepared him to help solve those problems. The letters were so well written that almost every one resulted in a job interview.

There are many ways to differentiate between market segments. Criteria vary considerably from person to person. Some job seekers differentiate by industry, others by geography, and still others by job category. Your choices will depend on your career objective. What is most important is that you take the time and make the effort to research the thousands of prospective employers in this country to find those whose needs have the best potential of matching your career objective. Realize that you cannot possibly develop an effective marketing campaign to reach all potential employers. Many people spend months mailing resumes to and filling out applications for companies for which their services do not meet any need. Your search is more likely to be effective if you focus your marketing efforts.

Once you have differentiated the larger market into homogeneous segments, be prepared to develop a variety of marketing plans. Each segment will, by definition, have distinct needs that you must address. The real value of segmenting and targeting your market is that it enables you to tailor your marketing efforts (modify your resume or take a different approach in interviews, for example) to appeal more directly to the needs of each segment.

HONESTY IN MARKETING

The misperception that marketing is by its very nature dishonest, manipulative, and deceptive is common. Perhaps it is this misunderstanding that prevents us from effectively marketing ourselves. Even though it is true that marketing has often been abused, it is not true that marketing is abusive by nature. We are all too familiar with the used car salesman who sells junk or the pushy insurance salesperson who won't leave or the TV commercials that lie or stretch the truth. Somehow, marketing seems to carry with it the image of con men. But in the purest economic sense, marketing is nothing more than the process by which our economy operates. Without marketing, the exchange of goods and services would be difficult. Therefore, it does not follow that in order to market yourself you must be deceitful.

In fact, marketing in an effective job search requires complete honesty. In no instance should you lie, mislead, or overstate anything during any stage of your job search. There is no room for a dishonest resume, a lie in an interview, a forged transcript, or even an embellished answer. Even seemingly harmless things such as fluff or stretching the truth have no place. Nothing will lose you a job faster than a recruiter's discovery that you have misled him or her in order to win a job. Most companies are reputable and simply do not want to employ individuals who are dishonest in any way.

You will have many opportunities during your job search to make untrue statements—on a resume, in a letter, or in an interview—that have little likelihood of being verified. The temptation to embellish or overstate qualifications is great. It is also very difficult to know how far is too far when you're selling yourself. As a general rule, don't take chances. Be conservative. Most people grossly underestimate what they have to offer an employer, so there is usually little reason to stretch the truth or to lie about anything.

Use this simple test to help you decide on the appropriateness of what you say in selling yourself. When you are considering a statement for inclusion in a resume or letter or when you are preparing an answer for a possible interview question, imagine being confronted by an employer about the statement you're about to make. Will you be able to look that employer directly in the eye and with confidence answer, "Yes, that is true"? Do you feel yourself needing to soften or apologize for the representation that you have made? If so, you may have gone too far. If you notice a sinking feeling in your stomach, a slight nervousness, sweaty palms, or any other indication that you cannot handle that representation, avoid it. Never make any representations that you cannot support wholeheartedly. To do so could have damaging consequences for your job search.

To effectively market yourself, you should present yourself in the best possible light, fully stating your accomplishments and potential. You are entitled to play up your strengths and assets, while minimizing your weaknesses. That approach is not dishonest. Nowhere is it written that you must reveal all of your shortcomings and minimize your strong points. Everyone has weaknesses as well as strengths. Sell your strengths. Lead with your strong suit. Focus the employer on what is good about you, not on what could be wrong. Just be careful that you don't cross that fine line between fully stating your strengths and misrepresenting them.

OVERCOMING THE PERSONAL BARRIERS TO EFFECTIVE MARKETING

There are many barriers to overcome during the job search process. Included among these are personal inhibitions. The three most common problems that job candidates face are the fear of rejection, the inability to think and speak highly of themselves, and feelings of inferiority (being intimidated by interviewers and prospective employers). Success in the job search requires that you master your discomfort and fears.

Nobody Likes to Be Told No

I have often wondered how many job seekers fail because they are afraid to risk rejection. Who among us likes to be told, "No, we don't want you"? All of us want to be liked and highly regarded, and we all want to be the candidate selected to fill the job opening. We need to know that our peers and our colleagues respect us and our professional capabilities. Yet, the job search demands that we expose our egos to scrutiny and possible criticism and face the chance of being rejected. It isn't easy, because being told no hurts.

There is no way to avoid the risks of the job search. Some of your efforts are bound to end in failure or rejection. However, don't personalize every rejection. It is clear that most people are much too sensitive to the no's of the job search. These people see every interview they don't get, every job offer they don't receive, and every letter that goes unanswered as a personal put-down. For them, the job hunt is an extremely scary personal proposition because they allow it to become a test of their self-worth.

Let's propose an alternative to this approach in keeping with our marketing concept. Marketing is the process of bringing together a service that a job seeker is selling with a need that an employer is trying to fill, so a rejection for a job opening only indicates the inability of the seller's product to meet the buyer's needs. Most of the rejections that you receive are not, in fact, rejections of you as a person. Employers may warm to you as an individual but perceive that your professional qualifications are not suited to their needs. In my experience, the vast majority of rejections simply testify to a mismatch of the job seeker's abilities and the employer's needs. Unfortunately, rejections take the form of negative phrases such as "you aren't," "you need more," and "we don't want." Don't let these rejection statements destroy your confidence and self-esteem. You need to prepare yourself for rejections (you will get many before you land a job). Realize that you can't match up with every job.

Of course, rejections are not always the result of mismatched abilities and needs. You will be competing against very qualified people, and it can be a "cold, cruel world" at times. Some of you will find yourselves losing jobs to candidates who are better qualified than you are for a specific position. You simply can't avoid that risk when you compete in the business world. However, if you have put forth your best effort to be the best candidate you can, you will find a place in the business world. You may have to alter your expectations slightly, but somewhere there is a match. Guard yourself against assuming that the reason you didn't get an interview or a job offer is that you are not good enough. Honestly evaluate each situation, and don't be so quick to put yourself down. Have confidence in yourself, and give yourself the benefit of the doubt.

The following example should help you to understand rejections from the employer's point of view. Recently, I served on an interview team assigned to fill a position for the college. From a long list of applicants, we chose to interview five people. The team thoroughly enjoyed talking to all of the candidates. All five were very bright and likable. When we made our final choice, we rejected three candidates: one had great potential but needed some more experience, another had too much experience and was clearly overqualified for the job, and the third lacked experience in an area critical to the performance of the job. We would have been very satisfied with either of the remaining two, but one candidate had somewhat stronger work experience, so we recommended hiring that person. We passed by (rejected) four candidates, although we liked them all and knew that any one of them would have been acceptable. We chose the candidate we perceived to be the best match for our needs.

Let's suppose that the worst case comes true and an employer says that your professional background and your education are not good enough, simply that you as a candidate do not rate highly enough. Has that employer's assessment touched your self-esteem? No, because the company is still only rejecting your *professional qualifications,* not you as a person. Your feelings of self-worth should not depend on your success as a professional. Regardless of that success, you have worth as an individual. Focus the rejection where it truly belongs—on your qualifications, not on you as a person—remembering that what an employer knows of you as a professional is limited to some impressions gathered during a few short interviews. Rejection will never be easy, but it will be much easier if you don't internalize the inevitable rejections.

The bottom line is that during the job search you cannot avoid the risk of rejection. Even though you can minimize the risk through an effective marketing campaign focused on a clearly defined market segment, you will not be able to remove the risk entirely. It is up to you to approach the job search process with a mature understanding of rejection that enables you to hold on to your self-confidence and self-esteem. Don't worry about failing. Worrying will only cause you to miss out on opportunities.

"Don't Brag!"

Most of us grow up hearing our parents tell us, "Don't brag," "Be humble," and, "Don't be conceited." We're taught that we're not supposed to boast about ourselves, and, consequently, we learn to label people who talk highly of themselves as vain. These attitudes can create a significant psychological hurdle that must be overcome if you are going to sell yourself effectively. Now is the time to amend some of these childhood dictates.

A job search is your time to brag about yourself, your time to discuss your accomplishments and abilities with confidence and pride. It's your time to stand up and say, "I'm the best person I know to hire!" Of course, you don't want to overstate your strengths, but the fact is that most people grossly underestimate their value as an employee. Give yourself complete credit. No employer will criticize or reject you for honestly and assertively presenting your case.

There is a key distinction between the harmful vanity we were taught to avoid and "honest sales." Some people boast of themselves to put others down. They want to prove themselves better than others, not in a healthy, competitive way, but in a game of one-upmanship. They devalue someone else to raise their own stock. This approach is clearly wrong and will not earn points with employers. Honest sales means selling an employer on your accomplishments and abilities. For the good of your career and job search, you must learn to think and speak highly of yourself as a professional. Avoid the "aw-shucks" approach and do not apologize for your successes. So long as your intent is not to disparage another person and your representations about yourself are honest and believable, it's okay. You will not be perceived as conceited.

The secret to "bragging" about yourself successfully (i.e., not sounding overly boastful or creating a negative response in the listener) is to use your accomplishments and successes as evidence of your claims. For example, telling a prospective employer that you are a good producer may sound hollow. But if you add to this claim the information that you improved the productivity of your work group by 20 percent last year, no employer will object to your original characterization.

Earlier, in the section "Honesty in Marketing," I mentioned a test that would help you to determine the appropriateness of selling statements. You should be aware of one caveat. You may feel uncomfortable with a selling statement not because it misrepresents the facts but because you are uneasy with the idea of aggressively promoting yourself. If the latter is true, ignore your uneasiness. It is a false reading. Remember that embellishing the facts is wrong, but that simply presenting yourself in the best possible light is the *essence of marketing*.

Lesser Than Thou

The job search can be a terribly intimidating process, particularly for the MBA with little or no work experience. Your fears can lead you to perceive every employer (or employer's representative) as an obstacle in your path to meeting your objective—getting a suitable job. You believe that the person sitting across from you has control of your future. After all, he or she has the power to reject you for the position you are seeking. Your mind whirls as you try to decide how you should behave in order to be accepted. In this state, it is very easy to fall back on behavior patterns that have worked in the past. The role of student is probably very familiar to you. For two years (or more if you attended an MBA program part-time), you have been in a "one-down" position in relation to professors and administrators. They control the university, and their power and authority are much greater than yours are as a student. This is the norm, and, after years of existing in that environment, students tend to become accustomed to not asserting themselves.

Understandably then, many students and graduates enter the job search with a "lesser-than-thou" attitude. They are intimidated and feel beholden to the employer. Sometimes, their feelings border on fear. Projecting a sense of inferiority is a sure way not to get hired. The successful job seekers are those who can overcome their intimidation and approach employers as equals, letting respect and courtesy guide their interactions. Remember that there is a big difference between showing the employer respect and courtesy and approaching him or her with a one-down, lesser-than-thou attitude. Respect and courtesy are required in every relationship, regardless of the relative power and authority of the people in that relationship. Be careful to distinguish deference from respect. Some of the common symptoms of a lesser-than-thou attitude include using too many "sirs" or "ma'ams," being afraid to ask questions, not identifying the job wanted, and showing too much gratitude for the interview. As a job candidate, you are required to demonstrate that you can behave properly, not submissively.

Try to see the interview as the employer sees it. The employer doesn't expect you to be grateful or excessively polite. When I speak with an employer who is extremely enthusiastic about a job candidate he or she has recently interviewed, invariably I hear the employer describe their interview as "just like talking to one of my colleagues." Of course, many factors are needed to create this feeling, including similar interests and values. But it is clear that a good colleague-type relationship is not based on intimidation. Associates do not feel inferior or superior to one another. The employer wants to hire someone with whom he or she can imagine working. If you can walk into an interview and have a professional discussion as if you were already on the payroll and had an office down the hall, you have bettered your odds of getting the job. One of the surest ways I know to impress an employer is to make him or her forget that you aren't already an employee. You will give the impression of a confident and mature professional. The interviewer will walk away thinking that you're that company's kind of employee.

You won't be able to have that type of an impact if you are intimidated by the process and the employer. You have to break free of the one-down student role and overcome your fear of the job search. You must believe that you are a competent professional. You may lack certain skills and experience, but you don't lack ability and intelligence. You are good or you could not complete an MBA degree. You are on a par with the employer, at least in terms of professional worth. You could be the interviewer's colleague tomorrow. In a few short weeks, he or she could be coming to your office to get information from you, and, in several months, you could be making recommendations on important issues to that person. Just because you are a student or a recent graduate does not mean that you should be intimidated by an employer. Go to the interview with the attitude that you are neither better nor worse than the interviewer. You are two professionals about to discover whether a match of interests, skills, and values exists between you and the employer's company. Don't allow yourself to feel inferior to the employer.

THE KEYS TO MARKETING YOURSELF SUCCESSFULLY

To be an effective marketer, you must focus on employers' needs. However, you shouldn't have the impression that only their needs count. Your needs and your objectives are as important as the employers' are. Throughout this process you will be evaluating employers on whether they meet your needs. Each party is responsible for satisfying his or her own needs. You control this process as much as the employer does. The employer chooses whom he or she wants to interview; you choose for whom you want to work. Since you are the seller, it is your job to persuade the buyer (an employer *you* have chosen to approach) to purchase your services. To make the sale, you need to show the employer that you can fill one or more of the company's needs. But, remember, you are deciding who your prospects are and to whom you will market yourself.

The following guidelines should help you market yourself. Together, they provide a summary of practical procedures for the job search process:

Develop a plan. Develop a marketing plan well ahead of time and follow it.

Target your campaign. Focus your marketing efforts on those companies that need candidates with your qualifications. Do your homework beforehand, so that you find high-quality potential matches.

Position yourself in the market. Don't try to sell yourself for jobs for which you aren't qualified. Recognize your strengths and weaknesses and market your strengths.

Know your customer. Research your target companies, and create an appropriate sales pitch for each. Remember that each company is unique.

Package your product well. Present yourself as a top-notch candidate. Write a good advertisement (resume), wear clothing appropriate for business, and behave in a professional manner.

Focus on your strengths. Constantly remind the employer of what you have to offer.

Focus on the employer's needs. Show how you can contribute to the company and fill *its* needs. Persuade the employer that you will be an asset.

Be aggressive. The aggressive candidate usually wins. Take the initiative, pursue all leads, and follow through. Push, but do so with tact and class.

Know what sells. Know what your competition has to offer so that you know what to sell.

Essential to the job search process is the exchange of information. There will be many opportunities for you to collect the information that you need to make your decisions. You should feel free to ask any question concerning the company and the position sought. In fact, most employers will think less of you if you don't ask questions. But your questions should not be phrased in such a way as to make the employer responsible for your needs. Too often, students go into interviews and talk about their objectives and fail to show how they meet the employers' needs. Remember that you will achieve your objectives only if you sell your services effectively to the employer.

MARKETING WORK SHEET

Use the following exercise to help you implement the concepts and strategies presented in this chapter.

GIVEN: I am a product.
               Employers are my customers.

OBJECTIVE: I have to sell me.

What can I do for an employer? (List specific skills and tasks.)

For what jobs am I most qualified?

Why should customers buy my services?

Which employers are most likely to need my skills and talents?

How am I going to sell my product to this market segment? What will be my marketing plan?

How will I package myself to my advantage?

What should my sales pitch be, and how will I alter it for different companies?

How does my product compare with that of my competitors?

Chapter 5

Managing the Career Planning and Job Search Process

There are two stages in the process that leads from graduate school to the workplace: career planning and the job search. These phases are inextricably tied together. Each, however, is quite different and requires a very different set of skills. You must be adept at both to be successful in meeting your professional objectives.

Career planning is the first phase of the process. During this phase, you devote your time to discovering your own values, needs, and ambitions and to defining your options in the world of work. Most of your work in this phase ends when you reach a decision on what job objective(s) you wish to pursue in the marketplace. This phase is a period of introspection, research, and analysis and is best characterized as an *exploration* stage.

The second phase, the job search, includes most of the steps traditionally identified with job hunting, including the writing of resumes and interviewing. During this stage, you and the employer come together in the marketplace, hoping to establish a match of needs and objectives. This phase concludes with the acceptance of a job offer and is best characterized as the *marketing* stage.

Both phases call on you to use skills with which you may be unfamiliar and that may prove difficult to master. Succeeding at this process requires you to make extensive use of the following skills:

- *prioritizing*—the art of determining what is most important
- *compromising*—learning that you can't have it all
- *analyzing*—probing and questioning to collect data and make decisions
- *self-disclosure*—being honest and objective about your own needs and goals

- *being disciplined*—following a systematic method to reach your goals with no motivator but yourself
- *researching*—learning how to find information
- *decision making*—making choices based on the information you collect

If you find yourself weak in any of these areas, you'll need to take steps to improve your abilities. There is no substitute for these skills.

Let me warn you of a potentially disastrous mistake. The number one reason that students fail in their job search (either not finding a job or not liking the one that they find) is inattention to career planning. Most students (and most adults) want to bypass the career planning stage and go straight to the job search, ignoring the best advice of counselors and placement professionals. These individuals begin their job search with little understanding of where they want to go and where they can go in their careers. Don't make this mistake. If you want to succeed in your job search, you must spend a considerable amount of time and energy preparing for the job search phase. You simply cannot be successful in your job search without a thorough grounding in career planning.

A WORKING MODEL

The figure on page 85 illustrates the career planning and job search process. The model establishes a framework for your professional development journey. It will take you from not having a job objective to securing a job in the field of your choice. You should plan to proceed through all of the steps shown in the model in the sequence shown, from left to right and from top to bottom.

Every job seeker begins the process at a different stage, depending on his or her level of career development. And even though everyone passes through all of the stages outlined *at some point,* not everyone needs to explore each part of the process at the beginning of every job search. For example, some MBA candidates need to begin with self-assessment, while others may already know in which field and in what type of corporate environment they want to work. Others may know fairly well how to find a job but are confused about their career objective. The first step, then, in any job search is to evaluate exactly at which stage you need to begin the larger process.

The model is also limited to the extent that it implies that each step is a finite stage, with discrete starting and stopping points. In fact, each stage really blends into the next. The starting point for one stage may overlap with the ending point of a previous stage.

Model Overview

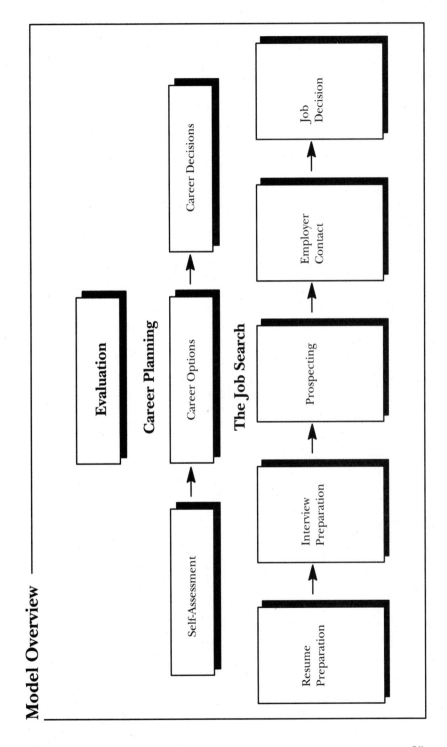

For example, it is quite common for people to complete the self-assessment stage and begin researching career options only to discover that they failed to evaluate themselves as completely as they should have. In such a case, researching career options causes the student to reassess the accuracy of his or her earlier self-assessment. If you find that as you learn more you are returning to earlier stages and rethinking your conclusions, you are on the right track. Expect some reevaluation as you go through the process, but complete most of each stage before the next is completed.

The steps in the process are conceptualized as three levels. These levels are *evaluation, career planning,* and the *job search.* At each level, you will need to ask yourself certain questions. By answering them, you will be able to determine approximately where you stand in the career development process.

The First Step—Evaluation

Before you start any specific steps in the career planning and job search process, you need to evaluate where you are in the process and what work you have to do. Evaluation is a critical step. I encourage you to begin it very early, preferably with the help of a counselor. You need to answer these questions:

- Where am I in the career development process?
- What should my plan of action be?
- What is my timetable for completing each step?
- What resources are available to me, and where are they?

Phase I—Career Planning

Self-Assessment. You cannot begin to make progress in career planning until you understand who you are as a person and where your talents and interests lie. During this phase, you will answer the following questions:

- Who am I?
- What are my personal goals?
- What is important to me in a career?
- What strengths do I have to sell?
- What weaknesses do I have to work on before my job search?

Career Options. Once you know what your personal goals are, you have to test them against the reality of the marketplace to see whether you can find a satisfying career in the business world. You will develop answers to these questions:

- What generally are the career options in business?
- What qualifications are required to enter specific business fields?

- What would it be like to work in certain career areas?
- What is the advancement potential in each of these areas?
- What type of person would enjoy working in each area?

Career Decisions. What a critical stage! At this moment in the process, you are formulating your professional objective. This objective (or objectives) will be central to the entire second stage. Answer the following questions very carefully:

- Where will my experience fit best?
- Where will my interests fit best?
- Where will I be happiest?
- What do I really want to do?

Phase II—The Job Search

After you have determined what you want to do, you need to find an employer who will let you do it. You are going to have to market yourself to employers to find a job that will help you achieve your goals. The job search phase consists of five steps.

Resume Preparation. The resume is the promotional tool that job seekers use to obtain interviews and employers use to decide whom they will interview. There is one basic question at this stage:

- What will I sell?

Interview Preparation. The interview brings employers and job seekers together. As you plan for interviews, ask yourself:

- How will I sell myself?

Prospecting. You are now ready to go forth and find a job. Your questions at this juncture:

- To whom should I market myself?
- What company will offer me the opportunity I seek?
- What type of corporate culture will suit me?
- How do I contact high-potential companies?
- What contacts can I make to help me?

Employer Contact. All of the planning up to this point is simply preparation for this step—marketing yourself to your prospects in search of a job offer. There are no questions to answer; just sell yourself.

Job Decision. If you have done a good job selling, you will have one or more job offers. At this step, you must decide which offer to accept. The question is straightforward:

- Which company is best for me?

TIMETABLE WORK SHEET

This entire process depends on your planning ahead and starting early. Some of you will need to start immediately; others will be able to wait a while. Regardless, you must determine as soon as possible at which step you need to begin the career development process. At that time, you should develop a plan indicating what work you need to do and by when you need to have it done. This section contains a work sheet that will help you get started developing your career planning and placement strategies. Of course, a plan is only useful if you follow it. Once you develop target dates, stick to them. Be disciplined. Remember, the evidence is crystal clear: the most successful job seekers are those who plan early.

Let's follow a typical student through the evaluation and career development process. It's September 1989. Eileen has just begun an MBA program full-time (she expects to graduate in June 1991). She goes to the university's MBA career planning and placement office to seek guidance in creating a career development plan. After talking with her, a counselor can clearly see that Eileen knows what she wants from a job, at least in generic terms. She has done some research into career options but is still uncertain about

Eileen's Timetable

Stage	Step	Needed? (Y or N)	Start Date	Target Date	Completed
Phase I— Career Planning	Self-Assessment	N	—	—	
	Career Options	Y	1/1/90	5/1/90	
	Career Decisions	Y	5/1/90	6/1/90	
Phase II— The Job Search	Resume Preparation	Y	4/1/90	9/1/90	
	Interview Preparation	Y	4/1/90	9/1/90	
	Prospecting	Y	6/1/90	9/1/90	
	Employer Contact	Y	9/1/90	3/1/91	
	Job Decision	Y	3/1/91	4/1/91	

where to find a job that will meet her needs. The counselor suggests that she research career options more thoroughly to help her solidify her objective. Together, she and the counselor have determined her starting point. Now they need to create a schedule for the necessary career steps.

Eileen tells the counselor that she wants to have a job by graduation. In order to facilitate a possible career-required relocation, she prefers to make a job decision by April 1. She fills in 4/1/91 as the target date in the job decision box (see the sample work sheet). With this date established, she can begin to work backward to complete her career timetable. The earliest date that Eileen can begin contacting and meeting specific employers is probably the September before she graduates. Since she is aggressive, she wants to set 9/1/90 as her start date for this phase. She needs to have her prospect list ready at that time, and the counselor suggests starting work on that list by 6/1/90. She should have her resume ready and be prepared for interviews by the employer contact date of 9/1/90.

Since most of the resource people needed to help her with those steps are available in the spring, she will have to start working on resume and interview preparation by 4/1/90. And since Eileen wants to start prospecting by 6/1/90, she needs to have a career objective by then, and the counselor recommends that she begin that work on 1/1/90. By simply knowing the approximate date by which she wants to accept a job offer, Eileen and her adviser have created a career schedule that will put her on course to meet her objective.

Notice that although Eileen has almost two years before graduation, she needs to start the whole process within four months of entering the MBA program and then has only eight short months before coming face-to-face with an employer in an interview situation. This schedule is typical for most full-time students in an MBA program (part-time students will need to develop a plan with respect to their individual schedules). As you can see, there is little time to waste.

Now that you have an idea of the typical timetable for the career planning and job search process, you should begin to create your own plan using the blank table provided.

SUMMING UP

The first five chapters of this book have focused on a variety of basic concepts that form the foundation for successful career planning. All too often books like this are quick to focus on the how-tos and forget the fundamental concepts, the whys of what you will be doing. MBA job hunters need a basic conceptual understanding of the process, a perspective on it, before charging ahead. In fact, one of the characteristics of successful MBA candidates is how well they understand the concepts presented in these chapters. A large part of what MBA employers are willing to pay top dollar for is contained in the advice in these chapters. Maybe you would rather have jumped right into the nuts and bolts of finding a job, but if you had, you would have had only part of the package.

Let's review for a moment what has been covered that will help you come out on top. First, you now have the *facts* about the true value of MBAs in the job market, some of the realities of the working world, what is expected of a top MBA candidate, and what is involved in a good career planning and job search process. It is imperative that you use these facts to develop a realistic perspective on your position in the MBA job market and realistic expectations about the job you are looking for. You should now understand the *attitudes* that MBA employers look for in their top candidates. You should understand what attitudes are needed to be effective in your job search, and also the attitudes MBAs often develop that keep them from being hired. You now know that MBAs with a healthy balance of confidence and humility are highly sought after.

Along with attitudes, you can now see that certain key *skills* are needed to be successful in your job search. The most important of these is the ability to sell yourself. One whole chapter has been devoted to the concept of the job search as a marketing process. This entire book is built around the premise that your job search is basic marketing and every step of it should be planned accordingly. It can't be said too many times: you must learn to sell yourself! MBAs who not only understand this (that's the easy part) but also fully absorb it will find themselves miles ahead of their classmates who use a more traditional approach.

Finally, these chapters have discussed many *criteria* with which to evaluate and select different life and career options. As you plan your career and look for a job, each decision will be weighed against certain fundamental questions, such as "What does success mean to me?" "What role will a career play in my life?" and "What rewards should I expect from a job?" These chapters have helped you understand realistically what to expect from your job and how to make good decisions that work for you.

With these concepts firmly in mind (reread the chapters if they aren't), you are ready to move on. The next part of the book focuses on the more introspective and developmental aspects of career planning. The most important question for your personal well-being and happiness is "What do you want to do with your life?" The only "right" answer is one that works for you. It turns out that having a strong focus on career goals is also one of the keys to a successful job search and, surprisingly enough, something that is not very well developed in many MBAs. Using the foundation built in the last five chapters, the next three chapters will help you develop your career goals. The result—a good career objective—will put you on the right track to finding a good job in which you can succeed and prosper.

Your Timetable

Stage	Step	Needed? (Y or N)	Start Date	Target Date	Completed
Phase I— Career Planning	Self-Assessment				
	Career Options				
	Career Decisions				
Phase II— The Job Search	Resume Preparation				
	Interview Preparation				
	Prospecting				
	Employer Contact				
	Job Decision				

PHASE I:
CAREER PLANNING

Chapter 6

Self-Assessment

Wait! Don't skip this chapter! I know, self-assessment sounds like touchy-feely psychological mumbo-jumbo, right? Well, it's not. I'm not talking about getting in touch with your innermost feelings, joining encounter groups, or doing anything like that. What I have in mind is a basic process of identifying yourself—learning who you are in terms of your attitudes, values, skills, etc., and discovering your own path and style in the world. Now you're probably thinking, "I know who I am." Yes, but there is a world of difference between having a general, gut-level sense of who you are and having a thorough enough understanding that you can discuss it articulately and can use the information to develop your personal strategic plan for your life and career. Think of it this way: after you read a case in an MBA course once, you probably have a pretty good sense of what's going on. But you wouldn't dream of going back to class without doing more thorough fact gathering, analysis, and developing of alternatives, would you? Of course not. If you did, you'd be lost if called on in class, because you hadn't done your homework. That's what this chapter is all about—doing your homework.

WHY SELF-ASSESSMENT?

Self-assessment is one of the most important things you can do for yourself. As Richard Bolles says in his book *What Color Is Your Parachute?*

> You have got to know what it is you want, or someone is going to sell you a bill of goods somewhere along the line that can do irreparable damage to your self-esteem, your sense of worth, and your stewardship of the talents that you have.
>
> Remember this: you live half your life at your job whatever it may be. The world already has more than enough people who can't wait for 5 o'clock to come, so that they can go and do what they really want to do. It doesn't need us to swell that crowd. . . . It needs people who know what they really want to do, and who do it at their place of work, as their work.

What you learn at this stage will determine the career options you explore, how you write your resume, and your interview strategy, among other marketing considerations, and generally how effective you are in selling yourself to employers.

Who are you? What do you want? Have you ever *really* stopped to think about it? Most of us live with a general sense of where we're going and what we want, but far too many people fail to take a careful look at themselves and clearly define their goals and values. As a result, many of us go through life living a series of roles, trying to meet other people's expectations and adapting our life to fit someone else's goals. We become socialized into certain patterns of behavior and expectations but fail to reach beyond that to achieve what truly makes us happy. Why? Because we don't really understand who we are and what we want.

Failure to evaluate their needs and objectives plagues many job hunters. Many people operate under the assumption that they can adapt themselves to a job by developing the skills and motivations needed, whether these fit the individual or not. This is wrong! Although people are capable of learning and adapting, each person has a core of basic characteristics and desires that is well developed, even by the time bachelor's degree studies are completed. Someone leaving graduate school, particularly someone who doesn't have much work experience, is especially vulnerable to this myth of infinite flexibility. Students frequently say that they will use job interviews and research on career options to define professional objectives. But many job opportunities exist, and each one will probably seem exciting and glamorous. The temptation to let each new opportunity pull and shape your career objective is very great. You become like Proteus, changing form to fit each job. You need to fight that urge. Your challenge is to find a job that fits you, not a job into which you must squeeze yourself.

Of course, job information is important. I don't want you to underestimate its value in shaping your career objective. However, you must begin the career planning and job search process with a foundation, a strong core of knowledge of who you are. Then, as each opportunity presents itself, you will have something to test it against to see whether it's viable. With the first approach, you are defining yourself as you go along. More often than not, this approach results in a self-concept that is, in fact, a hybrid of your "true self" and occupational stereotypes, your perceptions of the best type of employee for the job (or jobs) into which you are trying to force yourself. Your self-concept gets more muddled with each new position you consider. If you take the time to develop a strong self-concept first, you are much more likely to end up working at a job that really fits you. "You" are not a job or a company. The self-assessment phase leads you to think about yourself outside the constraints of job descriptions and companies. A firm definition of who you are will be a major factor in guiding you toward a rewarding career.

The evidence is clear that career satisfaction and personal happiness are most likely to be achieved when your career fits your self-concept. Self-concept means not only your skills but also your attitudes, values, character, ambitions, etc. You are probably accustomed to thinking about finding a good match for your skills but not so much about finding a fit for the whole of you. A good *total* fit is what leads to a career for which you have a passion, as opposed to one that you just tolerate.

I find the imagery used by one career author—Anna Miller-Tiedeman—particularly compelling. She talks about finding your career compass, that intuitive sense of what career is good for you. Your career compass serves as a guide, helping you navigate the maze of career opportunities and getting you back on track if you're lost. Your foundation of self-knowledge will serve as your career compass. It's not only personal satisfaction that makes self-assessment so important. Earlier you learned that effective marketers must know their product. Self-assessment is the process whereby you learn your product. It's worth repeating that you can't possibly sell yourself in an articulate and concrete fashion unless you know yourself well. What you learn here will determine which career options you explore, how you write your resume, what your interview strategy will be, and how effective you are at all of these. It can easily make the difference between winning and losing a job.

THE PROCESS: WHAT TO EXPECT

The self-assessment process is relatively straightforward. However, you will need to begin it in the proper frame of mind. Set aside large, uninterrupted blocks of time in an environment conducive to thought (most people prefer quiet). Equip yourself with plenty of paper and a couple of pencils. Be prepared to reflect upon yourself and your past and to dream about your future. When you are ready to begin, you should turn to the self-assessment workbook in this chapter. But before you do, familiarize yourself with the work sheet, identifying the tasks involved and placing them in the context of the self-assessment process.

The workbook exercise will ask you to consider yourself in relation to ten topic areas. You will be asked to think about your past, present, and future as they relate to your family, your friends, your activities, and your work. Let your mind roam freely and actively, using the workbook to focus your thoughts. Spend as much time as possible on each question. Remember, this process can be productive only if you are committed to it.

After you have explored all of the questions under each topic area, you will need to convert your answers into a form that will be helpful in your job search. If you look closely at the information you have gathered, you should see some patterns emerge. It is possible to detect a pattern of skills and interests even in the earliest years that grows stronger as people develop. Human development charts the process by which interests become abilities and abilities become accomplishments. If you can identify a pattern in the activities that have been the most rewarding in your life, you will have a very valuable clue to determining your future professional happiness.

Be warned that this process may be difficult for you, even though it requires skills that you use all of the time. Self-assessment runs counter to much of the quantitative, problem-solving training MBAs receive. It is "softer," closer to organizational behavior than finance. Perhaps some of the trouble MBAs have with self-assessment stems from a fear of honesty. You might be afraid to be honest with yourself, afraid of uncovering terrible inadequacies, failures, and weakness or simply of finding that you have no strengths. Remind yourself not to make value judgments; there are no right or wrong answers to these questions. This workbook is a tool to help you realize your niche in the business world. Attack it as you would a business case, the most important assignment you've ever done. Remember, no one but you has to know the results.

SELF-ASSESSMENT WORKBOOK

The exercise outlined in this chapter is especially designed for MBAs. It assumes that most MBAs have a *sense* of who they are and what they want. Experience, however, has shown that most MBAs have never paused to research and analyze it. This exercise should assist you with your evaluation, resulting in your being able to articulate to yourself, and to employers, the essential you. The process assumes that you have the information that you need but that you just have never collected it in the way that you need to for good career planning.

This book is not a comprehensive guide to understanding yourself. It is not designed to present a complete system capable of guiding MBAs who don't have at least a general sense of who they are. For that type of assistance, students need to investigate more complex and lengthy counseling techniques (see the section titled "Other Resources" at the end of this chapter).

As you begin to complete this exercise, you will notice that the categories covered in the workbook go beyond those usually found in career books and job-related exercises. These books generally focus on skills, ignoring the importance of the job hunter's individual personality and career needs. But the job hunter brings much more to the job search process than skills and area-specific knowledge. The job seeker brings his or her values and ambitions as well. These other elements contribute to the person's total employee profile. The workbook that follows incorporates additional self-assessment categories to reflect a more balanced approach. Use this workbook as a tool to discover better lifelong career matches.

Instructions: Review yourself in relation to the following ten areas. It is important that you understand yourself in each of these areas. Complete the statements under each section with an eye toward furthering self-knowledge. Don't be put off by the content of the workbook. It isn't meant to be patronizing or simplistic but is designed to make you reconsider aspects of your life that you might take for granted at present. Don't make judgments of right or wrong; simply put down ideas. Sample responses lead off each section to help prompt your thoughts.

Personal Traits

Each of us possesses certain traits. The combination of these traits makes us unique individuals. How would you describe yourself, and how would other people who know you well describe you? Are you sensitive, shy, businesslike, aloof? Evaluate yourself honestly, making a list of your traits.

I am . . .

creative	casual
a good organizer	a helpful neighbor
a fast learner	friendly
attractive	a hard worker
meticulous	aggressive

---

1. The good things about me are . . .

2. The not-so-good things about me are . . .

3. My family would describe me as . . .

4. Friends would describe me as . . .

5. People who work with me think I am . . .

Happiness

Life is made up of preferences. Think about the things in life that give you that wonderful feeling of joy and happiness. What makes you happy, what makes you laugh, and what are the things that you look forward to doing?

I am happy when I am . . .

working	playing sports
relaxing at home	reading
accomplishing a project	traveling
shopping	helping another person
programming a computer	studying

---

1. I get excited about . . .

2. In school I loved to study . . .

3. In school, I hated to study . . .

4. Among my extracurricular activities in school, I really enjoyed . . .

5. If I had my education to do all over again, I would . . .

6. In my previous jobs, I was happiest when I was doing . . .

7. In my previous jobs, I hated doing . . .

8. If I were financially secure and could choose any job I wanted, I would work at . . .

Happiness is like a crystal,
Fair and exquisite and clear,
Broken in a million pieces,
Shattered, scattered far and near.
Now and then along life's pathway,
Lo! some shining fragments fall;
But there are so many pieces
No one ever finds them all.

—Priscilla Leonard
From "Happiness"

Values

As we grow, we each begin to adopt certain values. Around these beliefs, we structure much of what we do and how we live. We also establish priorities in our lives in reference to our values. Some of us place a top priority on earning money, some on community service, and others on family. What values are central to your belief system? Discover what thing or things matter most to you.

I believe in . . .

God	family
wealth	patriotism
kindness to people	community service
self-gratification	work
freedom	success

---

1. My top five priorities in life are . . .

2. If I lost the following things, life would have no meaning for me . . .

3. To me, a career means . . .

4. My ideal life would be . . .

Dreams and Ambitions

Most of us daydream a bit about the future. Many of us harbor secret dreams and ambitions but are embarrassed to reveal these thoughts. Forget your guilt or discomfort, and ask yourself where you would like to be in your life. What things do you wish would happen to you? Dare to dream about what you would like to be. Don't be afraid to discover what you are striving for.

In my dreams, I . . .

scale mountaintops	make a million dollars
run my own business	own a mansion
live a life of leisure	become a vice president
am an expert in my field	find a cure for cancer
have four kids	am a financial genius

---

1. If I could have a job that enabled me to indulge in my favorite activity, I would . . .

2. If I had the necessary talent and could be anybody in the business world, I would be . . .

3. When I imagine my success, I see . . .

4. In five years, I would love to be . . .

5. When I retire, I would like to have . . .

6. When I have complete control over my time, I like to . . .

7. When I close my eyes and imagine my career, I see . . .

8. If I had a crystal ball and could see into the future, it would reveal . . .

Accomplishments

Review what you have achieved in the past. Try to discover things in which you have excelled and things you are proud of having done. Look for things that made you feel good when you achieved them and things that you fondly remember doing. Think back to the time that you won an art award in grammar school, pitched a no-hitter in Little League, or wrote a poem for your high school literary magazine. Compile a list of as many of your accomplishments as you can remember.

It may be you . . .

won a sales contest
led the league in scoring
wrote a prize-winning essay
acted the lead role in a play
were promoted ahead of
your peers

catered a large party
programmed a computer
won a scholarship
built a cabinet
helped a person out of
trouble

---

1. My greatest accomplishments in life include . . .

2. I have been rewarded for . . .

3. I feel pleased with myself when I (list accomplishments) . . .

4. I have produced these positive results . . .

5. I have overcome these challenges, difficulties, and barriers . . .

Motivations and Rewards

In our personal and professional lives, we are motivated by rewards. Some of these are tangible, and others are intangible. Ask yourself why you do the things that you do. What drives you to be your best? Are most of your motivations internal or external? Learn what motivates you and what you consider your on-the-job rewards to be.

I am motivated by . . .

money	good times
benefits	power
a sense of achievement	a plush office
being given responsibility	professional contacts
the sense of serving a cause	experience

---

1. I really get motivated at work when . . .

2. At the times I wanted to give 110 percent of energy and enthusiasm to a project, I was . . .

3. Of all the rewards I get from work, I most value . . .

4. I would be willing to work for less pay if I could have . . .

5. I would be willing to risk failing on the job if I could have . . .

Roles

We all have an image of ourselves and the roles that we fill in our lives. Who are you? What labels do you apply to yourself? Which roles do you like, and which roles don't you like? We all act in certain capacities, such as teacher, spouse, manager, and parent. Learn how you label yourself. Determine what roles you try to fill and which ones you wish you could fill.

I have assumed—or would like to assume—the following roles . . .

spouse	professional
parent	manager
friend	leader
coach	mentor
community volunteer	counselor

---

1. I see myself most strongly as (use labels such as "a student" or "a boss") . . .

2. I like to be thought of as . . .

3. I would like to become (use labels) . . .

4. My role models are . . .

5. The person I most admire and would like to emulate in the business world is _____. I would like to emulate this person because . . .

Strengths and Weaknesses

We all have areas in which we excel and areas in which we are weak. It's OK to have weaknesses as long as you know them and discover your strengths. What are you especially good at, and what are you not particularly good at? People who spend their lives trying to conquer every challenge and be everything to everybody eventually wind up abandoning this strategy or being consumed with frustration. Learn what your limits are, and discover in which direction your potential lies.

My strengths	My weaknesses
I handle details well	I am not very creative
I am outgoing	I am too methodical
I am perceptive	I am unassertive
I work well with numbers	I am not a good salesperson
I am concerned about my fellow workers	I often unintentionally hurt people's feelings

1. In my previous job, I really excelled at . . .

2. At this stage in my career development, I excel in . . .

3. I wish I were better at . . .

4. I am not very good at . . .

Skills

There are two types of skills: *transferable* skills and *content* skills. Transferable skills are those that can be put to use in any job, such as people skills, communication skills, and planning skills. Content skills are those that can be applied only to specific areas. These would include analyzing statistics, drafting, and writing computer specifications, for example. What skills do you have? Take a complete inventory of everything that you have to offer an employer. Most people grossly underestimate their marketable skills and are stunned to realize all of the things that they know how to do. Determine your skills, and think about how they can be transferred to a variety of jobs.

My skills include . . .

researching	forecasting	reporting
defining	administering	summarizing
evaluating	directing	recommending
interpreting	developing	coordinating
estimating	training	enlisting
designing	counseling	maintaining
programming	delegating	reconciling
persuading	negotiating	improving
promoting	inspecting	stimulating
implementing	expediting	updating
communicating	organizing	analyzing
planning	writing	instructing

1. I am happiest when I am using these skills . . .

2. I hate using these skills . . .

3. My strongest skills are . . .

4. I wish my skills were better in the following areas . . .

Environments

Although most of us are marvelously adaptable when we have to be, we usually find that certain types of environments motivate us to be our best. What environments suit you best? Learn what circumstances enable you to work up to your potential.

I work best . . .

in a comfortable office
in a fast-paced environment
in a small company
in an office with many
coworkers
in quiet surroundings

under close supervision
with people I like
in a large corporation
in a formal setting
when I work independently

---

1. I really performed well when I was at (e.g., a particular school or job) . . .

2. I would love to work for a company that . . .

3. My favorite bosses were (describe traits) . . .

4. My ideal boss would be (describe traits) . . .

Looking for Patterns

Instructions: You have now completed the fact-gathering section of the workbook. It is time to review your answers to the workbook questions to try to detect patterns or recurrent themes. The following questions are designed to help you uncover these patterns.

1. What personal traits emerge most often?

2. What types of things make you happy or give you a sense of satisfaction?

3. What values reappear frequently (e.g., a belief in the intrinsic value of work, the need to lead a balanced life, the desire to help others)?

4. What rewards are you motivated by (e.g., a large salary, power, a sense of achievement)?

5. What do you enjoy working with most (e.g., people, data, ideas)?

6. What skills do you use most often (e.g., management skills, analytical skills, creative skills)?

7. In what environment do you perform best (e.g., a structured or an unstructured environment, a competitive or a noncompetitive setting)?

8. What other patterns do you see emerging?

Developing the Job Objective

Instructions: This is the stage in the self-assessment process in which you develop your job objective. Use the self-analysis you have just completed to think about your ideal job—your purpose is finding employment that is right for you, your ideal job or a job similar to that ideal. For now, don't concern yourself with whether the particulars are realistic. This question will be answered once you have begun investigating the job market. Remember that the creation of the job objective is the culmination of all of your earlier exploration. Use it to dream about your ideal job.

1. If I had my ideal job, I would be doing . . .

2. I would be filling these roles . . .

3. I would be able to utilize my skills in . . .

4. I would be able to accomplish . . .

5. Achieving this ideal job, I would feel . . .

6. I would be rewarded with . . .

7. I would have opportunities to become . . .

8. The people I would be working with would be . . .

9. I would be working in this type of environment . . .

10. I would work for a company that . . .

11. The criteria that I will use to decide what job to accept are . . .

12. At this point, I would state my job objective to be . . .

OTHER RESOURCES

By now, you should have a good idea of the dominant themes in your life and a sense of direction toward your career. Imagining your ideal job has enabled you to create a job objective that will provide a foundation for the next steps in the career planning process.

If you have completed the workbook and are confused (or if you skipped over the workbook section), you should probably investigate a few non-MBA-specific self-assessment tools.

Tests, as a group, are one of the least understood resources in the self-assessment process. For a wide variety of reasons, people are often uncomfortable with the idea of taking psychologically based tests. But these tests can be useful to you in a number of ways, so don't allow unfounded fears to persuade you to ignore their importance. The best self-assessment tests are based on extensive research and have been widely tested and used.

Self-assessment tests can help generate ideas and directions for career research. For many MBAs, these tests are confidence builders, the results confirming what the job hunter already knows about himself or herself. For others, the test findings are more surprising. After reviewing the results, some test takers come to the conclusion that they need to reassess themselves entirely or that they need to investigate certain areas overlooked in past assessments. These tests can also provide the job hunter with a broader perspective on his or her place in the world of work, which affords a helpful framework for self-evaluation. In addition, the words and labels learned through the testing process can help job candidates build up a self-assessment vocabulary, enabling them to articulate in an interview situation who they are and what they want.

The tests do have their limitations, however. Some job hunters take a self-assessment test with unrealistic expectations, believing that it will yield *the answer* to career dilemmas. Others overreact to the tests, feeling themselves limited by the results. You must understand the purpose of this type of test in order to interpret and apply the results properly. These tests were created to give you clues about yourself and to indicate possible career directions. Seen in this light, they will be a valuable tool. If they do nothing more than confirm what you already know or supply you with the words and phrases with which to describe yourself, they pay for themselves. Remember that psychologically based tests will not tell you the "right" thing to do—they cannot make your career decisions for you. You are the only one who can determine what is really right for you.

To help you understand the philosophy behind these tests and to allay your discomfort, let's look at some of the most popular tests. The four most common tests are the Vocational Preference Inventory, the Self-Directed Search, the Strong-Campbell Interest Inventory, and the Myers-Briggs Type Indicator. The first three are based on the career work of John Holland, the fourth on the work of Peter B. Myers and Isabel Briggs Myers.

Holland's career theory was first developed in the late fifties and is still widely used today. It is based on six personality types that can be used to describe people and work environments: realistic (manually, mechanically, and technically oriented), investigative (scientifically and mathematically oriented), artistic (oriented toward artistic creativity), social (human relations–oriented, e.g., involved in activities such as teaching or nursing), enterprising (management-oriented, e.g., possessing leadership and interpersonal skills), and conventional (task-oriented, e.g., possessing clerical, computational, or business systems skills). Using this system, each person is characterized by his or her primary, secondary, and tertiary preference for work activity and then matched to work environments that are of the same type. (Over 12,000 occupations have been characterized by their type.) Holland believes that people make vocational choices based on the match between their personality types and work environment types.

His theory gave rise to several assessment tests. Holland himself developed the Vocational Preference Inventory, a test that determines a person's type. Later, he created the Self-Directed Search, an easier-to-use version of the earlier test (it can be self-scored). The results of these two tests are interpreted by using the vast amount of career information that has been categorized by Holland types, matching test taker with complementary occupations. The Strong-Campbell Interest Inventory is also based on Holland's work. Like the Vocational Preference Inventory and the Self-Directed Search, this test screens the job hunter by type identification. However, the individual's responses are then compared with those of other people from a variety of occupations (their responses form a large database). The results tell the test taker how similar he or she is to people in particular fields, thereby identifying possible career paths. Remember that all of these tests will provide *clues*, or *directions*, for the career search. Be prepared for some odd career matchups. You determine whether the information the search reveals on particular career choices is valid for you.

The Myers-Briggs Type Indicator is quite different from Holland-based tests. It focuses on personality traits. The test taker answers a series of questions. The responses are measured on four continuums relating to personality: a preference for the outer or inner world (extroversion vs. introversion), how you perceive things (sensing vs. intuition), how you judge things (thinking vs. feeling), and how you deal with the world outside (judging vs. perceiving). These preferences do not entail value judgments of right or wrong or good or bad, but by having their inclinations in these four areas analyzed, people can become more attuned to the way they deal with their surroundings and with others. This test is predicated on the belief that by understanding type in general and one type in particular the test taker increases his or her awareness of self and is better able to make a career choice.

For the person who is unclear on answers to general career and self-assessment questions, these tests (and others like them) are of great value. Plan to use self-assessment tests in consultation with a counselor. This type of test is based on extensive research and relatively complex theories, and interpretations should come from someone qualified to give them. Professionals trained in counseling can be found in university career centers as well as in private agencies.

Books on the basics of career planning can also be helpful. University and local public libraries are bound to have many of these titles. A careful library search will probably turn up *What Color Is*

Your Parachute? and *Where Do I Go from Here with My Life?* I heartily recommend both of these titles.

What Color Is Your Parachute? by Richard N. Bolles is an excellent resource for those who need more work on identifying skills. This book has become the job hunter's bible. It offers sound advice and is straightforward, fun to read, and easy to use. Bolles's approach to career planning stresses the analysis of skills and accomplishments.

Where Do I Go from Here with My Life? by John C. Crystal and Richard N. Bolles presents the career planning system that provides the basis for *What Color Is Your Parachute?* Although fairly lengthy, the system outlined in this book is especially helpful for those job seekers who are particularly confused about the type of career they want. It describes an in-depth life-career planning process.

Remember that the work of self-assessment is crucial. Use every tool at your disposal to help you establish your base of knowledge of self. Explore and reexamine until you have found a flexible foundation for the next stages in the process of finding that MBA-level job that is just right for you.

Chapter 7

Researching Career Options

Isn't it exciting! An MBA can choose from among so many different career options. There seems to be something for everyone. Everywhere you turn, you hear stories about how much fun a certain job is for someone. But how do you find out what is fun and right for *you*? Completing the self-assessment process you learned in the last chapter is part of the answer. The other part is thoroughly researching your career options.

There are volumes of material that provide general background information about careers, but few that give the detailed in-depth information you need to decide what is best for you. (Some particularly good ones are listed in "Career Resources," the appendix.) In general, locating the information you need requires a great deal of patience and persistence. This chapter will help you develop a strategy for tracking down solid information about your career options.

A word of warning: at this point, career options means general occupational categories like marketing research, financial analysis, manufacturing management, management information systems, and investments. It's much too early to be talking about career paths in specific companies. So, if you use specific company information, use it only as a base from which to generalize. Stay focused on general paths. Later, you will refine your research to the more specific company level.

LAYING DOWN A STRATEGY

Your career research progresses through three stages, each with a different objective. Stage One is *orientation*. Your objective here is simply to gain a general idea of what various career options are really about and then identify a few areas that you want to investigate in more detail.

Stage One information is easy to find and quick to read. Particularly good resources are introductory and survey-type books, corporate literature, and professional associations. Also, many of the books listed in the appendix contain useful introductory chapters.

Stage Two is *in-depth research*. Now is the time to check out the career areas you have identified in Stage One. Your objective is to obtain enough information about a career area to be relatively sure it is for you. When you complete this stage, you should be about 75–80 percent sure of your final decision. Your best resources for Stage Two are in-depth books (like those listed in the appendix), articles, and periodicals.

Career Research Stages

- Stage One: Orientation
  Output—Career Areas to Investigate
- Stage Two: In-Depth Research
  Output—One or Two Career Areas
- Stage Three: Information Interviews
  Output—Career Decision

Stage Three is *information interviews*. This stage is vital but is the one people most often leave out. It consists of interviewing managers, executives, faculty members, and alumni who are working in the career areas to which Stage Two points you. With the additional information gained from Stage Three, you should be confident enough to make a decision about your career objective.

There is a wealth of information available to help you progress through these stages. Good sources are:

Career resources centers. Career resources centers, often found in university counseling and placement offices, are an excellent source of introductory information and broad overviews of most career areas. They usually offer career testing as well as career counselors to help you get started. You will find them quite helpful in Stage One but less so in Stage Two. Most have such a large clientele that they cannot stock enough materials for complete Stage Two research in any one area.

Corporate literature. Major corporations spend large amounts of money developing recruitment literature that fully describes their job opportunities and career paths. You can usually obtain it from your MBA or university placement office or directly from the company. This literature provides a wealth of information about available career options. It's a superb resource for Stage One and early Stage Two.

Professional associations. Part of the mission of a professional association is to encourage young people to choose its members' field as a career. Most have literature available to introduce the field to you. Typically, it is just introductory material, suitable only for Stage One research. Some associations, however, offer more extensive information, appropriate for Stage Two.

Books and articles. Libraries are full of books and magazine articles about specific career areas. These provide both introductory material and in-depth analyses. Most of your Stage Two research will take place here.

Professional journals. Every profession has journals that discuss the topics and concerns of that profession's members. By surveying these, even though you may not want to read all of their articles in depth, you can obtain an excellent feel for the challenges you will face in that career area. Professional journals are excellent Stage Two material.

Career fairs. Many colleges, universities, and professional organizations sponsor career fairs. Employers set up tables or booths, and you can wander among them to learn about career opportunities and drop off your resume. Fairs are great places for Stage One research and often lead to contacts for Stages Two and Three research.

WHAT TO LOOK FOR IN YOUR RESEARCH

Good resources are worthless unless you know what you're looking for. If you have done a good job of assessing yourself, your values, and your priorities, you should know exactly what to pay attention to. Everyone's list will vary somewhat, since everyone's priorities are a little different, but what follows is a list of concerns that all MBAs should heed. Feel free to add your particular concerns and interests to it:

What tasks will you perform? Know what the content of your job will be and what tasks you will perform on a daily basis.

What skills will you need? Each job requires different skills. Be sure you know what skills are needed to perform the tasks well.

What will the work environment be like? What will the people you work with be like? What will your hours be? What type of facilities will you be working in?

What salary and benefits can you expect? Each industry and career area has a different compensation structure; check it out.

What other rewards should you expect? Each career area offers a unique set of rewards that draws people to it. Be sure you know what they are.

What life balance is required? What degree of commitment, time, and energy will you have to invest, and how much will be left for personal endeavors?

What is your growth potential in this area? Where can you go, and how fast can you get there?

What qualifications are needed to enter this area? Be sure you know what degrees, certifications, and experience are needed.

What does it take to succeed? Beyond acquiring the skills needed, what will you have to do to succeed in that career over the long term?

What is the daily work life like? Although every job has its excitements and challenges, each also has its daily grind. Be sure you understand the daily life in the job, not just its peaks and valleys.

In what parts of the country can you find jobs in this career area? The best opportunities in some jobs are restricted to certain regions in the country. This could make a difference to you.

What kind of positions must you take in the first five years? Many careers require that you "pay your dues" in a variety of entry-level positions before achieving the goal you seek. Know what the early years will be like as well as the later ones.

What are the future prospects for this job function? Some types of jobs are expected to take off in the future; others are grinding to a halt. Don't hitch your car to the wrong train.

INFORMATION INTERVIEWS

The unique information that you can obtain in an information interview is the personal experience of a real person. Books, articles, and videotapes are all great, but there's no substitute for hearing it from a person who is actually doing a job that you are considering. That's why these interviews have a section to themselves.

But Stage Three is perhaps the most unfamiliar, difficult, and intimidating part of your research. Information interviews can be a tremendous help in your decision process if done correctly. They can also fail miserably and embarrass you if you don't do sufficient groundwork.

True worth is in being, not seeming,—
In doing, each day that goes by,
Some little good—not in dreaming
Of great things to do by and by.
For whatever men say in their blindness,
And spite of the fancies of youth,
There's nothing so kingly as kindness,
And nothing so royal as truth.

. . . .

We cannot make bargains for blisses,
Nor catch them like fishes in nets;
And sometimes the thing our life misses
Helps more than the thing which it gets.
For good lieth not in pursuing,
Nor gaining of great nor of small,
But just in the doing, and doing
As we would be done by, is all.

. . . .

—Alice Cary
From "Nobility"

Before you embark on an information interview, be sure that you have done all the other research you can possibly do. Most of the people you will contact for advice are busy professionals with careers of their own. You will typically find them happy to help you since they have all been in your shoes before. You will also find that they will lose that desire quickly and become impatient if they discover you have not done your homework beforehand. You cannot walk into a person's office and ask a broad question like "What is marketing?" Don't expect your interviewee to lead you by the hand or tell you everything. Do all your research beforehand and use the interview to find out things you cannot find anywhere else. The people you interview will respect you for not wasting their time, and you will get the maximum benefit from the time you spend with them.

When you approach someone for an information interview, be careful to explain that it is only an information interview, not a job interview. Never use an information interview as a way to get through the door and ask for a job. You will find that there may be some follow-up by the employer after an information interview if you have made a good impression, but you will never get a job by deceit. In addition, you may ruin the chances of future students ever getting an information interview with that person. Let the employer initiate the follow-up. Do not leave your resume unless requested to do so.

When you telephone a prospective interviewee, use this approach:

"Hello, my name is _____. I am in the MBA program at _____ and am researching career options as part of my career-planning process. I have done much research into the field of _____ and am very interested in this field as a career. Would you be willing to meet with me for an hour to help me answer some open questions and to give me your experience and opinions about this field as a career?"

Since you requested the interview, you will be responsible for directing it. Let's be honest; you may be a little nervous or intimidated by the person you're talking to. Decide what you want to know before you go to see the person and write it down. The written questions may save you some embarrassment.

Many interviewees will offer you a tour of facilities and perhaps the opportunity to spend some time observing the workplace. By all means, take advantage of these opportunities. If you develop a good rapport with the interviewee, don't be afraid to ask to see people at work.

In general, talk to as many people who are working in the job you are considering as you possibly can. They will give you insights, stories, and advice that are invaluable. No other resource can replace it. Stages One and Two are valuable in building the foundations for conducting a successful information interview. A successful informational interview in Stage Three is a key to being completely confident about your career choice.

WORKBOOK

Perform the following exercises for each career option you are considering. Although it is often very difficult to predict what a profession will really be like to work in, you should obtain the indicated information to the best of your ability. The information is available if you look for it.

1. I will usually be performing these tasks as part of a typical job in this career:

2. I need these skills to be successful in this profession:

3. I can expect my salary to be:

　_____ starting

　_____ after 2 years

　_____ after 5 years

　_____ after 10 years

　_____ after 15 years

4. In addition to salary, I will probably receive these benefits as part of my compensation:

5. I expect that these parts of this profession will be most rewarding to me professionally and personally:

6. In a typical career path, I would progress as follows:

Year 1:

Year 2:

Year 3:

Year 5:

Year 7:

Year 10:

Year 15:

Year 20:

Year 25:

7. On the average, I expect to work _____ hours per week.

8. The people I will be working with can be described as:

9. I will need these qualifications (experience, education, etc.) to have a reasonable chance of getting a job in this profession:

10. Other than the skills and qualifications I listed above, I will need the following to succeed in this profession (e.g., contacts, money, a mentor):

11. I will most likely be working in these parts of the country (list cities, states, or regions):

12. A typical day on the job could be described as:

13. The prospects for this profession are:

_____ fantastic—a real growth career

_____ good—still moving up

_____ average—hard to tell where it is going

_____ poor—declining job market

_____ terrible—real lost cause

14. I would describe the environment in which I would be working as:

15. The person who would be happiest in this job would likely be described as:

16. The bad news about this profession is:

Chapter 8

Determining Career Goals

You now know a considerable amount about your skills, qualifications, objectives, and values. You've spent a great deal of time looking at different opportunities; a few may even seem like natural fits for your interests. Now comes the tough part: you must decide which options to pursue.

CHOOSING THE RIGHT CAREER OPTIONS

One of the scary parts about a job search is that you must make a number of decisions that will have a great impact on your life. The first of these is choosing the career option that matches you best. Making that choice involves a series of attempts to match your interests with the job market. Some careers will fit a little, some not at all, and a few very well. Your challenge is to find the career that meshes with your interests well enough for you to be happy—don't be too much of a perfectionist.

Your expectations will play a big role in how good a decision you make. Most of us want quite a bit from our job—rewards, esteem, power, and so on. There is a pervasive myth that a perfect job exists for each person, one that will satisfy all your work-related needs. Believing this myth will drive you crazy as you try to find the perfect job. All jobs will have some shortcomings and mismatches with your interests. Choosing the right one is a matter of setting priorities and making trade-offs.

It can be very disheartening to discover that no career option or job matches your skills, objectives, and values perfectly. This is especially true for first-time job hunters, who usually have to accept that the career option they choose may not satisfy more than 80 percent of their career goals in the best case. This can prove a tough pill to swallow.

Look for the career option that satisfies *most* of your career goals. Most of us must seek outside interests to satisfy the rest. You

125

must be prepared to compromise and accept a less-than-perfect fit.

Remember, too, that in a first job out of school it is quite common to spend the first year or two in training or apprentice positions. Entry positions are rarely your ideal job. Be careful not to focus too hard on the entry position, and look at your opportunities from a longer-term perspective.

DEVELOPING A GOOD CAREER OBJECTIVE

What is a good career objective? You know that you are looking for a career that meshes well with what you know about yourself, but how do you translate that into a career objective that gets you what you want and is marketable? Sometimes it seems impossible to do both. Employers seem to want very precise career objectives that limit you too much. You want a broad objective that maximizes the number of opportunities available to you. In fact, it's not too difficult to develop an objective that is flexible and marketable—if you understand what a good objective is.

Think of the career options in the world of business as slices of a large pie. Through career planning, you are trying to find a slice that suits your particular interests. Your first dilemma is how big a slice to consider. How many career options can really fit you, and how many can you realistically search out?

You should understand that the slices are defined by generic *categories*, not job *titles*, by characteristics such as values, work type, skills required, and rewards. In fact, there is a big difference between job titles and generic categories. There are many job titles in each category. Each of you will likely consider many jobs, and that's good. But one broad category, or slice of the pie, probably fits you best *right now*. Your values, preferences, skills, and abilities will likely point clearly to one category while leaving lots of flexibility to choose among different titles, companies, and industries.

The worry is that you will attempt to pursue several *categories* of jobs, categories that define significantly different types of people. Employers often perceive a person who focuses on dissimilar career areas as an undirected person who has not paid enough attention to career planning and will therefore not stay with the company very long. Furthermore, you are gambling with your personal satisfaction by not narrowing your objective to a category that fits you. No one will be concerned if you pursue several different job *titles*. As long as the jobs require the same *types* of knowledge, skills, abilities, and interests, you should have lots of flexibility and no trouble marketing yourself.

For example, suppose Jan Smith is looking for a job as a portfolio manager, equities analyst, bond analyst, investment analyst, or

Sometimes
the decision
to do
nothing
is wise.
But you can't
make a career
of doing
nothing.
Freddie Fulcrum
weighed everything
too carefully.
He would say, "On
the one hand . . .
but then, on the
other," and his
arguments
weighed out so
evenly
he never did
anything.
When Freddie died,
they carved
a big zero
on his tombstone.
If you decide
to fish—fine.
Or, if you decide
to cut bait—fine.
But if you decide
to do
nothing,
you're not going
to have fish
dinner.

   —"Decisions, Decisions"

financial planner. Is her career objective too broad? No. All of these jobs are analytical, numbers oriented, and concerned with financial concepts. Jan has identified a category, a slice of the pie, that fits her knowledge, skills, and abilities, and all these jobs have these common characteristics. She has a good career objective that includes multiple job titles. Now, if she added sales management to this list, that would require a whole different set of skills and abilities, and her career objective would be more risky.

At the other extreme is the danger of defining your objective too narrowly. Very restricted objectives can work very well, but they too carry considerable risk. Employers love to see people who know exactly what they want to do and exactly why. Those people are likely to stay with a company as long as they are treated well and are likely to be very happy employees. Specific objectives certainly make your job search much easier and will be very effective in an interview because of your enthusiasm. The risky part is that you may prevent yourself from being considered for any other positions, some of which may fit you very well. There are two sides to the coin. One, a very specific objective says you know exactly what you want. But two, it also says you don't want to do anything else. Don't be discouraged from pursuing precisely the career you want, but be forewarned: you run the risk of a longer job search because of fewer options.

This raises the question of *balance* in your career objective. There are four basic elements of a career objective:

- what type of work you want to do
- compensation you require to do it
- geographic location
- industry or company to work in

Anytime you define one of these elements narrowly, you restrict the opportunities available to you. If you decide to make all elements very specific, you will have only a few target employers, and the odds of your being hired will get much smaller. To be realistic, you should balance your objective, particularly early in your career. Whenever you define what you want in one element narrowly, be prepared to broaden what you will accept in other elements so that your total "opportunity pool" remains essentially the same. To do that, you will have to assign priorities to the elements of your career objective.

Here is an example to show you how this works.

Sam Brooks came to me seeking help with his job search. After several months of looking, he was frustrated because he had made little progress. When I asked him about his career objective, he said that he wanted to work as a brand manager for one of the top five consumer products companies and would like to stay in the Northeast. He wanted to earn at least $40,000 per year to start. He had restricted his job search to date using these criteria.

He had restricted it so much, in fact, that his chances of being hired were very low. He was absolutely correct in trying it for a few months. I asked him to prioritize what he wanted. He said he definitely wanted to be in brand management, as he thought that was his niche. He also had a large school loan and likes money, so $40,000 was a strong second priority. His wife's parents live in New York and she would like to be close, so that was his third priority. Finally, he wanted the prestige and training of a large company.

When Sam realized his career objective was unrealistic (his futile search was evidence), he began to modify his objective. He decided to continue to look for a brand manager's job, but to consider any consumer products company in the Fortune 500 (hardly small), to include Midwestern and Mid-Atlantic states, since they are still within a day's drive of New York, and to lengthen his loan repayment schedule so he could accept a salary as low as $35,000. With that modified objective, he was able to find a very satisfactory job because his opportunity pool became larger.

In summary, there is no reason why your career objective cannot be flexible enough to provide you lots of opportunities and be well received by employers to whom you will market it. The trick is to define the slices of the pie not by job titles but by generic and homogeneous job characteristics and to be sure to balance narrowly defined elements of the objective with broadly defined elements. The result should be a very effective career objective.

Multiple Objectives

Before we leave the subject of career objectives, multiple objectives deserve one further comment. It is quite common to see college students trying to maximize their opportunities by pursuing several divergent career paths (that is, slices of the pie). The idea is to look at everything and then decide, hoping to keep options open for fear of not finding a job. That may sound good in theory, but in practice it usually doesn't work. The real reason for choosing multiple career objectives is often that students have not set priorities for their values, needs, and objectives or have not taken the time to know themselves and research their career options adequately.

Employers view this as laziness and immaturity.

What happens is that most students have only a limited amount of time to devote to career planning and placement. When they try to pursue divergent objectives or look at everything, they usually spend less time preparing themselves for interviews and do less career research on each area. They end up with breadth of knowledge, not depth. Instead of increasing their opportunities, their lack of preparation actually decreases them.

Generally, the most successful job hunters are those who have narrowed their career objective to one career category (maybe two) through sound career planning. Those people have such enthusiasm and confidence that a look-at-everything job seeker with minimal preparation will almost never win out over them. The formers' interview performance will be so much better that their chances of being hired are greater despite their smaller prospect list.

Of course, it is *possible* to be a legitimate candidate with multiple objectives. Furthermore, what is right for you will probably change throughout your life. You may well have several successful careers during your lifetime, particularly with a degree as versatile as an MBA. It does seem, however, that at any particular point in a person's life there is one option that is better than the others. For every combination of life-stage, needs, and preferences, there is usually some career option that will work best.

If you are in fact considering several career objectives, be sure that:

- You really have more than one legitimate target and are not just playing the field.
- You have carefully analyzed yourself and each of those career objectives.
- You can confidently justify to an interviewer why each of the career paths meets your objectives and why you would be good in each career.
- You can explain why you are the rare individual who can pursue more than one career option.
- You anticipate the doubts and objections of the employers.

PHASE II:
THE JOB SEARCH

Chapter 9

Planning Your Job Search Campaign

You have finished the introspective part of this process and are now ready to turn outward and develop your marketing campaign. Most companies launch new products with intensive, systematic campaigns, and you will need one too. This portion of the book discusses the major elements of a step-by-step method you can use to plan your campaign.

LAUNCHING YOURSELF

An effective marketing campaign requires a thoughtful plan and plenty of preparation. While you cannot predict the exact course your campaign will take, neither can you afford to wander aimlessly. A systematic, well-planned approach will greatly improve your chances of success.

What you must envision is a focused and very concentrated campaign. It should be a well-coordinated, purposeful series of events impelling you directly toward a new job. You must take time to research it, design, it, and prepare for it. It's just like planning a long trip, writing a term paper, or developing a new product: you can't just dive in.

At this point, you have already built some of the foundations of your campaign. You have completed your product research (self-assessment) and identified what you have to sell. You have researched your market (career options). And you have selected your target market (chosen a career objective). Now you need to plan the next steps.

First you must assume the right *attitude*. Reread the sections on the characteristics of effective job hunters and on selling yourself. Get into an aggressive frame of mind, brace yourself for rejection, and be ready to ignore it. Bring energy from other activities and focus it here so that your job search becomes a top priority. Practice picturing yourself as a success. Get fired up!

Your next step is to develop a *prospect* list. Prospects are the companies that you think have the potential to be a good fit for you. Then you will have to plan a *strategy* to market yourself. Next, you'll have to develop effective *resumes* and *cover letters* to advertise your availability. *Interviews* will follow, requiring you to do *company research* and hone your sales pitch. The result? Good job offers.

A job search can be a full-time occupation in itself and takes time to develop. Don't expect to execute the entire search in a few weeks. Plan waves of contacts so that you are approaching new prospects every week, starting with your highest priorities. That way, each week you will be doing some cold calling, some new prospect work, some follow-ups, some interviewing, etc. This spreads the work out, keeps you fresh and interested, and keeps your spirits up, since it's always encouraging to make new contacts.

If you think you are beaten, you are;
If you think you dare not, you don't;
If you'd like to win, but think you can't,
It's almost a cinch you won't.
If you think you'll lose, you're lost.
For out in the world we find
Success begins with a fellow's will;
It's all in the state of mind.

If you think you're outclassed, you are;
You've got to think high to rise.
You've got to be sure of yourself before
You can ever win a prize.
Life's battles don't always go
To the stronger or faster man;
But soon or late the man who wins
Is the man who thinks he can.

—Walter D. Wintle
"The Man Who Thinks He Can"

WHY RESEARCH COMPANIES?

Every good salesperson knows that you not only have to know your product but you also have to know your customer before you can sell your product. You will be most successful in your job search if you can show employers—your customers—how you fit their needs. Good company research is therefore vital.

Yet employers tell tales of MBAs who come to an interview without knowing even the basic business of a company. Neither these employers nor I can understand how MBAs can be serious about a career and not research companies they interview with. Serious job hunters want to be sure companies they are considering will be a good match and offer the right kind of opportunities.

Company research will be important at a variety of steps in your job search, including prospecting, preparing for screening interviews, targeting your marketing strategies, developing your sales pitch, and making a good job decision. Early on, while you are prospecting and developing marketing strategies, you will need only limited information about a company. As you progress, you will need more and more. Each step raises new questions and new issues, sending you back to your resources for new information. The closer you get to a job offer and the more likely it becomes that you may work for a particular company, the more important good research becomes. By the time you reach the point of making a job decision, you will want to know the company intimately.

The amount of detail you need to go into should reflect the stage you are at in the job search. It doesn't make sense to do more research than you have to, given the large number of companies you will consider and the limited amount of time you have. Focus on just the essential information, increasing the detail at each step. With this approach, it's easy to fit company research into even the busiest schedule.

COMPANY INFORMATION SOURCES

There is no reason not to be well-informed about companies whose stock is publicly traded. Some of the common sources of information on public companies are:

Company publications. Most companies of any size produce large quantities of publicly available publications, including recruiting literature and sales material. Company personnel and investor relations offices will be happy to mail such material to you if you call for it. Most placement offices and some libraries have large collections. A caution—all of this is from the company's perspective; check other sources to eliminate any "sugar coating."

Corporate 10-K reports. All publicly held companies must file a "Form 10-K" with the SEC each year. This document includes a complete annual report, a business plan, a description of product lines, information about potential problems, and much more. Most large university and public libraries have extensive collections of 10-Ks, and they are also available from the company. These reports are a rich source of company information.

Investor publications. Moody's, Standard and Poor's, Dun & Bradstreet, and Dow Jones are the leading publishers of financial data and business forecasts for investors. Most large libraries have extensive collections.

Business press. Major business publications, such as *Fortune, Business Week, Forbes,* and *Barron's,* regularly include articles about corporate strategies and performance. The *Reader's Guide to Periodical Literature,* which indexes articles by subject, provides quick access to most business publications. InfoTrac and Dow Jones News/Retrieval Service are two computerized database services that provide similar information.

Alumni. Alumni contacts employed by the firm in which you are interested are an excellent source of information on "how it really is" and may be your only source for small companies. Your school may sponsor an alumni placement network. Check with your MBA placement office or alumni office for a directory.

Faculty. If you are an MBA candidate, don't forget that your faculty has worked with, observed, and studied, often in considerable detail, a number of companies in which you are likely to be interested. Faculty members will often have firsthand knowledge through their consulting activities or previous students.

If you are considering a small company, it will be much more difficult to find information. The only resources from the above list that are likely to be of help are alumni and faculty members. You can also contact the local Chamber of Commerce and Better Business Bureau, competitors, and other local businesses. Local newspapers and city or state business and commerce magazines may also have information.

WHAT TO KNOW ABOUT AN EMPLOYER

There is an overwhelming amount of material to absorb about any given company. Remember, though, that you're not trying to impress the employer with how much you can memorize or with your knowledge of obsure facts about the company. MBAs in particular should not appear to be know-it-alls. Try to get a basic understanding of what the company is, something of its history, and where it is headed. Demonstrate your knowledge by how effectively you sell yourself and by asking intelligent questions that ask for clarification and expansion of what you already know rather than basic information.

Never (and I mean *never!*) go to an interview without taking time to learn something about the company in question. Employers do not expect to answer questions that are answered in their published literature. They are looking for serious employees. To them, not researching the company is a sign of laziness and indifference.

You should focus on the following key items, where appropriate, to prepare for an interview:

- relative size of firm in the industry
- potential growth for the industry
- annual sales growth trend for the last five years
- array of product lines or services
- potential new markets, products, or services
- various price points in product or service line
- who the competition is
- how the company ranks against the industry
- organization structure—by product line, function, etc.
- geographical locations
- number of plants, stores, or sales outlets
- short-term profit picture
- training structure
- recent items in the news
- annual growth trend of earnings per share
- current price of stock
- recent sale or acquisition of business lines
- strategic direction of the firm
- compensation levels
- reputation
- people you know in the firm
- typical career path in your field
- name of recruiter

PROSPECTING

The first thing you're going to need to start your campaign is a list of prospects to approach! Unfortunately, lists of companies in directories and such seldom give you the information you need to identify high-potential prospects. If you prefer the "shotgun" approach, you'll find more prospects than you have time or money to contact. Because many MBAs find it difficult to develop a good prospect list, they end up with untargeted and ineffective job campaigns.

To develop a prospect list, you need to do "brief research." The central question to ask at this point is "Is it worth my time to approach this company?" This isn't the time to do extensive research, and you won't have time for it if you are looking at as long a prospect list as you should. All you need to establish is whether a company is a possible—not probable but possible—candidate. Many MBAs waste time at this point trying to determine whether a company is a probable candidate. You will never know for sure whether a particular company is one for which you would like to work until you have a chance to interview and usually not until you have an in-depth hiring interview. There will be only a few companies that you can get to know well before you interview, and those are the ones in which you have friends or family working. Thus, if you apply a "probable" standard at this point you will end up with too small a prospect list.

Students are usually much too quick to judge a company or a job. So often students tell me, "I don't like that," or "I don't think that is for me," based on very little information. Usually, that information is nothing more than a few pieces of recruiting literature or, more commonly, rumors on the student grapevine. Other times, students rule out a job on the basis of nothing more than their *perception* of what the job title means. I don't understand how people can be so quick to judge a company or a job. Why not take a 30-minute interview or send a resume? So what if you have to get dressed up in your suit or spend 25 cents for a stamp. Why not at least try to talk to the company to learn the *facts* directly from them? Experiment: Drop your resume in the placement office of companies you've never heard of. Go to career programs for companies that have not requested your concentration. Look at a job title different from the ones you normally do. Take advantage of every opportunity you can to get an interview or make a contact.

Don't worry if you can't see the obvious connection in the beginning. It's like putting your hands into a pond. If you reach down and churn the bottom, all sorts of things will float up. If you don't churn the waters, you'll never see what's hidden. So it is with your job search. You have to try everything you can. Eventually something will float up for you. I'll almost guarantee you that you'll find good jobs and companies that you might have ruled out on the basis of first impressions.

It might seem that I am contradicting what I said earlier about limiting your market to high-potential employers. I'm not at all. I don't mean to suggest that you should pursue prospective employers that you know little about instead of those that you know are high-potential prospects. But the fact remains that most MBAs limit themselves too much. When an unfamiliar company comes on campus, interview anyway. If you look in a directory indexed by career area to develop a mailing list and you spot unfamiliar companies, send a resume anyway. Put some priority to your efforts, but be open-minded and creative. You know far less than you think about most prospects and may be surprised at what results from a "shot in the dark."

The basic questions at this point are:

- What is the size of company?
- What are its industry and products?
- Does the company hire MBAs?
- Does the company operate in your discipline or interest area?
- Where is the company, including its various divisions and local operations, located?

If there is a match with even some of these items, it's worth at least a resume in the mail, if not a more involved strategy. But more about that later.

Now, where do you actually find the names? There are many sources that identify companies doing business in the United States and abroad. They provide much of the information you will need, but most are not indexed in a manner particularly useful to job seekers. Some of the more popular include:

- *Forbes* 1000 and Report on American Industry
- *Fortune* 500
- *INC.* 500
- Dun & Bradstreet's *Million Dollar Directory* 500
- Dun & Bradstreet's *Middle Market Directory* 500
- *Directory of Corporate Affiliations*
- Standard & Poor's
- Thomas' *Register of American Manufacturers*
- Moody's
- *Directory of American Firms Operating in Foreign Countries*

Many others focus on specific disciplines and industries (see complete resource listing in back of book). Consult *Klein's Guide to American Directories* to find a directory that focuses on your interest area.

Some directories do focus on providing indexes and information to help job seekers target their job search. Those that identify specific MBA job opportunities include:

- College Placement Council *Annual*

- *Peterson's Business and Management Jobs*
- Association of MBA Executives *MBA Employment Guide*

Finding prospects in a specific geographic area is not as difficult as it may seem. Each of the above resources includes some geographic information. The most valuable sources (usually overlooked) are the local Chambers of Commerce and Economic Development Offices. Almost all of them compile lists and directories of employers in their areas and will gladly give them to you or sell them to you cheap. Local classified ads and the phone company yellow pages are also good sources. A series of books entitled the *National Job Bank* by Bob Adams Inc is quite helpful. (See the resource listing for more geographic area directories.)

Knowing who to write to in the company can be as important as knowing which company to target. Generally, you want to go to as high a level in the company as you can, as long as the person to whom you write has some direct responsibility for your interest area. That means you don't always write the CEO! Try to obtain the name of the hiring manager or manager directly responsible for the area of the company in which you wish to work. The reason is simple: these people have the power to hire you, so they are the ones you want to impress. Personnel people can only recommend or refer. Furthermore, personnel staff almost always have more resumes to sift through than do the hiring managers, so your resume is less likely to get lost.

That's not to say that personnel people cannot provide valuable assistance. The personnel department enjoys a broad view of the company and can slot you into other departments if the department you have requested or applied for has no opening. Hiring managers usually know only their own department or a few departments at best. It's also often easier to get an appointment with the personnel department, and frequently the only name you will be able to find easily is that of the personnel director or employment manager. Often, they are the ones who initiate the hiring process. So if your objective is broad or your interest is focused on the company rather than a specific department, personnel may be your best first contact. Otherwise, contact the hiring manager.

Try as hard as you can to obtain *somebody's* name. Letters that start with "Dear Sir" or "To whom it may concern" are not nearly as effective. One obvious way to get the appropriate name is to call the company and ask. The annual report and 10-K also list the officers and upper-level executives in the company. The College Placement Council's *National Directory* lists the primary employment contacts for member firms, which includes most large firms in the

United States. Friends, faculty members, and alumni are excellent sources of names too. Remember, though, that publications (including the 10-K) are only reliably accurate as of their publication date.

CHOOSING A STRATEGY

Once you have compiled a list of your prospects, you are ready to develop strategies with which to approach them. There are a number of job search strategies that you can adopt to find the job that fits your career objective. This section discusses the most common methods: on-campus interviews, job listings, "friendworking," mass mailings, classified ads, and employment agencies. It outlines the pros and cons of each and rates each one low, moderate, or high on four scales:

- cost—the out-of-pocket expenses you can expect to pay
- probability of success—the chances of your securing follow-up interviews with this method
- time—the amount of time that you must invest
- scope—the variety of employers and, therefore, job objectives that can be met

You should realize that finding a job is a very imperfect process. No one strategy can easily be labeled the best. Which ones you choose will depend heavily on the combination of job objective, type of prospects, personal style, time and money available, and other circumstances. Each has its unique advantages and disadvantages, and all have been used successfully in different situations.

There are two basic principles. First, always look for the strategy that has the highest probability of reaching your prospects effectively. All too often MBAs choose methods that are low-cost and take the least time—they look for the most convenient way. In fact, this is an alluring trap that may lead to a frustrating job search because the most convenient strategies often have the lowest probability of success. If you had unlimited time, I'd say just try all the strategies you can to reach your markets. Given that you don't, though, you will find a job more quickly if you choose methods that have the highest probability of success *with your target market*.

The second principle, which offsets the first, is the need to diversify your strategies. Quite simply, you shouldn't bank on any one strategy alone. MBAs should always be working a variety of angles, watching the classifieds, mailing out resumes, interviewing on campus, etc. You will be making a foolish mistake if you limit yourself too much. What this means is that for any given company you approach, you should be able to identify one or two strategies that will be most effective, molding the approach strategy to the target. Effective campaigns combine all strategies to a certain extent.

A final consideration, of course, is practicality. Just about every person seeking a job has some limit to his or her resources. Unemployed people have plenty of time but not much money. Working people have money but usually not much time. Students are usually short of both time and money. Thus, it's impossible to conduct the "perfect" campaign. You must do what is practical within the resources available to you. Don't be too limiting, though, or use practicality as an excuse to take the easy way out. At the MBA level, the salaries and the level of opportunities are too high to let time and cost be a major factor. Also, remember that every job hunter has some kind of limit, so really you are no worse off than your competition.

I will persist until I succeed.

—Og Mandino
From *The Greatest Salesman on Earth*

On-Campus Interviews

If you are fortunate enough to have access to a good college placement office, you have a real gold mine. Such offices do much of your work for you by making employers convenient for you to reach. It is the only job search strategy that is highly convenient, takes little time, *and* has a high probability of success. College placement offices usually have on file a wealth of names of employers and contacts that can be invaluable to you. Never in your life will it be so easy to obtain an interview as it is through your college placement office while you are completing your MBA.

Once you leave school, your real challenge is getting your foot in the door if you should decide to seek employment again. I have seen graduates work for months and even years to obtain as many interviews as you can easily get while still in school. In a college placement office, the employer actually comes to you. Although you still must earn the interview based on your qualifications, it is a great deal easier than it would be if you were dependent on only a cover letter and a resume.

Think of it this way: when you send employers a resume through the mail, they do not have to interview you. The only way they *can* interview you is to bring you to the job site, which is fairly expensive. But in a college placement office, employers will interview twelve to fourteen people each day. Generally, they will fill the schedule, even if only a few of the candidates are of the caliber that they would invite to the job site after receiving an unsolicited resume. The employers are there to interview and will take maximum advantage of the situation. It is economical for them to interview all candidates in whom they have any potential interest. Thus many students receive interviews on campus who would not be considered if they mailed in a resume.

Clearly, the on-campus interview process is an absolute gem of an opportunity; the time investment is minimal and the potential is high. Yet I see student after student let numerous opportunities slip by, perhaps because placement offices lull students into believing it will be easy to get more. It won't be; don't pass it up.

However, you should not rely exclusively on the on-campus strategies to find your job. There are thousands of positions available that will never find their way onto a college campus. College placement offices cannot possibly recruit all those employers or provide opportunities to fit every student's objective. So plan to devote time to other job search strategies in order to maximize your job prospects.

Strategy: On-Campus Interviews

- Cost: low
- Probability of success: high
- Time: low
- Scope: high

Job Listings

Many employers choose not to make personal visits to campuses, usually because of cost and time considerations, but they do recognize college placement offices as valuable sources of talent. College placement offices usually develop good working relationships with these employers, who in turn notify the placement offices whenever they have openings for which a college graduate may be qualified. These job listings and contacts are a valuable extension of the placement office's function. Yet, they too are often underutilized. Once again, the employers are coming to you, the student, to notify you of openings instead of your having to chase them. You should pay very close attention to the job listings and make contact on each one that has *any* potential match with your objectives.

An employer has two options for follow-up on a job listing, neither of which is very desirable. A few companies will interview you by telephone. However, such interviews can be awkward for people who feel uncomfortable speaking on the phone. Phone interviews also provide only limited information compared with face-to-face interviews. The other option is to bring you to the job site for an interview. Unless you happen to be in the same city, this is quite expensive. Employers are forced to spend a substantial amount of money based on nothing more than their impression of your resume. The result is that the yield from this method will be substantially lower than from campus interviews.

So how can you be most effective with this method? You must make your application stand out from the crowd. It is absolutely essential that your resume be the best possible, since that is all the recruiter has to judge you by before spending money on you. The most successful candidates using this strategy also write very good cover letters. Their letters are usually a little longer and more detailed than the average, since they need to do some of the selling that they would normally do in an interview. They will probably sound more aggressive than your normal letters, but you have to get the employer's attention. A highly effective strategy is to offer to make the trip to the employer's office for a screening interview at your own expense. A phone call to discuss the position may help make your name stand out. Finally, a personal reference from the placement office or a faculty member will get the employer's attention.

Strategy: Job Listings

- Cost: low
- Probability of success: moderate
- Time: low
- Scope: moderate

Friendworking

The most effective approach by far to an off-campus job search is through personal contacts. Most MBA candidates either know or can find people in all types of industries who can help with a job search. They may not be able to give you a job, but they can help. I call this approach "friendworking" instead of networking, since networking often connotes the use of high-level contacts that most students don't have. It takes some hard work and creativity, but you can make contacts. Don't assume that just because you don't know a lot of people right now you cannot use contacts to find a job.

The basic principle on which friendworking is based is that any resume or referral received by a company with the recommendation or sponsorship of an employee of that company will get considerably more attention than an unsolicited resume received in the mail. Employers want to make the best decision possible, and they feel more confident when somebody already employed by them knows a candidate. Most companies even have special handling procedures for resumes received through employees.

Master of human destinies am I.
Fame, love, and fortune on my footsteps wait,
Cities and fields I walk; I penetrate
Deserts and seas remote, and, passing by
Hovel, and mart, and palace, soon or late
I knock unbidden, once at every gate!
If sleeping, wake—if feasting, rise before
I turn away. It is the hour of fate,
And they who follow me reach every state
Mortals desire, and conquer every foe
Save death; but those who doubt or hesitate,
Condemned to failure, penury and woe,
Seek me in vain and uselessly implore—
I answer not, and I return no more.

—John James Ingalls
"Opportunity"

Your ultimate objective is to find the person who has the power to hire you. Usually, you cannot find that person immediately but will have to use a more indirect approach. Your immediate objective for friendworking should *not* be to find people who have jobs to offer. If you approach friends asking them if they know anybody who has a job opening, most will say no. A more circumspect and effective approach is to find a person who works for or knows somebody who works for a company that you would like to work for and has the power, or can refer you to someone who has the power, to get you an *interview*.

This objective is achievable. Since you are looking for an interview, not a commitment to hire, you are much more likely to succeed. The approach is simple:

Friendworking Sources

friends	classmates
teachers	relatives
neighbors	acquaintances
colleagues	members of professional
club members	associations

1. Make a list of everyone you know (relatives, friends, associates) who works for—or might know someone who works for—a company in which you might be interested. List only those with whom you have more than a casual acquaintance.
2. Call these people. It's more personal than writing a letter, and it doesn't force them to spend time writing you a letter.
3. Tell them you are finishing or have finished your MBA, are looking for a job, and need some help in getting interviews.
4. Ask them: "Do you know anyone in your company, or do you have a friend, who could help me get an *interview?*" Make it clear that you do not necessarily mean someone who can grant you the interview—another contact will be fine.
5. If the response is positive, ask them: "May I use your name when I contact that person?"
6. If you feel comfortable with the person at this point, ask: "Do you have any friends or associates who might refer me as you just did and would not mind my calling?"
7. If the response is positive, again ask: "May I use your name?"
8. Thank them.

There are some key principles that you must pay attention to in order for this to work:

- Do not look directly for people with jobs to offer you. Remember that you are looking for leads to get your foot in the door.
- Always shoulder the burden of work yourself. Do not ask your contacts for return letters or to make the calls for you. Limit their work to what happens during your phone conversation unless they offer more.

- Let your contacts be noncommittal. Don't make them stick their neck out. Be clear that you want an opening to *sell yourself,* not for them to sell you.

Congratulations—you are now friendworking! Time and again this process has worked to direct students to the right people to talk to inside companies. Often, people you contact will appreciate your initiative so much that they will actually sponsor you for a job in their company.

Don't be intimidated by friendworking. It is not the type of process that enables you to predict in advance the path it will take. All you need is one person to start with. That person will lead to several more, who in turn will lead to still more, and so on. You simply have to get started. Pick up the phone and make a call. Be creative.

Strategy: Friendworking

- Cost: moderate
- Probability of success: high
- Time: moderate
- Scope: high

Mass Mailings

Probably the most frequently used and the most frustrating job search strategy is mass mailings. At one time or another, everyone seems to try this process of sending out volumes of mail in hopes of being invited to come in for an interview. This is probably the easiest job search strategy to implement. It is extremely simple to find a list of companies that you want to contact. As computers and word processors have become more prevalent, it has become even easier to develop a mailing list and mass-produce cover letters.

The problem with mail campaigns is that corporate personnel offices usually receive hundreds of resumes each day. Reviewing them is a grueling process, and after a while they all begin to look and sound alike. While most companies will at least glance at each resume, the odds of any of them standing out are low. So your resume and cover letter have to almost dance on the desk to catch the recruiter's attention.

Many mail campaigns are untargeted and use cover letters that are written generically in order to appeal to every possible company. Such letters are usually uninspired and don't sell well. Unless you have a very unusual set of qualifications, this type of campaign is unlikely to yield any results for you. The only mail campaigns that seem to work are those that are carefully targeted and those where

Strategy: Mass Mailings

- Cost: moderate
- Probability of success: low
- Time: low
- Scope: high

special effort is put into the cover letter. Campaigns that are targeted at high-potential companies and use a tailored cover letter often result in some interviews.

You need to take responsibility for follow-ups if you want this strategy to work. Most cover letters I see say something like, "I would like an interview. Please call me to arrange a time if you are interested." The logic is sound: *if* the employer likes you, you will be contacted. But you'll get better results if you take the initiative and say, "I would like to request an interview. I will call you in two weeks to see if we can arrange a mutually convenient time." It seems that the combination of removing the burden from the overworked recruiters and taking the initiative to follow up leads to a higher success rate. It also gets you an answer a lot sooner.

At best, you can expect a low response rate from this strategy—probably around 1 or 2 percent. But since the time investment is low, this is not bad. While mass mailings can be a valuable supplement to other strategies, job seekers who rely exclusively on them are likely to become very frustrated. If you are not going to take the time to target your campaign, I suggest you save your money.

You should plan to do a well-targeted mass-mailing campaign for four specific purposes: (1) to broaden your prospect list when you are making maximum use of on-campus strategies and friendworking, (2) to look for a relatively specialized job within a small market, (3) to look at small companies that do not have large recruiting staffs, and (4) to focus on a specific city.

Names of companies to write to are relatively easy to find (see the appendix). You will find thousands of companies that you may wish to contact.

Your cover letter and resume must be extraordinarily well printed and developed. For mail campaigns, some advisers recommend that you choose colored stationery to stand out from the pile. There is little merit in this advice, so don't change the paper color just for the mail campaign. It is more important to have a good word processing service print your letters so that they will be of high quality.

Classified Ads

Most job hunters peruse classified ads in the work areas that they are interested in. National business publications, such as the *Wall Street Journal* and *Barron's,* as well as all major newspapers, contain extensive employment listings that may be quite valuable to you. They are a good source of leads, but there are thousands of people who will see the same ad, so the volume of replies is likely to be very high, particularly if the job is attractive. In addition, only a small

Strategy: Classified Ads

- Cost: low
- Probability of success: low
- Time: low
- Scope: high

percentage of the jobs available in this country ever make it to the classified ads. Most major employers place an ad only after they have exhausted other sources of filling the job. If you rely totally on classified ads, you are missing the majority of the job openings. However, it takes little time to peruse the ads and to respond, so use them. At the same time, don't pass up a majority of the job openings by not seeking those that are never advertised. Use the classifieds but don't make them the cornerstone of your job search.

Employment Agencies

Employment agencies are most commonly used by job seekers with some job experience and not by those coming straight out of college. For MBAs who have significant professional work experience, they are a viable alternative. For the new college graduate without work experience, employment agencies will not likely have positions.

Employment agencies operate as a broker. They maintain lists of candidates and openings from employers. They earn their money by charging a fee of 10 to 20 percent of your starting salary, which may be paid by you or by the employer. Some employment agencies may even charge an up-front fee to list your name. They are most valuable for targeting a specific geographic area and for higher-level positions. Employment agencies do have better access to small companies and are typically able to blanket a specific geographic area very well. Experienced students and those forced to restrict their job search to a specific geographic area should consider using employment agencies.

Unfortunately, there are some good agencies and some unscrupulous ones. If you are asked to sign a contract, be sure to read it thoroughly. Some contracts may restrict your job search flexibility and freedom. For example, if you sign a contract with an employment agency and subsequently take a job with a company that

---

Strategy: Employment Agencies

- Cost: high
- Probability of success: moderate
- Time: low
- Scope: low to moderate

---

happens to be a client of that agency, you may owe it a fee even if you did not obtain the contact through the agency. Also, the effectiveness of employment agencies is somewhat mixed. Large organizations tend not to use employment agencies because they find it more economical and less trouble to maintain their own in-house recruiting function. Smaller companies find it is smarter to use employment agencies than to incur the overhead of having their own staff.

Creative Strategies

One thing you quickly learn when devising job search strategies is that sometimes it's best to ignore all the rules and try something different. Anything can work anytime, given the right combination of circumstances. The attitude a person has plays a bigger role in determining success than do specific strategies. The only constant is that there is no limit to the creativity and ingenuity of aggressive MBAs. What follows are some of the less common but more creative approaches to the job search:

- **Volunteering.** Find an organization doing things similar to what you want, or doing things for someone you want to work for, and volunteer. It'll give you a chance to demonstrate your skills and acquire marketable experience, and it might just get you an offer.

- **Temping.** Signing on with a temporary help agency for professionals while looking for a job is a good way to get your foot in the door with companies, try out some jobs, demonstrate skills, get experience, and pay the bills. Most employers find it hard to let good talent go.

- **Joining civic organizations.** Civic organizations are a great place to network since most businesspeople join them to show community support. At a lunch or banquet you might just find yourself sitting next to a person with the power to hire you.

- **Placing work-wanted ads.** These ads are rarely effective in broad, national publications (*Wall Street Journal, USA Today,* etc.) since usually only desperate people place them there. However, they can be effective in professional journals and trade publications, particularly if you are in a specialized or narrowly defined area.

- **Pounding the pavement.** If you can stand lots of rejection, cold calls to employers may work. They take guts and initiative, and some employers admire that. You also get the chance to present yourself in person instead of just on paper. With a little luck, the secretary will be out and the personnel director will be greeting visitors personally.

- **Joining professional associations.** These organizations usually have a job search bulletin board or some other means of helping members network.

Chapter 10

Resumes

Preparing a resume can be a puzzling and frustrating task for new job hunters as well as experienced ones. Yet it is one of the most important steps in a job search. Without a well-prepared resume, you will never get your foot in the door. This chapter will help eliminate some of the mystery surrounding resume writing and enable you to prepare a resume that will be an effective tool in your job search.

CONCEPTS

The Art of Resume Writing
Resume writing is an art, not a science. Despite what others may tell you, there is no one correct way to write one. Each resume is an individual statement that reflects a person's unique personality, education, experience, and career objective. The "art" of resume writing is in the assessment of the portfolio a job hunter has to market and the selection of the right material to paint the best possible picture of that person. It should be your personal advertisement to help you find the job you want.

This may run counter to the way you have learned to write resumes. Typically, resume writing is taught as the filling out of a personal data form, where the emphasis is on collecting facts to present your professional history accurately. This may work at the undergraduate level, but it won't work for MBAs. Resume mechanics are important, but the best resumes bring forth your unique qualities, your individuality. There are no formulas (beware of those who say there are). There are some accepted practices and guidelines, but you should view these only as tools to help you craft your personal statement.

Resume writing is hard work. A truly good resume generally takes longer than a few days or a weekend to prepare. It requires countless hours of thought, writing, and editing. Picking over the exact word, experimenting with different formats, and producing many drafts before one finally seems right is very common. Then, you may find yourself revising the finished resume over and over as you gain experience using it and receive feedback on it. It should continue to evolve throughout your career. Be prepared to invest a lot of energy and time in it.

The Purpose of a Resume

A resume is not a fact sheet, not a job application, not your life history. It's just a special form of advertisement. It's little different in concept and execution from a magazine ad or a television or radio commercial. When you create any kind of ad, you are trying to tell customers that a product is for sale and to entice them to take a closer look at it and consider buying it. You want to make a positive impression on prospective buyers that will encourage them to take one step further in the buying process.

It's not that you should dress the resume up with neon lights and make it look like a billboard—but you have to think of it as a promotional tool. Too many MBAs approach their resume as if it were a data sheet or job application. Its purpose is to help you sell yourself. If you think of it as a marketing tool, you'll find yourself writing a totally different resume from the one you would otherwise write.

Remember that what you want to sell is yourself, but understand the limits of what a resume can achieve for you. All you really want it to do is to win you an *interview*. It's extremely rare that anyone gets a job offer just by putting nice words on paper. A resume can go a long way toward creating a positive atmosphere, but it won't get you a job by itself. Too many MBAs try to put everything in a resume that they would want to say to an employer face-to-face. That's impossible, and it's counterproductive. All you want to do is to put enough highlights in the resume to get the employer's attention and get an interview. Then you can tell the rest of your story.

The Resume Reader's Perspective

A well-prepared resume makes a subtle but strong psychological impact on the reader. Exactly what causes this impact is difficult for the reader to pinpoint. Even professional recruiters, who read resumes all the time, often say they just know intuitively when they have a good resume in hand. In its overall effect, the resume conveys the professionalism, confidence, and capability of the writer. It is easy to read, looks nice, says important things, and somehow just seems to flow.

It is important to understand that it is not the mechanics of the resume per se that make the difference but rather the overall impact and impression that they help create. No recruiter is going to say, "I really like this person but I do wish he had used one-inch margins and capitalized headings." A recruiter may comment on obvious errors, such as misspellings or sloppiness. But for the most part the guidelines and mechanics presented here are simply tools that work as a package to sell you and create a good feeling in the reader. They work at a more subtle, subconscious level to create an overall impression.

. . . Wisdom is born out of experience, and most of all out of precisely such experience as is brought to us by the darkest moments. It is in the meeting of such moments that are born new insights, new sympathies, new powers, new skills.

Such conflicts as we are in the midst of today cannot be won by any single stroke, by any one strategy sprung from the mind of any single genius. Rather must we pin our faith upon the inventiveness, the resourcefulness, the initiative of every one of us. That cannot fail us if we keep faith in ourselves and our future, and in the constant growth of our intelligence and ability to cooperate with one another.

The memory of Americans' . . . glory in Valley Forge tells us the truth which echoes upward from this soil of blood and tears: **the way to greatness is the path of self-reliance, independence, and steadfastness in time of trial and stress.**

—Herbert Hoover
Valley Forge, 1931

Let me tell you how I know a student has written a good resume. When I go to lunch with an employer who has seen that student's resume, all I hear the employer talking about is the student and how wonderful he or she must be. The employer is so excited about the student that not a single word is uttered about the resume itself. But what does the employer talk about when the resume is not well done? The resume—usually because it is boring and doesn't tell him what he needs or wants to know. It's sort of like watching television commercials. (You know how bad some of them are!) The product may be terrific, but all you have to go on is the information that's in the commercial. If that's not done well, you give up. You may not know much about developing commercials (or at least don't take the time to think about it), but you certainly know the good ones when you seem them. It's the same way with resumes.

When recruiters read a promising resume, they can feel the excitement building inside them. Everything in the resume is "meaty" and tells something good and important about the writer. The more they read, the more they want to read. When they've finished, they can't wait to interview the person. Some of the excitement comes from good qualifications and skills (no resume "trick" can make up for that). But many a well-qualified student has failed in the job market because his or her resume failed to sell and excite the reader. A well-written resume can make the difference.

The message of a good resume is clear and unequivocal. The writer takes the burden of drawing conclusions and pointing out qualifications explicitly, remembering that employers hate to have to work to find an important detail or to have to assume something about the writer's background.

It is very difficult for you to be objective about your resume. To determine what kind of impression it makes, you should test-market it. Ask friends, colleagues, and counselors to read your resume and react to it. Find out what creates positive and negative reactions for them and why. Use the feedback from them to see if your message is really getting through.

Static

As a promotional tool, your resume is designed to communicate a message. All of the concepts and tools in the rest of this guide are designed to help the reader receive your message clearly. It is much like a radio broadcast—you want the signal to be received loud and clear without any static. So as you read about type size, copying, white space, layout, supporting the objective, eliminating extra words, etc., remember that "static" is anything that obscures your central message or makes it difficult for the reader to "hear." You should work to "boost the signal" so that your message is strong, and eliminate any static interference. Some common causes of static include wordiness, redundancy, poor layout, poor typing, poor copying, ineffective highlighting, and poor organization.

The Job Objective

One key to a well-written resume is your job objective. The objective defines your target market and determines what information you include. You should never write anything until you have developed the objective, because that is what gives your resume its focus. The reason why so many people struggle when writing their resume is not that the mechanics are difficult but that they themselves have no focus, so they can't figure out what to write in the resume.

Everything in the resume should support in some way your basic contention that you would be a good person to hire for whatever your job objective says you want. If it doesn't do that, take it out of the resume. Effective sales-oriented resumes present a tightly woven series of facts that maintain a direct link to the job objective. This is quite different from the more commonly used approach of presenting all of your professional qualifications to every employer and letting each one figure out which apply. That's not good selling.

Creating one general resume doesn't work, because in its breadth it will become so diluted as to lose its ability to sell effectively. Ideally, you should tailor a resume for each job and employer with whom you interview. A more practical approach is to create different resumes for categories of job objectives and for industries where the required qualifications significantly differ. Most job hunters need at least two or three resumes.

For example, suppose your prior training is in nursing and you have worked as a nursing supervisor. Now you want to interview for hospital administration and nursing positions. You will need one resume to focus on medical experience and skills and another to focus on administrative and supervisory skills. Because the job objective for each is different, the body of each resume should also be different.

Keep in mind that some facts, although only distantly connected to your specific objective, may still make helpful statements about you. An unrelated job may indicate your breadth of experience or initiative. Volunteer work may demonstrate your skill with people or civic-mindedness. So, don't be too harsh in judging whether an item in your resume supports your objective. Simply be sure that anything you include in some way makes a statement about you, has a purpose, and will support your objective.

Some advisers prefer to see the job objective stated in the cover letter instead of the resume. While I generally disagree with this advice, it can be appropriate. But regardless of where it appears, your resume needs the focus of a well-defined objective.

Ordering the Details

Your resume should contain those items that sell you best and make the strongest case for your being fully qualified to do the job.

There simply is not enough room on the paper to say everything about yourself that you may want to. Your challenge is to select your most valuable strengths and assets. You will be forced to make trade-offs as to what to include. The resume should begin with the most important and proceed to the least important details. You want the excitement to start as soon as the reader picks the resume up. If you bury your strengths near the bottom of the page, the reader may lose interest. If you have a considerable amount of education or are just coming out of school, your education may be your most important qualification and should appear early in the resume. On the other hand, if you have extensive work experience and that is your strongest qualification, it should appear first.

Similarly, it is important for you to effectively arrange the data within "Job Experience" and "Education" sections. What you lead with will have a great deal of impact. Consider what it is you want most to sell. In your education section, do you want to sell the degrees you have earned, or where you went to school? For work experience, your title(s) will say much about the type of skills you've learned, while the company you worked for will say much about the quality of experience. Lead with the one you want to emphasize most. You must decide which supports your objective and sells best for you.

How to Say It

The basic goal of a resume is communication. Consequently, it should be written so that anyone can read and understand it. You should never include technical terms or jargon that may be unfamiliar to the reader. And you must think very carefully about each fact, word, or phrase that you put in the resume. When well thought out and well written, every word can accomplish something for you. Don't worry if you spend considerable time debating the use of a word simply because it doesn't feel right. You are trying not only to tell the facts but to create in the employer a positive, enthusiastic feeling about you.

Make your statements concise. Employers read so many resumes that they appreciate those that don't waste their time. Complete sentences are not necessary; phrases will do nicely. You don't need to use personal pronouns, such as "I," since they are implied and just take up space. Double-check every phrase or sentence to see if there is a more succinct way to say it. Be direct, and don't waste the reader's time with unimportant words.

Avoid redundancy both in words and in thoughts. For example, a skill mentioned as part of your work experience should not be repeated in a "Skills" section.

It is also important that you pay close attention to technical English skills. Abbreviations of titles and names should be used consistently and accurately. There should be no misspellings or grammatical errors; they indicate ignorance and leave the reader with the impression that you don't care about your career.

Your resume must flow. The reader should not be dragged through a disjointed, jumbled, and halting discourse of unrelated facts. If your resume is well thought out, everything in it will be directed toward the objective, and no errors in writing style will mar it.

DESIGN AND PRODUCTION

Most employers comment that they are amazed at the number of people who fail to take the time to create a positive, professional image when they produce their resume. Employers cannot understand why a job candidate is not interested enough in his or her career to learn from any resume book what needs to be done to craft an attractive resume—to take the few extra minutes to go to a first-rate copy center or to pay a few extra dollars to get the resume professionally typed. Would you wear a stained shirt or a wrinkled suit or go with uncombed hair to an interview? Of course not. Then why use poor-quality paper or a cheap typewriter to produce your resume?

In this section you will learn some simple approaches that will help you design and produce a resume that says, "I am a great person," and, "I care." If you do your job well, nobody will notice what production techniques you use—but they will invite you for an interview.

Appearance

Appearance is a key factor in producing an effective resume, and it is the aspect of resume writing most often discussed. Although everyone knows that resumes should look neat and professional, far too many still have a messy, disorganized, hurriedly-put-together look. On the other hand, there is no reason to produce a resume looking like a formal prospectus for a stock offering or a glamorous spread in *National Geographic*. Unless you are applying for a graphics design position or some other job where demonstrated creativity is important, it is a waste of time to take more than the few simple design steps outlined in this section.

The only thing you need to pay close attention to is the *overall* appearance of your resume. Recruiters won't care what layout you use, whether you capitalize or underline, whether you use pica or elite type, or whether your margins are large or small. But they will be influenced by the resume's visual appeal. A resume that is visually attractive can work to your advantage by conveying an image of professionalism and competence. Remember that your resume is only a piece of paper, but it must create in the recruiter's mind as favorable an image as you would hope to create if you were being interviewed in person.

Companies invest a lot of time, money, and energy in maintaining and building their public image. They maintain the staff and office equipment necessary to present themselves to the public and their customers as professional, well-run organizations. If you want to join them, you must take the same approach.

. . . Then a ploughman said, Speak to us of Work.
And he answered, saying:
You work that you may keep pace with the earth
and the soul of the earth.
For to be idle is to become a stranger unto the
seasons, and to step out of life's procession, that
marches in majesty and proud submission towards
the infinite . . .

Always you have been told that work is a curse
and labour a misfortune.
But I say to you that when you work you fulfil a
part of earth's furthest dream . . .

—Kahlil Gibran
From *The Prophet*

Readability

Another key factor is readability. The reader must immediately understand what you are saying. If you were in an interview, you would speak clearly so the listener could hear and comprehend you. Your resume should do no less. Readability means type size and style, paper color, physical organization, heading placement, reproduction quality, etc. If readers have to strain in any way to understand your words, you are not speaking clearly and will not create a positive impression. Even the best-written resume will not be fully effective if the quality of reproduction is poor, the type style is difficult to read, or the color of the paper detracts from the message. The reader should be able to glide through the resume smoothly from beginning to end.

Once again, the mechanics are not as important as the reader's ability to sail smoothly through the resume. You want the reader to feel comfortable, relaxed, and content while reading the resume. You want the words to jump off the page by looking crisp and clear. They should work to broadcast your message, unencumbered by static interference. Make your resume difficult to read so the reader becomes impatient or frustrated, and you are only encouraging him or her to move on to another resume.

To test appearance and readability, hold your resume at arm's length and examine it as a physical object. Look at the overall arrangement and the balance. Is it symmetrical? Does the type run off center on the page? Examine the resume at closer range. Are the words sharp and clear? Do the sections stand out distinctly? Are the reproduction and paper quality good? Now begin reading. Do the words stand out as you read, or do you have to strain to see them clearly? Only if you can answer all these questions favorably does your resume pass this simple test.

Skimmability

Most resumes receive only a very quick reading. Estimates vary from 20 to 60 seconds. Employers have too many resumes to read each one in depth, so they skim them for a few important pieces of information. First, they check the objective to see if it matches their openings. Then they look for degrees, GPA, and work experience. Only then do they decide whether the resume is worth a complete reading.

Your resume needs to make its impact quickly and to entice the reader to look at it in more depth. "Skimmability" is a design and production concept that will help get your resume read in detail by an employer.

Skimmable Data

- objective
- degrees/major
- GPA
- job titles
- places of employment

Be sure that each of the bulleted items shown in the accompanying box stands out clearly in your resume. If employers can pick out these elements with a quick glance and your qualifications look good, they will be more likely to read your resume in depth. If they cannot locate key data quickly, they are more likely to pass it over. I favor a resume that uses bold print, underlining, and capitalization to direct the reader to the most important information and that invites the reader to peruse the resume in a logical sequence.

Length

Resume counselors disagree vehemently over the proper length of a resume. The great "one-page controversy" continues to rage furiously among both counselors and recruiters. One school of thought says that a resume should never be longer than one page. "If you can't say it in one page, it doesn't need to be said" is the argument. Recruiters in this group do not want to have their time wasted by a second page and generally need only the briefest amount of information to decide if they should interview a candidate. At the opposite extreme are academic resumes, where one must tell his or her life story and the length says as much as the content. Job hunters are caught in a vicious tug of war, and, unfortunately, so are resume counselors as they listen to conflicting opinions from employers.

There is general agreement that a resume should never exceed two pages outside the academic world. There is also general agreement that a resume should be as short and concise as possible. Whether it is one page or two, it should be as economical as you can possibly make it.

I believe that length is not the overriding consideration and that two pages are perfectly acceptable. Frankly, I think the whole argument is unnecessary. There are simply more important considerations in constructing the resume than to establish a finite length from the beginning. Also, many employers like to see more information than will fit on one page. If the resume is well constructed, the employer will be glad to read the second page. Pay close attention to all the other resume design principles *first*. If you end up with two pages, it must be because you have something good to say.

It is true that some recruiters will react negatively to a second page. We have all heard the stories about those who tear off the second page and throw it away. That may be true in a few cases, but what most recruiters object to is not the fact that there are two pages but that many applicants abuse the second page. The second page often is just a license to become wordy and sloppy or to throw in irrelevant information. Some advisers simply use the one-page rule as a convenient means of forcing applicants to write a concise, well-constructed resume. That's the real reason for the one-page rule.

But many MBAs may in fact need a second page to do an adequate job of selling themselves. Don't ever undersell yourself just to fit on one page. (However, one page is usually sufficient for students without work experience.) Because a few employers may have a negative view of a second page, do be doubly sure that what you say there needs to be said and adds something important to the resume. And be sure to put your most important information on the first page.

If you have information that you feel the employer should know and that will force your resume to go *beyond* two pages, it should be included as an addendum or on supplemental data sheets. Examples include course work, transcripts, a reference list, and extensive volunteer work.

Layout

Three basic layouts are commonly used for resumes. They are shown on pages 182, 184, and 186. Unless your situation is exceptional, one of these layouts will be fine. All of them are generally accepted by recruiters. The key difference among the three is the placement of the section headings in relation to the text.

The resume on pages 182–83 shows the *block layout,* where the titles are offset to the left of each section. It is widely used and is attractive to the eye. The organization is clear and easy to read and follow. Although it may be the best layout for legibility and appearance, it takes up a lot of space. Your information is actually written on only two thirds of the width of the page, so you simply cannot get as many facts on one page. Therefore, the block layout is not very desirable if your resume is bordering on two pages and you want to reduce it to one page or if you are having trouble fitting your information on two pages..

The resume on pages 184–85 shows the *centered layout,* where the titles to each section are centered on the page. This layout allows for maximum use of the width of the page and therefore gives you the maximum amount of information on one page. However, as the eye scans the resume, the section headings often are lost among all the other words, causing the resume to appear disorganized and to run together. Our eyes are trained to move from left to right across a page, not to the center and then to the margin, back to the center, etc. In practice, these resumes usually are the least attractive, are the hardest to read, and have the lowest skimmability.

The resume on page 186 shows the *indented layout,* where the paragraphs of the resume are indented under the section headings. This is an excellent compromise. It allows for much greater use of the space on the page than the block layout while being more readable and appealing to the eye than the centered layout. This layout enables you to put a relatively large amount of data on the page in a clear, easy-to-read fashion.

I strongly prefer either the block or the indented over the centered layout. If space is not a problem, I have a slight preference for the block layout over the indented.

In addition to the location of the headings, you can also see from the examples the different effect of using a *bullet* or a *paragraph* layout for the information to be included in each section of the resume. The bullet approach (you can also use a dash or an asterisk) presents each point in the resume as a separate item. Because it uses punctuation to separate each major point in your resume, it heightens both readability and skimmability. The problem is that it takes up a lot of space. If you have a lot of good experience or a lot to say, this format can very easily force you to two pages.

The alternative is the paragraph approach. You use the same information but link the sentences together in a block paragraph. This approach uses space much more efficiently, but it makes the resume a lot less skimmable.

Each section of the resume is a candidate for the bullet or paragraph layout (see examples). Generally, you should be consistent throughout the resume. I usually prefer the bullet approach because it makes each point in the resume stand out so strongly. If you don't have much work experience, it also gives your resume better balance. However, most MBAs have more to say than a bullet layout allows space for and therefore adopt the paragraph layout. You'll have to make the trade-off, but the indented paragraph layout is the most common format for MBAs and can prove quite effective.

Printing

There is another great controversy over whether or not to have your resume typeset and commercially printed. Many counselors say that printing is not necessary and that it is a waste of time and money. I agree that it is not necessary. It is certainly acceptable to have your resume typed, or laser-printed off a computer, and then reproduced (a note on reproduction later). If you are going to type your resume or have it typed, be sure that it is typed on an IBM Selectric or a similar top-of-the-line business-quality typewriter. Do not under any circumstances type it on a portable or home typewriter or use a dot-matrix computer printer. The results look terrible. There is no excuse for not having the best-quality typewriter possible, since there are plenty of word processing and typing services that will give you a professional job for very little money.

Having your resume commercially printed is not a waste of time and money. Printed resumes attain a standard of clarity, crispness, and professionalism that cannot be matched by a typed resume. They always stand out for their legibility and eye appeal. Particularly for an MBA, the professional image they create is well worth the expense. No recruiter is going to subtract points for your not printing your resume, but the printed resume is better and will repay the extra cost.

Copying

If you type your resume, the copying service you use will be extremely important. There is every reason to buy the best quality of copying you can find. The stakes are a career and an entry-level job that will pay you $25,000–$50,000 a year; this is not the time to worry about $10. Cheap copying will ruin even the best-typed resume. So make sure you get crisp, clear reproduction.

Type Size

If you are having your resume professionally produced, select a type size that is large enough to be easily readable. Ask to see samples of different sizes, and see what looks right to you. If you are typing the resume, don't do it on large paper and then reduce it to fit 8 1/2 x 11. Small type is very difficult to read and may be ignored. (Keep in mind, however, that larger sizes take up more valuable space.)

Paper

Paper quality is also very important. As with copying, buy the best quality you can. At a minimum it should be 100 percent cotton bond paper; most printers stock such paper just for resumes. Generally, for a business resume the paper should be a neutral tone— white or buff colored. In business, conservatism, not extravagance, usually wins points, so it's a good idea to avoid bright colors. That means the old strategy of using brightly colored paper to make your resume stand out in a pile won't work. Alternative weave papers such as linen paper are also acceptable as long as they are tasteful and don't look like your grandmother's stationery.

WHAT TO INCLUDE

Formats

There are three basic formats that most students will use in writing their resume:

- chronological

- functional or skills
- combination

The *chronological* resume is the most widely accepted format and the one with which employers are most familiar. We will concentrate on this format, mentioning the others only briefly. The chronological resume itemizes all jobs, education, organizations, etc., in reverse chronological order—most recent first. Dates are important in each section and often begin the section. This format is the easiest to write (another probable reason for its popularity). It gives evidence of a steady job record and provides a convenient structure and flow since it uses dates and titles. However, it starkly reveals any gaps in experience and can highlight undesirable jobs while making skill areas difficult to emphasize.

The *functional* or *skills* resume is organized by the job hunter's qualifications for the job, not by dates of employment and companies. It stresses the skills you are trying to market and deemphasizes positions unrelated to your objective. It can also hide a spotty employment record. The biggest problem with this resume is that it does not provide employers with a complete work history. Many are suspicious of what you may be hiding. Also, it will not highlight companies or organizations for which you have worked (which may be good or bad). The functional or skills resume is generally not recommended for college students (except in special circumstances), since it does not provide all of the information most employers want.

The *combination* resume combines the best of both formats. It includes both a section laying out the special skills you have and a section showing your chronological work history. It allows you to highlight your skills while still providing information employers want. By altering the balance between skills and work history, you can change the emphasis. But be careful: this format tends to be longer and therefore must be especially well written. The combination format is very valuable in certain cases that are discussed in the "Skills" section later in this chapter.

While each format has its appropriate applications, the chronological resume is a standard and provides all the information an employer wants. The rest of this chapter is devoted to that format.

Top of the Resume

The top of your resume provides two pieces of information: your name and where you may be contacted. Your name should stand out. Center it, capitalize it, and put it in boldface type if you are setting the resume in type. If you have only one address, put that beneath your name. If you have a school address and a permanent address elsewhere, put both of them on the resume with one at the left margin and one at the right margin, as shown on pages 182–83. There is no need to use the words "personal resume" or "resume" at the top of the page. Also, do not put any personal data at the beginning. This is usually some of the least important information and therefore should go at the end.

Objective

The statement of an applicant's job objective is usually the first section of a resume that employers will look at after the applicant's name. As discussed, it dictates the entire content of the resume and may easily be the most important section. The first question in an employer's mind is: "Does this person want to do the job I have an opening for?" If your objective is not reasonably close to the company's needs, the employer will probably not even read the rest of the resume.

The ideal objective is written specifically for the given position, company, and industry to which you are applying. However, doing that is often impractical. Most job hunters will not know the positions that are open when they first send their resume to a company. Your objective must strike a balance between being nebulously broad and needlessly restrictive. If you remember the image of the jobs available as a large pie, then your objective should define a slice of the pie in which you are interested (see "Determining Career Goals" on page 125). "Poor Job Objectives" and "Good Job Objectives" give examples of poorly and well written job objectives. You need to define what you want to do narrowly enough for the employer to be able to determine the department of the company for which to consider you, but not so narrowly that you cannot be matched with any of the available positions appropriate for you.

The key to writing an effective objective is knowing what you want to do and stating it clearly. No employer expects you to know *exactly* what you want, particularly at the lower levels. But employers are afraid of hiring people who have little idea of what they want to do, spending thousands of dollars to train them, and then losing them after a year or two. They want to hire people with a clear vision of their career goals so that there is the greatest probability of retaining them.

If you are having problems writing a job objective, it is probably because you don't know enough about the field you wish to enter or don't know enough about yourself to decide what field is right for you. If you are struggling to determine what your objective should be, then you need to stop writing your resume and reread the chapters on career planning. *Writing* job objectives is easy; it's

Poor Job Objectives

1. Too Broad.
   - A challenging position in marketing, finance, or management.
   - A position in banking.
   - Responsible position in which to apply technical and management skills acquired through education and experience.

2. Too Vague. ("Fluff" Statements.)
   - A challenging and responsible position in finance with a progressive company in an innovative industry.
   - To effectuate the financial growth of a large financial institution with the cooperation of skilled operations and investment personnel.

3. Needs to Be Split.
   - Financial management or production management position.
   - To obtain a position in marketing or personal finance.

knowing what you want that's hard. The well-written ones that sell come from people who have a clear concept of where it is they want to go and what it is they want to do.

Three basic pieces of information can be conveyed in an objective, two of them important, one less so. First is the *level* of position you are seeking. One question an employer must answer is "Should I consider this person for an entry-level job, a management position, a specialist position, an intern position, summer employment, or chief executive officer?" The employer's evaluation of your skills will change depending upon the level of position you are seeking. For MBAs, this is particularly critical. One frequent rap against MBAs is their desire to jump straight into management positions without earning their stripes. It is often very effective to state "entry-level position" to head off any preconceived notions that you as an MBA want an immediate management position. If you are in fact seeking a management position, make sure that you are fully qualified for one.

The second piece of information given in an objective is the *type* of position you are seeking. For what kind of position should this employer consider you? Do you want to work in market research, finance, sales, operations management? Use generic words, not

Good Job Objectives

1. Well Written.
   - Entry-level market research position.
   - Entry-level position in human resource development and planning or related area.
   - A position involving analysis, design, and implementation of management information systems and using my experience in financial analysis.
   - Marketing position leading to a product management career.

2. Special-Interest Objective.
   - To obtain a management position in marketing; special interest in market research or industrial sales.
   - Financial analyst position; special interest in banking.
   - A position in a service industry; special interest in promotion or client development.

3. Narrow Objective. (Potentially risky—use carefully.)
   - A purchasing analyst position in a $100-million to $150-million manufacturing firm in Virginia.
   - Cash management position in a Fortune 500 consumer products company.

titles, since titles mean different things in different companies. Avoid industry jargon and industry-specific terms unless you know them very well and are using that objective for one industry. Don't leave any chance that the type of position you want may be misinterpreted. Research the field well enough to know what the generic labels mean and then use them. Terms such as "consultant," "financial analyst," or "market research" are good generic terms.

If you don't particularly care what the entry-level position is but are more concerned about what happens five to ten years down the road, that's fine; say so. Leaving out the entry-level position altogether and instead stating, "Entry-level position leading to a plant management career path" is not at all vague. It's precise and reveals a mature perspective. If that's what you want, say it. Make sure you avoid all "fluff" when stating your objective. The box below includes a list of fluff statements that have no place in an objective.

The third sort of information an objective may contain is special interests. This information is optional. An objective that says "an

Fluff Words

- challenging
- rewarding
- innovative company
- progressive
- responsible

- growth position
- leadership
- problem solving
- unique
- works with people

entry-level financial analyst position" without indicating any special interest is perfectly acceptable. However, if you have special industry, job, or career aspirations, it is useful to list some of them in the job objective. Keep in mind the previous discussion about the trade-offs between a narrow versus a broad objective. If these special interests are, in fact, limiting items, then clearly state them as special interests. On the other hand, if they are optional, clearly indicate it by using such words as "prefer." For most people, a narrow objective is best restated as a special-interest objective (see "Good Job Objectives").

It is acceptable to talk about growth potential or the type of opportunities for advancement you want. But be careful to keep those expectations reasonable. If you definitely want a career track that will lead to general management instead of financial management, then by all means say so. If you want a career track that will take you into management instead of a specialist track, say so. Just be reasonable in your expectations.

Don't try to mix several objectives on one resume to apply for jobs in two different fields. Combinations such as marketing and finance are like oil and water; they just don't mix. It is relatively easy to have your resume put on a word processor and to have different resumes printed with your different objectives. There is nothing wrong with exploring different fields (see "Determining Career Goals" on page 125), but you should not try to do it with the same resume.

Education

This section is relatively easy to write. Generally employers are interested only in the degrees you have received. There is no need to list the exact dates you attended a university; the degree date will usually do. You may make an exception to this if you spent a long period of time going to school and are concerned about gaps in your resume. If so, it may be appropriate to list the starting and ending dates. Don't give a long listing of educational institutions attended from which you did not receive a degree unless you have significant tenure at one of these schools or a very high grade point average that will help sell your abilities. The accompanying list of "Education Data" shows the data that should be included for each degree you have received (list your degrees in reverse chronological order, with the most recent coming first), and the "Education Format Sample" shows an acceptable arrangement of the data.

The biggest problem in this section is how to handle low grade point averages. Although it may be tempting to leave out any mention of a low GPA, doing so usually proves self-defeating. The absence of a GPA often raises a red flag in the employer's mind, a suspicion that something is wrong. You will not be able to hide it by leaving it off your resume; the employers will obtain it anyway. Some will not even talk with you if the GPA is not on the resume. For others, it creates an atmosphere of mistrust. It is better to be honest and straightforward and include your GPA, regardless of whether it is good or bad. As an MBA, you have to have a good GPA to graduate, which will help compensate for a less than brilliant undergraduate GPA. In fact, many employers do not care if your GPA is somewhat low, as they are evaluating you on a variety of criteria, but they do care if it is missing.

Education Data

- Degree received
- School you attended
- City and state of the school you attended
- Degree date
- Major(s)
- GPA
- Specialized courses (optional)

You should not list all of your course work, but make a transcript available to the employer if required. However, it *is* useful to include specialized course work that would not be apparent from your degree. For example, if your concentration for your MBA is management but all of your course work has been in personnel, it would not be apparent unless it were listed. However, an MBA with a concentration in finance who has had no specialized course work need not say anything additional. Listing course work may also be a useful way for career changers to emphasize their new skills.

Another excellent item to include here is a list of special projects you may have completed during school. Include them if they demonstrate significant accomplishments, show "real world" knowledge, or spotlight skills that are not included elsewhere in your

Education Format Sample

MBA, Virginia Polytechnic Institute and State University, Blacksburg, Va., June 1985. Concentration: Finance. GPA: 3.4/4.0.

resume. Employers seem to respond well to those who show "real world" experience and accomplishments.

Although you should write out all of your degree titles, use common degree abbreviations such as "BS," "BA," and "MBA." In fact, "MBA" is preferable to—and certainly more easily skimmed than—"Master of Business Administration."

Experience

One of the most critical parts of your resume is the description of your job experiences. This can make or break your resume. Generally, you must include at least one or two sentences describing the basic duties of your job. However, a lengthy description of job duties is generally not your most effective sales approach. Employers want to know something about the tasks and duties you were expected to perform, but they are most impressed with outstanding performance. Therefore, it is extremely important to use *accomplishment statements.*

If I had to pick one thing that marks the difference between an average resume and an excellent resume, this is it. If you write good accomplishment statements, your resume will really stand out. So many descriptions of jobs on a resume read like job descriptions in a personnel department: "Analyzed quarterly financial results, supervised two employees, wrote computer programs, etc." They drone on with task after task. Breadth and volume of tasks certainly say something important but not all that you want to say. All they really indicate is what the person is or was supposed to do. They don't say anything about whether the person is any good at it! As an employer, I want good people—great ones if I can find them. I want someone who can make something happen, solve problems, make money, and cut costs. I don't want to hire another person who's just average. So sell yourself. Write a resume that says, "I can accomplish something for you," and you'll generate the enthusiasm and excitement to sell yourself.

"Achievement Verbs" (page 174) is a list of action verbs that you can use to start phrases or sentences describing your accomplishments; "Performance Descriptors" (page 175) is a list of descriptive words you can use to describe your performance. Present a picture of yourself as taking initiative, being creative, and being a leader and innovator. Announce that you are able to excel, not just meet some minimum qualifications. List awards or recognitions you have received while on the job. Emphasize that, given the chance, you can be an outstanding performer.

Always try to quantify your accomplishments where possible. Give the employer something specific. Use percentages or some other measure that makes your accomplishment easy to understand. For example, it is better to say that the yield increased 20 percent than to say it increased by 50 tons. If you cannot quantify an accomplishment, at least support it with a concrete example. A statement like "Attained leadership role" is weak and imprecise, but "Achieved leadership role by managing project group to successful completion" is believable and strong. See the accompanying "Accomplishment Statements" for more examples.

You must make a trade-off as to how much work content to describe and how much to talk about your performance on the job. If you are applying for a new job directly related to your prior experience, then you will probably want to include a number of details showing the employer that you already have the background and skills to do that job. However, if the work content is unrelated, then it is more important to present your performance on the job and your abilities as an employee than the actual content of the experience you have.

In general, you should include full-time experience only. At the MBA level, never use high school experience unless it is high-level business experience or is professionally related and therefore sells for you. Part-time summer work in college may or may not be appropriate. If it is business or professionally related, such as internships, by all means include it. It's a judgment call, but basically, the further away you are from that job experience, the less appropriate it will be in your resume. If you have never held a full-time professional job, then summer experience is going to be very important for you, but work while in high school should not be included. If you have been out of college for a year or two and held one professional job, summer experience, if professional, is prob-

Achievement Verbs

accelerated	formulated	programmed	succeeded
accomplished	founded	promoted	summarized
achieved	generated	proposed	superseded
approved	headed	provided	supervised
began	implemented	purchased	terminated
built	improved	recommended	traced
completed	improvised	redesigned	tracked
conceived	increased	reduced	traded
conducted	innovated	reorganized	trained
consolidated	installed	researched	transferred
controlled	instituted	revised	transformed
converted	introduced	scheduled	translated
created	invented	serviced	trimmed
cut	launched	set up	tripled
delivered	led	simplified	uncovered
demonstrated	maintained	sold	unified
designed	managed	solved	unraveled
developed	negotiated	sparked	utilized
devised	operated	staffed	vacated
directed	organized	started	verified
doubled	originated	streamlined	widened
earned	performed	strengthened	won
edited	planned	stressed	worked
eliminated	processed	stretched	wrote
established	produced	structured	
expanded			

Performance Descriptors

sensitive	strong	challenging
mastery	responsive	dynamic
versatile	earning respect	attractive
sophisticated	responsible	imaginative
artful	perceptive	innovative
diplomatically	repeatedly	highly
readily	discreetly	broad
deeply concerned	outstanding	unusual
instrumental	successful	tactful
natural	creative	effectively
significantly	with candor	acuity
exceptional	reliably	driving
deft	quickly	uncommon
lifelong	vigorous	competent
adept	leading	objectivity
pioneering	honesty	highest
penetrating	initiative	warm
dependable	accurately	urgently
extensively	thinks well	trained
aware	outgoing	humanizing
strongly	firm	deep insight
open-minded	experienced	talented
expert	high-level	empathy
astute	easily	calm
diverse		

Accomplishment Statements

Each accomplishment statement is shown in mediocre, better, and best versions:

Mediocre
1. Managed office.
2. Increased profits.
3. Purchased inventory.
4. Managed manufacturing plant.
5. Developed new computer system.

Better
1. Managed office operations and staff of twelve.
2. Increased profits for three consecutive years.
3. Purchased inventory for four departments.
4. Managed textile manufacturing plant.
5. Developed new financial accounting computer system.

Best
1. Managed sales office operations and staff of twelve to record productivity.
2. Increased profits by 10 percent per year for three consecutive years.
3. Purchased $10-million of inventory annually for four departments.
4. Managed textile manufacturing plant; significantly exceeded profit and quality goals.
5. Developed new financial accounting computer system under budget and ahead of schedule.

Employment Data

- Title
- Dates of employment
- Company
- City and state in which the company is located
- General duties
- Accomplishments
- Skills/experience gained

ably still relevant. On the other hand, if you have been out of college for four years and held two full-time professional jobs, that is what will sell and you should ignore your internships. The two guiding questions are (1) does it support your objective? and (2) does it sell?

See the list of "Employment Data" for information that should be included for every job. The title you use need not be your official title, since titles often bear no relation to the job. But you must

---

. . . Nothing useless is, or low;
Each thing in its place is best;
And what seems but idle show
Strengthens and supports the rest.

For the structure that we raise,
Time is with materials filled;
Our todays and yesterdays
Are the blocks with which we build . . .

—Henry Wadsworth Longfellow
From "The Builders"

---

make sure that whatever you state as your title, whether official or functional, will be supported by the company that you worked for should your prospective employer contact it. Be careful when using a functional title to be sure that you are not overstating your role.

There is no need to include a full mailing address for each company. Remember, this is not a reference list but simply a statement of where you have lived and worked. If a prospective employer needs to contact the company, you can give a full address later. Also, there is no need to include your last supervisor; that information is for reference purposes, not to win the interview. Finally, do not include your salary. In some cases a company will specifically request that information, in which case you can provide it via cover letter. Salary negotiations occur much further along in the hiring process. You're just trying to get an interview.

Changing Fields

It is relatively easy to describe prior experience that is directly related to the position you are seeking. The bigger challenge arises from unrelated job experience. Don't discount such experience.

177

In any job there are skills you learn that are applicable only to that job or field. These are content skills. But no matter what you have done, you have also learned skills and gained experience that are transferable to a new field. If you are changing fields, your task in writing the resume is to focus the reader's attention on your transferable skills instead of your content skills. You must examine your objective for the skills important in that field and then match those to skills you have learned in your current profession. You should devote much attention to your transferable skills and accomplishments in that profession and limited attention to the description of duties. You *can* sell unrelated work experience to a new employer. There are no jobs that do not give you some transferable experience.

For example, if you were a nursing supervisor, you have learned two sets of skills. You have learned a good deal about health care and running a nursing shift; these are your content skills. But you have also acquired a number of transferable skills, such as budgeting, cost control, and managing people. If you are going to continue in your health-care career, both sets of skills are important to highlight. If you are changing careers to business management, your content skills may not be very helpful, but you can still sell the transferable ones.

Honors/Activities

It is important that you present yourself as a well-rounded, complete person, particularly if you are a college student applying for an entry-level job. Let the employer know that you are not a one-dimensional person. Show that you not only have technical skills and a good education but also are an involved person who is enthusiastic about many things, has a healthy life-style, and can be an asset to the organization as a person. Be careful, though, not to give the impression that you have so many outside activities that you won't have time for work.

Most people have received some type of award or honor or have been involved in clubs or civic organizations. This is important information to include in your resume. Awards and honors make strong statements about your above-average performance ability. Activities make statements about the type of person you are and your ability to get involved and be enthusiastic about something. Employers look for this type of information to give them clues about your character.

Include your honors and awards from college, graduate school, and beyond. Omit high school honors on an MBA-level resume, and if you have been out of college for some time, you should drop those honors as well and substitute more recent professional and civic ones.

Your activities can range from participation in school clubs, civic organizations, churches, and synagogues to contributions in professional and political organizations. Include any that make positive statements about you and your character. It is often useful to include the years of your involvement, though exact dates aren't necessary.

It is particularly important to stress your leadership role in organizations. Be sure to include all organizations in which you have held office or been active in committees. It is not necessary to have held an office to demonstrate activity. Statements about programs, committees, or ideas you generated or led are very effective.

In general, list items that make positive statements about you as a person and your performance. If you have an extensive list, do not include everything; choose the most effective things. This section provides supplemental information, and you should not devote a large portion of your resume to it unless you have no work experience.

Personal Data

It is illegal for an employer to use personal data such as age, sex, race, or marital status to screen you for interviews or as hiring criteria unless they are qualifications necessary to perform the job. Therefore, it is your right to exclude any of this information. However, most employers do generally like to see a minimal amount of personal data, often just so they can know you as a person a little better. To a certain extent, it is a tradition to include a small

Personal Data

- Age
- Marital status
- Height
- Weight
- Sex (if it is not apparent from your name)
- Interests and hobbies

amount of personal data. If such details are harmless (i.e., they would not prevent someone from hiring you), I advise including them. They are especially useful in direct mail job searches, since the employer has no physical picture of you. However, they are not needed and can be excluded. The decision is yours.

If you do decide to include them, limit yourself to the data shown in "Personal Data" above. Don't include health statements.

Employers assume you are in good health if you are looking for a professional job, and they will require a physical to verify it. Interests and hobbies can be useful but are not necessary. They often demonstrate to the employer that you are a well-rounded person who will make an interesting employee and be fun to work with. They can provide conversation starters for interviewers to break the ice and establish rapport with you. If you include them, keep them brief. List only a few without detailed explanations. Never add a second page strictly to provide personal data, and never include any information that may negatively bias your chances of being hired.

Skills

A skills section is useful if you have skills or experiences that are not obvious from the other sections in the resume. In today's business environment, this section is particularly appropriate for highlighting computer skills you may have learned while in the MBA program or elsewhere. But do not use computer jargon; use generic words that anyone can understand, even those not skilled in computer systems.

This section is also commonly and effectively used if you are changing fields and need to sell the employer on the fact that you have acquired transferable business skills in unrelated experience.

Skill Section Examples

- Familiar with Lotus 1-2-3, dBase run on IBM PC.
- *Administrative Skills*—organized, chartered, and ran a new 60-member student organization.
- Developed strong interpersonal skills through my experience as a volunteer student admissions interviewer.
- *Leadership Skills*—led two-year campaign to establish new zoning standards in my community.

Career changers would often be well-advised to make extensive use of a skills section in a combination resume format to bridge the gap between careers. Presenting work experience in skill clusters rather than by organization and title helps negate the predisposition against unrelated career experiences and highlights transferable skills.

This section is more often abused than used properly, however.

Don't simply recap what has already been said in your work experience, or state that you have "great listening skills," "great leadership ability," or "outstanding interpersonal skills." These types of value judgments standing alone are not believable. Any statement about a skill that you have learned should be written in such a way that it does not appear to be solely your opinion.

The same advice that was given for accomplishment statements applies here; make your statements specific. It is ineffective to say "developed strong leadership skills." It is effective to say "developed strong leadership skills by managing student professional organization." See "Skill Section Examples" on the previous page for additional statements that are effective.

RESUME EVALUATION CHECKLIST

An effective resume is a powerful tool in your job search. You have little hope of finding a good job unless you write a good resume. Here is a checklist to use in evaluating yours. Be sure you can answer each of these questions Yes.

Does it sell your:

    abilities and skills?_____

    experience?_____

    education?_____

    accomplishments?_____

    potential?_____

Does it look:

    professional?_____

    easy to read?_____

    easy to skim?_____

    balanced on the page?_____

    as good as you would look in person?_____

Will it:

    catch the employer's attention?_____

    represent you at your best?_____

    make a strong positive impression on the reader?_____

MALCOLM J. SCOTT

School Address:
117 E. Thompson Street
Blacksburg, VA 24060
703-555-9693

Permanent Address:
5396 Bluebird Lane
Washington, DC 20006
202-555-5542

Objective: An entry-level position in marketing leading to a career in product management.

Education: *MBA,* Virginia Tech., June 1989
Concentration: Marketing   GPA: 3.7/4.0

BS, Business management, University of Rochester, June 1987   GPA: 3.1/4.0

Projects:
- Developed a market forecasting model that was later applied to small businesses in Blacksburg.
- Used statistical analysis software to conduct a market research study.
- Researched sales techniques and consumer acceptance.

Work Experience:

5/88–8/88   *Marketing Intern,* General Electric Co., Roanoke, VA.
- Assisted in developing marketing plans for new product line.
- Wrote marketing plan for presentation to top management.
- Used computer system to analyze demographic data.
- Worked with field sales offices as sales support assistant.
- Received commendations for cost reduction.

9/85–6/87   *Head Resident Adviser,* University of Rochester, Rochester, NY.
- Responsible for coed residence hall of 400 students.
- Planned and coordinated new recreational program.
- Developed promotional campaigns for health and safety programs.
- Received outstanding performance evaluations.
- Administered business of the residence hall including room assignment, collection of student fees, and check-in.

Computer Skills:
- Knowledgeable about IBM mainframe computers and operating systems.
- Experienced with statistical analysis software.
- Proficient in use of Lotus 1-2-3.
- Extensive use of computer graphics software.

Honors/Activities:
- Dean's list four of eight semesters.
- Membership chairperson, MBA Association.
- President, Delta Epsilon fraternity.
- News announcer, campus radio station.
- Awarded Farm Bureau scholarship based on academic merit.

Personal:
- Married, one child.
- Enjoy swiming, boating, ballet, and stamp collecting.
- Available immediately; will relocate.

Is it:

complete?_____

free of unnecessary words?_____

focused to support your objective?_____

the best job you can possibly do?_____

honest?_____

Does it:

transmit your message loud and clear?_____

prioritize what's important?_____

make *you* feel good about yourself?_____

SAMPLE RESUMES

This section contains resumes that illustrate the principles described in this chapter. Do not try to copy them! Copying sample resumes and filling in your own data is an alluring trap. These samples are basic illustrations, and you will only cheat yourself if you copy them. Remember: no two resumes are ever the same. Learn and use the principles in the chapter and you will develop a personal resume to sell yourself better.

TIMOTHY J. POWNALL, C.F.A.

4321 Dartford Street
Greenwich, CT 06060
203-555-9976

Objective

A position in financial planning and analysis with opportunity for advancement to top financial management.

Education

MBA, Virginia Polytechnic Institute and State University, Blacksburg, VA, June 1989, Concentration: Finance, GPA: 3.5/4.0

BS, Finance, Georgetown University, Washington, DC, June 1983, GPA: 3.0/4.0

Experience

Graduate Assistant, MBA Office, VPI&SU, 9/87–present

- Coordinated three other assistants in office activities.
- Counseled and advised students on program policies and procedures and academic matters.
- Developed and administered student database system.
- Developed computer system to automate course timetables.
- Recruited new students for program; increased enrollment 10%.
- Used PC extensively for analysis projects.

Stockbroker, Tinos Securities Corp., Stamford, CT, 5/85–8/87

- Sold a wide variety of investment products including stocks, bonds, and mutual funds.
- Developed financial plans for high-net-worth clients involving extensive financial analysis.
- Received training in all aspects of investment analysis.
- Rated the top rookie producer in my office.

Financial Analyst, Lafferty Corporation, Danbury, CT, 6/83–5/85

- Analyzed and made recommendations on a division's $40-million capital expenditure program.
- Analyzed business results on a monthly basis and published a report to management identifying trouble spots.
- Developed computer models to increase efficiency of analysis process.
- Assisted in preparation of major debt refinancing program.
- Promoted from trainee to analyst ahead of schedule; ranked in the top 10% of training class.
- Streamlined capital investment reporting system, which resulted in significant cost savings to the firm.

(2)

Skills

- Received Chartered Financial Analyst certification in 1986.
- Experienced in PC programming and applications development. Software expertise includes Pascal, Lotus 1-2-3, dBase III, and statistical analysis (SAS).
- Completed Toastmasters public speaking program.

Honors/Activities

- Awarded R. B. Pamplin scholarship for graduate study.
- Received Rotary International award for civic service.
- Member, Rotary International.
- Member, MBA Association.
- Member, American Association of Chartered Financial Analysts.

Personal

Interests include horseback riding, gardening, fishing, and Civil War history.

CAROLINE A. HOBBS

72 St. Paul Street
Islington, OH 45472
614-555-1984

Objective:

A technical management position with opportunity for progression to general management; special interest in the textile or chemical industry.

Education:

MBA, William and Mary, June 1989, GPA: 3.45/4.0

BS, Chemistry, Texas A&M, June 1983, GPA: 2.9/4.0

Work Experience:

Marketing Manager, XYZ Chemical Company, Atlanta, GA.
September 1985–August 1987.

Responsible for all marketing activities in the southwestern U.S. for corrosive chemicals. Developed strategies, expanded distribution network, and solicited customers. Took over new product line and penetrated established market. Increased sales to profitable level in only six months. Directed efforts of sales staff of four. Implemented first-ever advertising campaign to wholesale distributors resulting in 20% sales increase. Recognized within firm as the top marketing manager for 1986.

Manufacturing Engineer, Dow Chemical Co., Baton Rouge, LA.
August 1983–August 1985

Responsible for production line producing 10,000 pounds of dry chemical per week. Supervised 40 operators and foreman. Worked with researchers to develop more cost-effective production. Developed maintenance program that reduced downtime 50% to lowest in the plant. Promoted from one-year training program to engineer in only six months.

Honors/Activities:

- President, student chapter of American Management Association.
- Awarded American Chemical Society scholarship.
- Atlanta Chamber of Commerce award for professional contributions.
- Dean's list, three of eight semesters (undergraduate).

MARGARET H. LEWIS

School:
831 Forman Avenue
Newark, NJ 07102
201-555-1229

Permanent:
1856 Apple Drive
Atlanta, GA 38754
404-555-1452

Objective:

A position in human resource management; special interest in training and development and personnel.

Education:

MBA, Rutgers University Graduate School of Management, June 1989
Concentration: Management (personnel), GPA: 3.8/4.0

BS, Fashion Merchandising, Roanoke College, June 1983, GPA: 3.4/4.0

Career-related Courses:

Human Resource Management
Labor Relations
Grievance Administration
Wage and Incentive Systems

Organizational Behavior
Organizational Development
Equal Employment Policy

Skills:

Administrative. Chairperson for high school fashion merchandising program. Directed all aspects of the program including staffing, production of clothes, organizing curriculum, and scheduling. Assisted principal in reorganization of administrative staff.

Leadership. Supervised two teachers and staff of four. Initiated idea for the curriculum and developed it into the fourth largest in the school for women. Developed poorly performing teacher into one of the top teachers in the district.

Marketing. Promoted curriculums to students and faculty. Sold products made by students to local businesses. Taught marketing principles to students.

Communications. Taught courses to adults and high school students. Frequently gave speeches at local civic events. Wrote and edited articles in newsletters and newspapers.

Public Relations. Maintained relationships with business clients to provide practical experience for students. Chaired Chamber of Commerce public relations committee. Received award for public image of program.

Training. Taught high school students for four years. Conducted training programs for area businesses for two years. Commended for outstanding teaching performance.

Employment History:

1985–87   Area Coordinator, Blue Mountain School, Atlanta, GA
1983–85   Instructor of English, Blue Mountain School, Atlanta, GA

College Activities:

Graduate:
- MBA Association History Committee chair
- Graduate Student Assembly delegate
- MBA Case Team Member

Undergraduate:
- Glee Club ('81–'83)
- Alpha Delta Pi sorority vice president
- Elected dorm representative in freshman year

Personal:

Enjoy bike riding, swimming, and classical music.

WORKBOOK

This section will help you organize the information you will want to put in your resume. Think carefully about each section, and refer back to the text discussions as needed. For each degree and job experience, repeat the questions as many times as you need to. Use this section to help you write the first draft of your resume.

Top of the Resume

Name   _____

Local Address   _____

Permanent Address
(if applicable)   _____

_____

_____

Job Objective

For each objective, answer these questions:

Required
- At what level would I like to start (entry level, manager, etc.)?

- What type of work do I want to do (finance, marketing, etc.)?

Optional
- What are my special interests in that area?

- What is my career goal for the next ten years?

Education

For each degree received, list the following:

Required
- Degree received (MBA, BS, etc.):

- Major:

- University or college:

- City and state of school:

- Date received or expected:

- Grade point average:

Optional
- Special course work not easily identifiable from your major:

- Special projects, reports, research, or thesis that will sell for you:

Experience

For *each* work experience you have had, answer these questions:

Required
- Dates (month and year):

- Official or functional title:

- Company:

- City and state:

- Description of duties (usually brief):

- List your major accomplishments (e.g., major projects, innovative ideas, outstanding performance, etc.):

- List special skills you learned:

- List special experience you gained that is not obvious from the job description:

Honors

- List your academic honors and awards (scholarships, recognition, etc.):

- List your professional honors and awards:

- List your civic honors and awards:

Activities

- List each of your college extracurricular activities with this information:

  Name of organization:

  Offices held:

  Committees:

  Year(s):

- List your professional activities (same information):

- List your civic activities (same information):

Personal Data (Optional)

- Age:

- Marital status:

- Height:

- Weight:

- Sex (if not apparent from your name):

- List three to five of your hobbies and leisure time activities:

Special Skills (Optional)

- List skills you have that are not clear from any of the items in this workbook so far (computer skills, skills learned in hobbies, etc.):

Publications (Optional)

- List each of your *published* (journals, proceedings, books) documents in bibliographic form:

Chapter 11

The Interview: Process and Principles

Until now most of your work has been done by yourself. If you have followed this methodology step by step, you now know what you want, know where you want to do it, have developed a marketing strategy, and have designed your resume as your promotional tool. Now it is time for the

JOB INTERVIEW

These two words strike fear in the hearts of even the most experienced job hunters. Now is the time that you must venture forth and make things happen. Job seekers are often frightened, anxious, nervous, and intimidated by the process that is used to bring employers and employees together. Like it or not, there is no way to avoid an interview in order to land a job. This section will help you reduce your anxiety and become more effective at the process.

THE MYTHS OF INTERVIEWING

There are four common myths associated with the interview process. Before moving on to discuss the process itself, let's dispel them:

Myth 1. Interviewing is an objective process. It is not. Although there is much objective fact gathering, interviewing is a very subjective process that has everything to do with the chemistry and rapport that you establish between yourself and the recruiter. It is often criticized as a recruiting tool because of the subjectivity involved, but, like it or not, it is the method by which employers and job seekers choose each other. As with the resume, much of the communication occurs on a more subtle, psychological level than is commonly thought.

Myth 2. You can outguess and outsmart the recruiter. Most recruiters will be able to see right through canned answers, bull, or flowery language. They know and dislike all the common tricks and gimmicks. You cannot mold yourself to be what the company wants. You must be completely genuine, or you will not succeed in the interview.

Myth 3. Interviews are for the company only. Actually, interviews are your opportunity to collect information as well. Yes, they have the jobs, and there are many candidates available. However, you have the right and the responsibility to make a good career decision for yourself. Do not be intimidated by the fact that they control the job opening. Their job and purpose is to hire you, not to reject you. They want to find a good match—one that will be good for the company and one that will be good for you. They respect and admire a person who can exchange information with them and takes the initiative to ask questions.

Myth 4. You cannot prepare for an interview. The fact is, interview preparation not only can be done but is essential to winning the job you want. The secret lies in the *right* type of preparation.

THE KEY TO INTERVIEWING

Many books have been written and hundreds of gimmicks proposed as "the solution" to interviewing. If you are looking for tricks in this book, you're going to be disappointed. There are none. While it is true that the job interview is a very subjective process, it is also true that it is a process run by professionals who have seen a hundred times every trick or gimmick you might try. There are some rules of the game that you need to know and will be told in this chapter, but there are no tricks that work. Even if there were, you'd only be fooling yourself. But, as you will learn in this chapter, there is a method that works.

The key to successful interviewing is *knowledge.* Effective interviewers will tell you that all you need to do to interview well is to know:

- yourself
- your career choice
- the company
- the interview process

This doesn't sound very glamorous, but it will win you a job.

There are no shortcuts to acquiring this knowledge. Only hard *work* and thorough *preparation* will do the job. The good news is that if you have done a thorough job up to this point in your career planning and job search process, you don't have much to worry about. Except for an understanding of the interview process itself, your career planning has already taught you all you need—most of your interview preparation is already done. All you have left to do is to learn about the interview process, and you will be ready.

There are two key reasons why this approach is so effective. First, most people who use it develop tremendous confidence in themselves before an interview. Much of the fear and anxiety about interviews usually stems from a lack of knowledge about yourself, your career choices, the company with which you are about to interview, and the interview process itself. If you are adequately prepared in these four areas, you have nothing to fear. You have no need to worry about the questions you may be asked or to prepare canned answers, because you have already answered all the questions while planning your career. With this knowledge have come the confidence and assurance to relax and converse with the interviewer as you would with a peer or colleague. Recruiters will feel and see the confidence that you exude and will respond favorably. It's that simple.

The second reason that this approach is so effective is more obvious. If you have methodically researched each area and used this guide and the workbooks, you should be able to answer just about any question that an interviewer may ask you. Not only will you answer it, but you will answer it accurately, completely, and in a well-thought-out manner. Such answers impress interviewers; prepared, thoughtful people score points.

Although good career planning is most of your preparation, you should do several other things. First, you need to understand what the interviewer looks at and listens for in an interview and learn how to be most effective in presenting your answers. Second, you should review lists of common interview questions to help you understand the way in which you will be asked to present what you know about yourself and the approach you will need to use to sell yourself. Understanding the rules of the game ahead of time will reduce your nervousness and enable you to deliver honest, genuine, and effective answers.

What is the alternative? Well, the approach that most students adopt is virtually to ignore this process until about two weeks before interviews begin. They study lists of interview questions rigorously. They ask counselors and friends what the interviewer is looking for as if they were chameleons who could change themselves overnight to provide whatever answer the interviewer wants to hear. They spend a restless night before the interview, worrying whether they can remember all the dos and don'ts and the list of answers to questions they have memorized. They hope the interviewer won't ask them the really tough questions, like "What do you want to do?" and they practice ways to bluff their way through. So they enter the interview room nervous, fidgety, and uncertain; survival is the first order of business.

Now contrast that with MBAs who recognize well in advance of the interview that they need to think through their career plans carefully. By the time the interview comes around, they are likely to be excited about their future career and perhaps a little anxious about whether their goals will be met. But they are excited about the companies that they will be interviewing with; they can't wait to tackle the jobs that they know so well. Answers to questions come easily and naturally. For them, interviews are just friendly exchanges with employers, the logical next step in the process. Their focus is on achieving their goals, not surviving the interview.

The really appealing aspect of this approach is that anybody can work hard and prepare well, and so anybody can interview well. You need not be intimidated by what seems like a mysterious or magical process. This calm, methodical approach works for *everyone*.

THE PURPOSE OF AN INTERVIEW

Whereas the resume is designed to win you the interview, the interview is designed to win you the job. It is primarily a sales forum. You, the candidate, are there to sell the company on your qualifications, your skills, and your potential to that organization. The interviewer is there to sell you on the company and the opportunities it offers. Both of you are there to better understand each other and to demonstrate how your goals can be met by joining forces.

The interview is also an exchange of information (an often-forgotten fact), particularly the initial on-campus or screening interview. You want to find out about the company, its products, its careers, and its job openings. The company wants to find out about you, your qualifications, your personality, and your interests. Both parties are there to collect and convey information about what they have to offer each other.

While interviews are terribly intimidating to most people, they are actually as much for your benefit as for the employer's. It is only through the interview that you will discover whether a particular employer is a good match for your goals and interests. How can you ever know if a job will be satisfying if you don't sit down and talk about it? Don't be hesitant to take advantage of the interview for your own purposes. Not only will you be better off for it, but this approach will also show your maturity as an individual.

THE INTERVIEW PROCESS

Once you have located a prospect and sent a resume, the interviewing process follows a fairly standard and predictable flow. Keep in

*You've failed
many times,
although you may not
remember.
You fell down
the first time
you tried to walk.
You almost drowned
the first time
you tried to
swim, didn't you?
Did you hit the
ball the first time
you swung a bat?
Heavy hitters,
the ones who hit the
most home runs,
also strike
out a lot.
R. H. Macy
failed seven
times before his
store in New York
caught on.
English novelist
John Creasey got
753 rejection slips
before he published
564 books.
Babe Ruth struck out
1,330 times,
but he also hit
714 home runs.
Don't worry about
failure.
Worry about the
chances you miss
when you don't
even try.*

—"Don't Be Afraid to Fail"

mind that the resume is an advertisement designed to win you an interview. If that is successful, your first interview will likely be a *screening* interview. If you pass that hurdle, you will be asked for one or more *hiring* interviews, usually held at the employer's location. The hiring interview is generally the last step in the process and is followed by either a job offer or a rejection.

Let's put this process in perspective. The *Northwestern Lindquist-Endicott Report 1989* surveyed 250 well-known companies and reported that:

- 27 percent of campus interviews led to a second interview.
- 59 percent of second interviews resulted in offers.
- 56 percent of the offers were accepted.

Put another way, approximately 1 in 4 candidates interviewed on campus received a second interview, 1 in 6 received a job offer, and 1 in 11 were actually hired. This means you'll have to do a lot of interviewing to get a job. These numbers do vary some by industry, as shown in the accompanying table. The data are combined for bachelor's and master's degree candidates.

Although the practice is not as common as it once was, some companies will include a testing step after the screening interviews and before the hiring interviews. The tests are generally of two types. Aptitude tests are similar to the GMAT or SAT, which you are familiar with. Psychologically based tests simply reveal who you are. Neither can be prepared for.

Let's take a look at screening interviews and hiring interviews to give you some needed context before we examine the nuts and bolts of successful interviewing.

SCREENING INTERVIEWS

Screening interviews act as a screen to select candidates who *appear* to have the right qualifications and the *potential* to be hired. I emphasize "appear" and "potential" because a screening interview usually takes only 30–45 minutes, and few interviews gather enough information to make a hiring decision in such a short time. The only decision the employer makes is whether to invest the time and money in a more extensive hiring interview.

Screening interviews are usually very congenial. They often take place on a university campus (especially for entry-level positions) but may be at an employer's office. Because they are so short, neither party has enough time to present a complete picture. The goal is simply to put forth enough information for both parties to know whether to move forward.

Recruiting Effectiveness—Selected Industries

The following data are the average number of students successful at each stage of the interview process per 100 screening interviews.

Industry Group	Campus Interviews	Second Interviews	Job Offers	Acceptances
Aerospace/Electronic	100	31	25	13
Automotive/Mechanical	100	21	10	5
Bank/Finance/Insurance	100	21	10	6
Building Materials/ Construction	100	30	17	11
Chemicals/Drugs	100	21	14	7
Electrical and Electronics	100	18	12	8
Food/Beverage Processing	100	22	10	5
Glass/Paper/Packaging	100	11	6	3
Merchandising and Services	100	20	14	7
Metals and Metal Products	100	26	13	7
Petroleum and Natural Gas	100	18	9	4
Public Accounting	100	31	22	11
Public Utilities	100	28	12	8
Research/Consulting	100	25	14	8
Transportation	100	15	8	5
Diversified Conglomerate	100	40	15	10
Miscellaneous	100	20	9	5
National Average	100	27	16	9

Source: *Northwestern Lindquist-Endicott Report 1989.* © Northwestern Lindquist-Endicott Report by V. R. Lindquist, Northwestern University.

Many MBAs feel that accepting a screening interview implies some sort of commitment. The thought process seems to be "If I accept the screening interview, then I'm saying I'm really interested, which means that if they offer the job I have to say Yes." That sounds ridiculous, but many MBAs won't take screening interviews unless they know beforehand that there is a pretty strong chance they would go to work for the company. That's absurd! Screening interviews are your best way of prospecting. Sure, neither you nor the company wants to waste time, but all you really need to establish is that a particular employer *might* be a prospect. Remember that you can always say no at any point in the process if you see the match won't work. Why not take all the screening interviews you can?

Your challenge in a screening interview is to find the right things to sell in a very short time to win a hiring interview. By the time the rapport building, company introduction, and other formalities are complete, you probably have only about 10 minutes of a 30-minute interview to sell yourself. You need to have ready a concise, effective sales pitch. You should be able, from your company research and what you have learned in the early stages of the interview, to isolate enough information to target your pitch. Try to present a few key points about yourself that will win you a follow-up interview. You'll probably come away thinking, "But there's so much more they don't know about me." That's OK, because nobody's going to make any major decisions; the interviewer's just out to identify good prospects.

The tough part comes after the screening interview is over—and that is the waiting. The amount of time companies need and the processes they use to make a decision vary tremendously. Some companies may recruit for immediate needs and react very quickly, while others may be recruiting for possible needs in three months. Some companies, usually large, anticipate their hiring needs well in advance of the scheduled interview process and can respond quickly. In some, the recruiting team has considerable influence in the decision process, while in others the recruiter must circulate a candidate's resume (with comments) to hiring managers in order to get a decision. This is a very unpredictable and changeable process. Be sure to ask the company what to expect and stay flexible, and waiting will be a lot easier. And no matter how well the interview goes or what the interviewer promises, keep looking at other companies.

It is a good idea to send a thank-you letter to the interviewer. It is a polite gesture that shows initiative and emphasizes your interest in the company. The letter need not be long or complicated. Thank the recruiter for the interview, and indicate your interest and enthusiasm. The follow-up letter also offers good opportunity for you to reemphasize points you have made during the interview or to add information that you forgot to mention there. If you did not handle a particular question very well or there was some confusion in the interview, use the follow-up letter to clear it up. (See "Letter Writing" on page 291.)

Although recruiters are, by and large, a very professional group of people, there are often mix-ups in responding. Given the amount of travel that the recruiters do and the volume of applicants they work with, it is not surprising that administrative detail sometimes slips through the cracks. Before you leave the interview, you should find out when to expect a reply. If you do not hear from the company in that amount of time, you have a right to call and ask where you stand. Allow whatever period of time the recruiter stated plus a one-week cushion and then call. Recruiters usually will not object, and, if there has been an error, they will be very glad you called. It will continue to show initiative and interest in their organization.

Waiting is tough and the anxiety can be a strain, but patience does pay off. Once you have completed the follow-up, there is nothing you can do to affect the process. No amount of worry will change what has happened or is going to happen or make the time go by any faster. Do what you can, as described here, and then forget about it. You'll be much healthier for it.

HIRING INTERVIEWS

If you are successful in the screening interview, you will be invited for a hiring interview. Your mission in a hiring interview is to win the job; this is where the serious interviewing happens. These interviews are almost always held at the employers' location (usually at their expense) and are often called "on-site" interviews. Employers do not invite you for an on-site interview unless they are very interested in you. It is the final step in the job search. During and after the hiring interview, the decision will be made, by both you and the company, about your employment. All of the interviewing principles discussed earlier still apply: the emphasis on knowing yourself, knowing the company, and knowing the interview process; the importance of communication (verbal and nonverbal); the emphasis on preparation; and the type of person the employer is looking for remain the same.

Structure

For the entry-level position, you will generally have only one round of hiring interviews. Whereas the screening interview was simply a get-acquainted information exchange to see if there was mutual interest in further talks, the hiring interview is the point at which you and the employer decide if there is an employment match. Although some of the questions you are asked will be the same, the intent and purpose of the hiring interview are much different. The employer will spend some time selling the company and considerable time looking closely at you. Similarly, you will be trying to sell yourself as a great candidate to hire while looking very closely at the company as a possible employer.

A typical on-site interview might be structured as follows:

1. 7:30–8:30   Breakfast: a get-acquainted meeting to orient you to the day—often low-key but sometimes a "live" interview

2. 8:30–12   Interviews: four or five interviews with a variety of people; a tour of the facilities is often included

3. 12–1:30   Lunch: usually with recent graduates; a time for you to hear what it's really like from those who are doing what you will be doing

4. 2–3:30   Interviews: more of them

5. 3:30–4   Wrap-up: a critical session, usually with the person who is hosting your visit

An on-site interview can be a long, grueling day. Depending on the company, you may see as many as eight people. You must be "on" all day. You will see people at many different levels of the organization who will each grill you for some of the same information and some different information. Most likely, you won't get to relax even while you eat lunch, as they will interview you then as well. So you must keep your adrenaline running all day. You cannot afford for any reason to let down during even one interview, as it may cost you a job. It can be intense, challenging, tiring, and boring. It is hard work. Be prepared: psych yourself up for it and get plenty of rest the night before.

Questions Recruiters Recommend

The following questions elicit information beyond what you researched for the screening interview that you should be sure to collect during the on-site interview:

- What do people who work there think about the company?
- What will you be doing on your first job?
- What type of salary range and benefits will the company offer?
- Where will you be located geographically? What are the opportunities to change career paths in the company?
- Find out what a typical day is like for a person in the job that you will be doing.
- Make sure you know exactly what will happen after you leave the interview that day.
- What is that city or county like to live and work in?
- What are the cultural opportunities in that area?
- How much travel will be expected of you in that job?
- Look carefully for clues that tell you that the values of the people in this company match yours.
- Why is this job vacant (promotion, left company)?
- What type of people will you be working with? For?

After the hiring interview comes—you guessed it—more waiting! The actual job offer may be made anytime from the last interview of your site visit to weeks or months afterward. It really depends on whether a company is a "see 'em all" type or a "hire 'em if they look good" type. The former wants to look at all candidates before it makes a decision; the latter will hire the first person it sees who meets the qualifications. Generally, you can expect an answer within two or three weeks after your hiring interview.

Watch Out for . . .

Some of the most common mistakes MBAs make during hiring interviews are:

- **Not collecting the information they need to make their career decision.** Remember, this is your day, too. Many students return from their on-site interview to find that they do not have sufficient information on which to decide whether they want to accept the offer (if they have received one). The on-site interview is your chance to examine employers as well as vice versa. Use this time; you probably will not have another look at them before you go to work. In fact, you will win points if you show them that you are looking them over very carefully. Just because they are paying for you to visit them does not mean that you do not have the right to use some of the time to learn what you need to know. Employers know that it is in their best interest for you to do so.
- **Letting down at the final interview.** There is a tremendous tendency to relax at the final interview with your host. The company will often appear to treat this interview casually, but it is looking for your conclusions. This is your time to close the sale. Stay on your toes and leave the company with a positive feeling; show your interest if you think you want the job. Don't let fatigue get to you; many jobs are lost by a lukewarm close.
- **Not selling themselves.** As with the screening interview, the passive candidate will not get the job. Remember to sell yourself—all day. Focus on the needs of the company.
- **Letting fatigue show.** You will get very tired during the day, but you must have the stamina and discipline to look and act as fresh at the last interview as you did at the first. Don't let fatigue take away your enthusiasm and smiles. Remember that the last interviewer (other than the wrap-up) will probably have never seen you before, so you need to perform strongly.

Tips from Those Who Have Done It

Here are some pointers gleaned from the experiences of successful job candidates:

- Make a trial run to the interview site before the morning of the interview. Don't be late because you got lost.
- Ask the company about expense reimbursement before the trip. Many companies will have flights and hotels billed directly to them if you are short of cash; some will give you an advance. Don't be afraid to ask, or say that you are short of cash, if you are unemployed or on a student budget.
- Be flexible and don't get ruffled. Traveling to a new area can be difficult and confusing; nothing ever seems to go the way you plan. Don't let it rattle you.
- Take an alarm clock. Hotels don't always wake you up on time.
- Don't be afraid to ask for a restroom break during the day; it seems like it's never in your schedule.
- Watch everything you say. This is no time to experiment.
- Don't eat too much at lunch or drink alcohol; you don't want to be groggy after lunch since there are more interviews.
- Don't say yes or no on the spot if you should get an offer. Always go home and sleep on it.

GETTING READY FOR YOUR INTERVIEW

Your interview is important, so you should take a little time just before the event to get ready for it. Make sure you know what you are interviewing for, and be able to converse easily with the interviewer about the company (see "Why Research Companies?" on page 134). Prepare a list of questions you want to ask the interviewer. And jot down a few notes on the key points you will make to sell yourself.

Put together your "interview kit" the night before and take it with you to the interview. Include:

- extra resumes
- three references (typed on separate pages)
- a copy of your transcript
- pen and paper
- a handkerchief or tissues
- notes on questions you plan to ask and sales points to make
- papers, projects, publications, etc., that might be of interest
- a folio or small briefcase in which to carry all of the above

There is some advantage in choosing your interview time carefully. Some employers say that the candidates they remember most are the first and last interviewed in the day and the one just before lunch. During the first interview, the employer is fresh and starting with a clean slate, so it's easier for that candidate to make an impression. All the ones who come later are compared with that one. If your interview comes just before lunch, the employer has a break to let what you've said sink in, undisturbed by another interview. Employers almost unanimously agree that their morning interviews are better. They aren't as tired then or distracted by later events of the day. However, some say that a strong interview at the end of the day leaves a lasting impression as they travel home. But timing isn't everything—good people always seem to get noticed. However, all other things being equal, you might as well pick one of these good times *if you can*.

Plan to arrive at the interview site early. The extra time gives you a chance to collect yourself, straighten your clothes, and comb your hair. If you can't find a parking place, the elevator gets stuck, or it rains, you will have a built-in cushion. A little extra time also gives you a chance to get yourself mentally ready for the interview. You need to catch your breath, turn your attention to the interview, review your plan, and give yourself a little pep talk. *Whatever you do, don't be late.*

PRESENTING YOURSELF

Many MBAs focus very hard on their answers to interview questions but forget that their physical presentation is just as important as what they say. Your dress, posture, eye contact, voice inflections, lack of nervousness, etc., can be a big help in presenting yourself as a polished, mature professional. While polish alone is not enough to win a job, mistakes made here can keep you from getting one. It's well worth the time it takes to pay close attention to how you present yourself.

Positive Image

Employers are looking for people who can project a positive and professional image. They want to see self-confidence and energy. How do you project that? First, look alive and happy. Sounds obvious, but you'd be amazed at how few candidates do it! Be upbeat and enthusiastic. Show that you have plenty of energy to devote to the job. Sit up straight, have a twinkle of excitement in your eye, and smile. Don't talk about personal problems or negative things, but focus on the positives. If you look relaxed and as if you're enjoying the interview (yes, you can), you'll project lots of self-confidence. Believe in yourself. Let your tone of voice and posture carry a "can-do" message. Put on your best professional manners to show you're not just a student (that means don't smoke, swear, or chew gum). All these contribute to the "feel" of the interview for the employer and can make the difference. Use your physical presentation and body language to reinforce the sales messages you'll deliver with your words. You have to look and act the part if you want the employer to believe you.

Dress

How you dress for an interview is extremely important. MBAs are expected to present themselves as businesspeople, and the "look" is just as important as skills and attitudes. A lot is written about interview dress, and I'm not going to try to repeat all the basics. However, all the analysis of interview dress misses the main point and unnecessarily complicates the issue.

There is a definite business "look," a look that is unmistakable and will clearly identify you as a serious businessperson. For all the discussion of what the "uniform" is, it boils down to neat, clean, understated, and conservative. Walk through the business district of any major city, and you will see that the look clearly differs from that of other professionals.

Your objective throughout the whole job search has been to convince employers that you will be an effective businessperson. Therefore, your only objective in dressing for an interview is to look like "one of them." Recruiters don't sit back with a check sheet and note if your shirt is a certain color, your tie silk, your shoes shined, your skirt made of the right fabric, and so on. All they want is to see a businessperson across the desk from them. What they *really* want to do is to ignore how you are dressed. Yes, ignore it. You see, if you are dressed just like the recruiter's colleagues, clients, and business friends, you will look as if you belong in the professional world. It's the same effect as if you were to walk into a college classroom wearing blue jeans and a T-shirt. The rule of thumb is very simple: dress so that 5 minutes after you leave the interview the interviewer will not remember what you wore, because the interviewer will remember your dress only if it looks wrong.

You want your appearance to be a completely neutral factor in the interview so that the interviewer can focus on your skills and abilities, not on how you look (particularly important for women). You don't want the interviewer to remember you because you are underdressed, sloppy, or dressed like a scientist instead of an MBA. Similarly, you don't want to be noticed because you are overdressed, too flashy, sexy, or fashionable. You just want the natural look of a businessperson.

Many MBAs object to this because they don't like to feel constrained to wear what they perceive as a somewhat dull uniform.

They want more flexibility in their dress. In fact, there usually is some flexibility once you're on the job. You will find that the dress code varies by geographic location, level of the organization, industry, specific company, and whether you are at headquarters or at a plant site. But you won't find out those specific rules until you are on the job. In addition, after you have worked for a while, you should have a good track record and people will judge you by results and be more forgiving about small variations in dress.

But in the interview the first thing the employer sees is your appearance, the first "statement" you make. You want that statement to be, "I am a businessperson," unequivocally. Since you don't know what the rules are for that company and what flexibility may be allowed, why take chances? Wear the "uniform" that is accepted anywhere in the business world so your dress won't affect your chances for a follow-up interview. Then, use the site visit to assess the dress code and see whether you can be comfortable on a daily basis. But if you don't play it straight in the interview, you may never get that chance.

What sort of attire will make the right statement? It doesn't hurt to repeat what might seem like common sense. *Neat, clean, understated,* and *conservative* are the key words. Suits are a must for both men and women. Choose classic business colors: blues and grays are right for suits, white for shirts, and white or off-white for women's blouses. Ties are required for men. Get your clothes cleaned, tie your tie well, tuck in your shirt, and shine your shoes.

Remember: understated, safe, conservative, classic business attire is the rule. If you want more detailed information about the business uniform, read John Malloy's *New Dress for Success* or *Women's Dress for Success.*

Eye Contact

Eye contact makes a big impact in an interview. Try to maintain good eye contact with the interviewer throughout the interview. Don't stare, but don't spend your time gazing out the window, at your shoes, or at the desktop either. Good eye contact denotes confidence and builds rapport with the interviewer. Poor eye contact generally denotes a nervous person who cannot handle interpersonal communications. If you have a problem with eye contact, work on it.

Posture

People can tell a great deal about your self-confidence and attitude by the way you carry yourself. Don't slouch in the chair during the interview. Sit straight and project confidence. A slight lean forward can indicate interest at appropriate times. Don't lean back in your chair or adopt any position that could indicate lack of interest.

Nervous Habits

Everybody is a little nervous in an interview, and most people have some habit they use to settle themselves, such as drumming fingers or playing with a pencil. Although interviewers know that you will be slightly nervous, such habits are often distracting and leave a negative impression on the recruiter. Try to control yours.

Voice

Your voice projects much information besides the words you speak. It tells the interviewer how nervous you are and the degree of confidence you have. Interviewers look for a person who has normal speech inflections during an interview. Exaggerated high and low tones or monotone speech indicates practiced answers and nervous people.

Interviewers also look for a normal pace of speech. Most people when nervous begin to talk fast or to stutter and have trouble getting words out. Be particularly careful not to start talking so fast that the interviewer has trouble following. A normal conversational pace shows confidence and poise. Also, "uhs" and "umms" and other fillers are distracting and indicate nervousness. Practice avoiding them.

Physical Space

Communications professionals talk about a concept called *physical space* in interpersonal situations. It concerns the degree of physical closeness that we allow different classes of friends and acquaintances to maintain with us. For example, we allow our spouses, boyfriends, girlfriends, and significant others to approach us very closely and to touch us affectionately. But close friends are expected to stay a little farther back, though not as far back as regular friends. We wouldn't dream of letting a complete stranger approach us nearly as close as a good friend. The potentially difficult part is that different people define their physical space differently because of cultural, regional, and personal preferences. You have probably met people who are always hugging and backslapping, even with the most casual friends, while others reserve those gestures for only their closest family. In some parts of the country business is done on a very casual, physically close basis, while in other parts a more strict formal space is maintained.

The implication for interviewing is that you want to maintain a physical space between you and the interviewer that is appropriate for a new professional relationship. This may seem trivial, but there are a number of reports from recruiters that students just don't understand this. A good distance to maintain is 2 to 3 feet. Don't lean across the desk or sit directly next to the interviewer. At a cocktail or wine-and-cheese party, don't stand too close to a recruiter or approach in too friendly a fashion. These invade the recruiter's personal space and, more important, show that you have little understanding of how professionals act. Look for cues from the recruiter as to what space he or she is comfortable with. If the recruiter ever moves to increase distance between you, don't try to close it up. The recruiter is telling you what an appropriate professional space is for this interview.

Overcoming Nervousness

The first step to dealing with nervousness is to realize that it is normal and that you will never get rid of it completely. Even the most experienced and best-prepared job seekers still feel some anxiety and have "butterflies" before an interview. Those job seekers have also learned that the nervousness usually disappears once the interview has started. Expect to worry a little about the interview; discard the belief that you should feel unconcerned about it. Don't panic if you feel a little uncertain. Prepare yourself well, and then trust that your preparation will carry you through the interview.

A moderate amount of anxiety before an interview is, in fact, healthy and helpful. It keeps you from becoming too casual about an important event. It helps keep you sharp and alert. Worrying a little helps force you to prepare for the interview. Let your anxiety work for you and stop fighting it.

The preceding comments apply to a moderate amount of nervousness that does not interfere with the interview once it has started. Suppose, though, that your nervousness is getting in the way of your success at interviews—then what? There are several techniques that you can use to help a bad case of the jitters:

- **Deep Breathing.** The simplest technique, and an extremely effective one, is a series of deep breaths. Many MBAs find this useful just before going into an interview. Simply take about ten deep breaths, holding each one about 5 seconds. Breathe deep from your diaphragm, letting your stomach expand as you breathe in slowly. Exhale slowly. Imagine that your tension is flowing out as you exhale.
- **Progressive Relaxation.** The mind has tremendous power to control the body if only we learn to focus that power. A useful technique is to progressively direct your attention to each part

of your body, starting at your feet and moving to your head. Check each part for tension, and focus on relaxing the muscles. Imagine that they are turning to Jell-O. When your feet are relaxed, move to your calves, then thighs, stomach, etc. Feel the tension and then feel the muscles relax.

- **"What's the worst that can happen?"** Very often our anxiety stems from overestimating the importance of an event. When the stakes are high, failure becomes a horrendous crisis and we become quite anxious about it. To combat this, ask yourself, "What's the worst that can happen?" To each answer, ask yourself this question again until you follow the chain of consequences. For example, "If I screw up this interview I won't get this job so I won't make lots of money so I won't get the great house I dream of so my spouse and I won't be happy and my MBA will be worthless. . . ." and so on. It sounds crazy, but articulating the thought process helps to reveal its absurdity. No wonder we get nervous. Relax. Realize that it's just one interview of many. So what if you don't get that job? The world *won't* end, and you'll move on to the next interview.

- **Purple Polka-Dot Technique.** This is a tried-and-true technique that is very simple. Imagine that the interviewer is sitting in the chair wearing purple polka-dot underwear and nothing else. Just try to stay nervous and tense with that image in mind! Too often we let ourselves get too serious about the interview or let the interviewer intimidate us. This technique simply adds a little private humor and makes the interviewer seem less threatening. Try it—it works!

Finally, don't be afraid to pause and collect yourself during an interview. If you find yourself talking fast, stuttering, rambling, strumming your fingers, or otherwise bungling the interview, STOP! Take three or four deep breaths (silently) and regroup. Don't worry about the silence. There is no need to fill every second with talk. Although 5 to 10 seconds may feel like an eternity to you, the interviewer will probably not even notice.

Being Human and Professional

Somewhere on our business school campuses there is a great rumor monster churning out all sorts of false rumors about the way businesspeople (and therefore business students) are supposed to act. No place is this more evident than in the interview room. Professional is often interpreted as a somber, serious facade. You've seen this type—tense, serious, unsmiling, formal, "all business, no play." The irony is that this demeanor will lose you the job. Employers constantly talk about the "confident, relaxed, pleasant" candidate that they can't wait to invite in or hire. Employers like to hire human beings, not robots!

The message from employers is very direct: "Be yourself." Organizations are groups of living, breathing people. Recruiters are people, too. What they want to hire is a person who is professional and whom other people like and like to be with.

How to Seem Human and Professional

Myth	Good	Gone Too Far
rigid posture	comfortable and relaxed	slouched in chair
stern, serious face	open, warm face with smiles	open mouth, guffaws
no laughter	pleasant, inviting laughter	telling jokes
monotone voice	normal voice inflections	screaming and shouting
calm (like a tree trunk)	enthusiastic	bouncing in chair
gets down to business	establishes rapport	mostly small talk
rigid eye contact	normal eye contact	counting cracks in ceiling

MBAs will likely be considered for management positions requiring excellent people skills. Everyone will be part of a team or group in an organization and will depend on others to accomplish their own jobs. Unfriendly employees disrupt organizations and lower morale. Rapport building, friendliness, warmth, and humor are all character traits needed to succeed in business. Forget the traditional stereotype of the business interview. Companies want to hire competent professionals who are nice people. Be yourself.

THE NUTS AND BOLTS OF THE INTERVIEW

Now let's get down to the nuts and bolts of the interview. Like any long-standing institution, it has developed its own idiosyncrasies, conventions, and rules. It is only human nature to fear that which we do not understand or know anything about. So I suggest that you devote some time to this section to learn what to expect in the interview. Unfortunately, 30 minutes with one individual can make or break your chances of a career with a company. It only makes sense to me that you not let your naivete or ignorance of the interview process cost you that career.

Most interview sessions can be divided into three parts: introduction, dialogue, and closing. This structure is typical of just about any interview you will encounter, whether it is on site or on campus. Let's explore each of these parts.

Introduction

The introduction is by definition the stage of the interview at which you and the interviewer meet. It may last anywhere from a few seconds to a few minutes, depending on the interviewer's style. However, don't be deceived by the fact that it is only a short period of time.

Since many encounters in business are based on only a short exchange or interaction, the introduction is your first important test in the interview. It usually consists of small talk to set a positive tone for the interview. The interviewer will try to help you feel relaxed and comfortable, since you are expected to be a little nervous. Your task is to develop some rapport with the recruiter by the time you complete the introduction (see "Establishing Rapport" on page 285). When the introduction is over, there should have been established an easy and comfortable but professional feeling between you and the recruiter.

The initial impression that you make on the recruiter can dominate the entire interview. It has been said that many interviewers decide in the first 5 minutes of an interview whether to hire you or not. Although this is exaggerated, interviewers do collect a tremendous amount of information about you at the first meeting, often before you even open your mouth. During the introduction the interviewer will be assessing:

- how you are dressed
- how you speak
- how you sit
- how you shake hands
- your confidence
- your social skills
- your general personality
- your eye contact
- how you handle pressure

You can easily see how the tone and comfort level that you establish during the introduction can affect the entire interview.

The key is to psych yourself for the interview before you walk into the interview room. Too many people occupy their minds with

Tips on Making a Good First Impression

- Begin the interview in a friendly manner. Smile when you enter and show that you are pleased to be there. People like to talk with those they feel comfortable with.
- Don't use the interviewer's first name unless invited to do so. Use "Mr." or "Ms." at first; the interviewer will respond with "Please call me Joan" if first names are appropriate.
- Your handshake is extremely important. A limp handshake leaves an awful impression on the interviewer. Make sure yours is firm and businesslike.
- Do not alter your handshake for women. Most career women prefer not to receive the more social half-handshake in a professional setting. Use the same firm, businesslike handshake.
- Pay particular attention to your nonverbal communication. Make sure you establish good eye contact at this point and convey with your body language that you are confident, relaxed, and friendly.
- Try to establish rapport with the interviewer so you will both feel relaxed and comfortable during the interview.
- Let the interviewer take the lead in moving from the introduction to the dialogue.

other thoughts while they are waiting, and it takes them a few minutes to get warmed up. By the time you get warmed up, you may have lost the job. Devote some time before the interview to preparing yourself mentally. Start strong: make that good first impression.

Even if your first impression is poor, there is still hope. Most seasoned recruiters will give you some time to make up for a weak start. Their advice is this: if you start poorly, take a deep breath, regroup, and make the best of the remaining time. You have nothing to lose, and there is no need to panic. It is much better to take 10 seconds to relax—perhaps even to comment to the interviewer that you have started poorly—and start over again. Say to the interviewer something along these lines: "Gee, I've really gotten off to a poor start. Can we sort of start over?" I don't recommend though that you depend too heavily on a recruiter's generosity for your interviewing success.

Dialogue

The dialogue is the heart of the interview. It usually consumes the bulk of the time and will last 15 to 20 minutes in a 30-minute interview. During this time, all of the information is exchanged, and you and the employer attempt to sell each other on your respective qualifications.

The recruiter's objective during the dialogue is to answer the three basic questions discussed in marketing yourself (see "Focus on the Employer's Needs" on page 64).

- What are you like?
- What can you produce for the company now?
- What is your potential in the company?

Remember that no matter how qualified you may be you must convince the company that you can contribute and have good potential before they will hire you.

These, too, are your objectives during the interview. You as a candidate likely want to know:

- What the company is like
- What it can do for you now
- What its potential is for you

You read at some length earlier in the book about selling yourself ("Selling Yourself" on page 66). This is where you do it! You will have only a very short time to convince the employer that you are the right person, so don't waste it. All of the knowledge and thorough preparation will be wasted if you don't use it to sell yourself to the employer. Students consistently forget to do this. It takes courage, but you have to do it.

The most difficult part about teaching interview skills is that no two interviews are alike. The issues and topics that can be covered are many (see "Common Interview Questions" on page 221). They depend on the company's culture, the particular position, the recruiter, and your own interests and qualifications. Sure, there are certain standard topics that every interviewer will cover, such as what kind of job you want and why, but the questions used to address these topics will vary tremendously. That's why the only effective preparation is good career planning.

The style of interviews also varies widely. Some like to control the interview; others like you to. Some are aggressive and ask tough questions; others take a laid-back, friendly approach. Some talk about the company a lot; others ask you lots of questions. You never know what style you will encounter. Every good salesperson knows that you have to approach each customer differently and in a style that fits the customer. It is your job to adjust your style to the interviewer's. Think of yourself as a mirror. Spend the first part of the interview reading the interviewer and adjusting your approach. That's not to say you can or should change completely. If you are a very aggressive person, you can never become laid-back, but you can tone down some. If you are a very low-key person, you can't magically transform yourself into a fire-breathing dragon, but you can become more assertive. You never know if the interviewer's style is representative of the company's culture or just a personal style. If it does represent the style of the company and you see that style consistently over many interviews, you can use that information to decide if you fit. If it is just the personal style of the interviewer, you don't want lack of rapport with that person to block your chances with that company. You won't know this until after the process is all over, so you want to stay flexible in the interview.

Remember to be yourself. Adjusting to the interviewer's style does not mean to change your personality or put on a show for the interviewer. You cannot be, with any degree of sincerity and confidence, anybody but yourself. You have prepared well, you know yourself, and you believe in yourself; so relax and *be* yourself.

I had one student who was an excellent student, a well-qualified candidate, and a very nice person. He received all types of first interviews but no follow-ups. I couldn't for the life of me figure out what the problem was, because he was a good communicator. I called him in to the office and said, "Let's have a mock interview. Pretend I'm the recruiter." Suddenly he changed completely. Gone was the natural, confident, enthusiastic MBA. In its place, as he later admitted, was what he thought he was *supposed* to be. I finally convinced him to loosen up and be himself, and within a month he had four job offers!

Employers hire people, not robots. Loosen up and be who and what you are.

Use a portion of the dialogue to get answers to your questions about the company, but be careful—this is your time to sell yourself, so don't take up all of the dialogue asking questions. In a screening interview (such as the on-campus interview), focus on answering their questions; you will have ample opportunity later to ask all of yours. Make sure you get enough information to know whether you want to investigate the company further, but devote at least two thirds of your time to selling yourself. Intelligent, thoughtful questions about the company do impress an interviewer, but it's your qualifications (and how you sell them) that will win you the interview trip or the job. Refer to the accompanying list

Questions Recruiters Recommend

The following general questions are appropriate for a screening interview:

- What are the opportunities for personal growth?
- Would you identify typical career paths based on past records? What is the realistic time frame for advancement?
- How is an employee evaluated and promoted?
- What is the retention rate of people in the position for which I am interviewing?
- Could you describe typical first-year assignments?
- Tell me about the company's initial and future training programs.
- What are the challenging facets of the job?
- What are the company's plans for future growth?
- Is the company stable and financially sound?
- What industry trends will affect this company in the coming years?
- How has this company fared during recent economic cycles?
- What makes this company different from its competitors?
- What are the company's strengths and weaknesses?
- How would you describe the company's personality and management style?
- Is it company policy to promote from within? Tell me the work history of the company's top management.
- What kind of career opportunities are currently available for someone with my degree and skills?
- What are the company's expectations for new hires?
- Describe the work environment.
- How can the company utilize my skills?
- What is the overall structure of the department where the position is located?
- Why do you enjoy working for this company?
- What qualities are you looking for in your new hires?
- Why should I want to work for your organization?
- What characteristics does a successful person have at this company?

Source: *Northwestern Endicott Report 1983.* © Northwestern Lindquist-Endicott Report by Victor R. Lindquist, Northwestern University.

for questions recruiters recommend that interviewees ask. Obviously, you can't ask them all in 30 minutes, so choose a few key ones.

A rule of thumb: do not ask questions that you could have answered by researching the company ahead of time, particularly questions that are answered in the recruiting literature or annual report. Recruiters expect you to spend some time doing your homework before the interview. Their logic is that if you really want to work for them and are really concerned about your career, you will study the literature before the interview.

Use the dialogue to build momentum. In a good interview you can almost feel the sense of anticipation building in both parties. Your challenge is to create some excitement in the employer early in the interview and then keep the impetus going. With good research, you can have an accomplishment, degree, skill, or honor that you think will be of interest ready to spring on the employer early. If you can get his or her attention with an exciting asset of yours, you're in a perfect position. Employers like to get enthusiastic about a candidate (since so many interviews are boring). That's one reason you should take references, transcripts, papers, etc., with you to the interview. It's more ammunition to keep your momentum building. You can almost bet that if you can get an interviewer excited about you, you'll get a second interview.

The recruiter will be testing your communication skills during the dialogue since, at any level in business, you must be able to sell your thoughts and ideas to another person. Although the questions may deal with different topics, a hidden message in each of your answers is how well you can think on your feet and put across your thoughts and ideas. Pay careful attention not only to the content of your answers but to the form in which you express them. You can easily have good answers to questions but fail the interview because you express them poorly. The interview, for all its shortcomings, is a fair test of your ability to communicate clearly and effectively.

In most interviews, let the interviewer run the show. Do not be long-winded; make your answers concise and to the point since the interview is short and you have much ground to cover. Remember that the interviewer is likely to be directing the interview to those topics that he or she considers important, no matter how mundane they may appear to you. If you want to sell yourself most effectively, you would be wise to follow those leads. Generally, if you take charge of the interview, you will be perceived as pushy.

Occasionally you encounter an interviewer who does not want to take charge of the interview. Often this is because the interviewer is

217

inexperienced, although some employers do it to test your assertiveness. Whatever the reason, you have to be sure you get the chance to sell at least some of your strengths. If the interviewer is constantly wandering to other subjects or keeps talking about the company instead of asking you questions, take control and focus the interview on selling your strengths.

Closing

At some point, the interviewer will start to close the interview. The interviewer will probably summarize, thank you for your time, and leave an opening for you to make a closing statement. Like the introduction, this seemingly insignificant part of the interview is in fact very important to your success. It is as important to make a good lasting impression as it is to make a good first impression. In fact, many interviewers will tell you that they cannot remember the exact content of your introduction (although they will remember their general feeling and any errors you made), but they can easily recall your closing statements since they are more recent in their mind.

Finish strong. Give the interviewer something meaty to take away. If the interview has been focused on your skills, your course work, or whatever, add something else in that area. If the interviewer has a very warm, friendly style, make sure that you leave in a warm, friendly way. In some way you should give the interviewer something important to help close the sale.

How to Close an Interview

- Ask questions about how the hiring process will continue with this company. You are entitled to know exactly what will happen with your application before you leave the interview room.
- If you feel good about the company and the opportunity offered, say so. This is the time to show your enthusiasm and interest in the job. Don't *assume* that the interviewer knows how you feel.
- This is also your chance to make any closing remarks or summaries or to provide any additional information that you feel is important. Make it short so the interview still ends on time.
- Leave with a warm, friendly, and positive feeling between you and the interviewer.
- Obtain a business card so you can follow up.

The most common error is to let down at the end. Wait until you have left the interview room before you breathe your sigh of relief. In track, runners will talk about running through the finish line. That is, they imagine themselves actually finishing about 10 yards beyond the finish line so they are still running at full speed when they cross it. Use that same concept in the interview. Run through the end of the interview. Imagine that it actually ends about 1 minute after it does. Stay psyched up and keep your best form. End as positively as you started.

As with the introduction, there are opportunities to recover if you blow it. It is always better to do it right the first time, and you may not have another chance to meet the interviewer face-to-face, but don't panic if you stumble in the closing. A good follow-up letter can help you recover from a poor closing.

Use the closing to find out what will happen after the interview. Feel free to ask the recruiter when you should expect to hear from the company again. Be sure to obtain a business card or the complete mailing address and phone number of the recruiter so you can follow up.

ANSWERING INTERVIEW QUESTIONS

What's a Good Answer?

There are hundreds of questions that you may encounter in an interview. Many of the questions may be answered in different ways, and all provide the interviewer with important information. Furthermore, most interviews will contain at least one atypical or unusual question. All of this makes it difficult to help a candidate prepare for interview questions. There is no way to use prepared answers. The best preparation, to make the point again, is good career planning; by the time the interview rolls around you should have found answers to almost all of the possible interview questions, for your own information as well as the company's.

No matter what question is asked, the interviewer will be collecting a considerable amount of data about you. Interviewers are trained to use all their senses to collect as much information as possible. You need to be aware that the content of your answer is only a part of the information you are transmitting to the interviewer. At all times you are being judged on your communication skills, confidence and poise, enthusiasm, maturity, ability to think on your feet, and professionalism.

Questions may be categorized as *closed-ended* or *open-ended*. Closed-ended questions are those that require a yes or no or simple answer. For example:

- Do you enjoy your major?
- What time is it?
- Who is your favorite professor?
- Did you pass accounting?

They are designed to collect a specific piece of information and are therefore easy to handle (you either know the answer or you don't).

However, interviews usually consist of open-ended questions that are designed to collect lots of information and force you to direct the answer and to think. Examples:

- Tell me about yourself.
- How does your experience qualify you?
- How did you choose your major?
- What did you think about the President's recent speech?
- What does success mean to you?

This type of question can be extremely intimidating, since it reveals very little about what the interviewer really wants to hear. However, several things may help you provide more appropriate answers.

First, you need to understand the general technique for answering interview questions:

- *Listen* carefully to the question. Try to answer it directly and avoid going off on a tangent.
- *Be concise.* Interviews are usually too short for long, rambling answers. Keep your answers brief but complete.
- *Sell yourself.* Use every opportunity to show the employer that you are qualified and a desirable person to hire.
- *Be enthusiastic.* Your confidence in yourself and interest in the job are contagious and will stir good feelings in the interviewer.
- *Be specific.* Don't give vague or ambiguous answers.
- *Understand the purpose of the question.* Consider the context in which the question is asked. Anticipate what the interviewer wants in the answer.
- *Don't dodge.* Never dodge a question—no matter how painful it may be, you must answer what is asked.
- *Watch the interviewer.* Watch for signs of agreement and pleasure, which say you are on the right track, and signs of boredom or impatience, which say you're blowing it.
- *Make each answer count.* Interviews are too short to waste time with a frivolous answer.

Second, students who understand the purpose for which an

interviewer *usually* asks a certain type of open-ended question can better direct their answers to it. Interviewers always have some rationale for their questions, even the seemingly irrelevant ones. One is to collect all the general information described in the beginning of this section. The other (and a very big one) is to collect some specific data about you. Your challenge is to figure out what the interviewer is really trying to find out. For some questions it will be obvious, but for many others it won't be so clear.

Let me give you an example. Suppose a recruiter asks you the following: "What books have you read in the last three months?" Now you know that the interviewer is not there to collect information for the Book-of-the-Month Club's top ten. So what *is* wanted? This question is usually asked to provide some insight into your personal values and intellect. Suppose you are widely read and enjoy everything from romance novels to joke books, from psychology to political science. What should you tell the interviewer? Now that you know the question is not intended to be casual cocktail party conversation or to elicit literally every title you have read in three months, you will know to leave out the junk books and use the answer to tell the interviewer something important about yourself and your interests.

To help you understand why questions are asked and to familiarize you with common interview questions, here is a list grouped by the *common and usual* reason they are asked. Note that many questions can have multiple purposes. When in doubt as to how to direct your answer to an open-ended question, use these categories to guide you.

Common Interview Questions

1. **Goals and ambitions.** What exactly are your goals, how ambitious are you, how far do you want to go, what do you want out of life and a career?
   - What are your future career plans?
   - Where would you like to be in five years professionally? In ten years?
   - In what type of position are you most interested?
   - How much do you hope to earn in five years? Ten years? Fifteen years? Twenty years?
   - What job in this business would you choose if you were entirely free to do so?
   - What goals, other than those related to your occupation, have you set for yourself for the next ten years?
   - What are your long-range career objectives?
   - How do you plan to achieve your career goals?

- What do you feel this position should pay?
- Why aren't you earning more at your age?

2. **Values.** What are your personal values?
   - How do you determine or evaluate success?
   - What are the most important rewards you expect in your business career?
   - Why did you choose the career for which you are preparing?
   - Which is more important to you, the pay or the type of job?
   - What two or three accomplishments have given you the most satisfaction? Why?
   - What is your philosophy of life?
   - What do you really want to do in life?
   - Who has exercised the greatest influence on you? Why?
   - What kind of people appeal to you most?
   - What books have you read in the last three months?
   - What public figures do you admire most?

3. **Personal assessment.** How well do you know yourself and your goals? What are you like as a person? How confident are you? How confident can the interviewer be in what you are saying? Do you have a strong character?
   - Tell me about yourself.
   - What are your greatest strengths?
   - What are your major weaknesses?
   - How much responsibility do you like?
   - If I were to leave right now, what do you think I would think of you?
   - How did you approach your toughest class?
   - What could you have done to improve your grade point average?
   - What do you do to keep in good physical condition?
   - Would you prefer on-the-job training or a formal program?
   - How do you perceive authority?
   - How do you handle your responsibilities?
   - What has been your greatest responsibility? How have you dealt with it?
   - What are your areas for greatest improvement?
   - Give examples of steps you have taken to improve yourself.
   - What conflict situations have you been in, and how did you handle them?
   - What methods do you use to overcome disappointments?
   - What motivated you to go to college?
   - What percent of your college expenses did you earn?
   - When you are annoyed or angry, what do you do?

- Do your friends ever come to you for advice? If so, what do you tell them?
- How would you rate yourself on a scale of one to ten?
- What was a difficult obstacle for you? How did you overcome it?
- What does competition mean to you?
- What are your spare-time activities?
- What is the most exciting thing that has happened to you?
- What will you do if you have no job offer after graduation?
- What kind of boss do you prefer?
- Do you prefer working with others or by yourself?
- Can you take instructions without feeling upset?
- What size city do you prefer?
- Will you fight to get ahead?
- What type of people seem to rub you the wrong way?
- How would you describe yourself?
- How do you think a friend or professor who knows you well would describe you?
- What motivates you to put forth your greatest effort?

4. **Qualifications.** What exactly are your qualifications to do this job?
   - Give me a detailed list of your accomplishments.
   - What supervisory or leadership roles have you held?
   - What skills and qualifications do you have that will help you in this career?
   - What successes have you achieved that will aid you in this career?
   - What organizational experiences have you had that will contribute to your success in this career?
   - What was your record in military service?
   - Do you like routine work?
   - Do you like regular hours?
   - Do you have an analytical mind?
   - In what ways do you think you can make a contribution to this company?
   - What is your previous work experience? What have you gained or learned from it?
   - How do you work under pressure?
   - Have you hired people before?
   - Have you fired people before?
   - What do you look for in hiring?
   - Are you a good manager?
   - In what ways would you change this organization?

5. **Sales.** Questions designed to give you the opportunity to sell yourself.
   - What strengths do you feel you can bring to an assignment with the company?
   - What can you do for us now?
   - What can I do for you?
   - Why should I hire you?
   - What characteristics do you possess that would cause me to make you my top selection?
   - What have you done that shows your initiative and willingness to work?
   - Expand on your resume.

6. **Communication.** Questions designed simply to examine your ability to communicate.
   - If you were the captain of the Dallas Cowboys and had to give a pep talk before the Super Bowl, what would you tell your teammates?
   - What media would you use to communicate an idea to a large group?
   - Give me an example of how you have used your writing skills lately.
   - What communication courses have you taken?
   - Describe the importance of communication skills in business.
   - Are you persuasive?
   - How do you obtain information from others?
   - What role does listening play in communication?
   - What do you think is more important in a conversation, listening skills or verbal skills?
   - How do you fit this job?

7. **Knowledge of career.** How informed are you about career alternatives and this company?
   - Why do you think that you might like to work for this company?
   - In what type of position are you most interested?
   - What do you know about our company?
   - If you were hiring a person for this position, what qualities would you look for?
   - What do you think it takes to be successful in a company like ours?
   - What do you know about the opportunities in this field?
   - What are the disadvantages of this field?
   - What interests you about our service or product?

- How would you plan a sales call?
- What do you consider the characteristics that a businessperson should have?
- Describe for me your perceptions of a day in the life of a person in this business?
- What traits or characteristics are essential to success in this job?

8. **Judgment and maturity.** How mature are you, and how sound is your judgment as demonstrated in your job search process?
   - What did you like best about your old job?
   - What did you like least about your old job?
   - Why did you leave your last job?
   - Why did you choose this company?
   - Why did you select us to interview with?
   - How do you organize or plan your current academic and extracurricular activities?
   - Why are you considering this career?
   - With the pressures you experience in college, how do you prioritize your time?
   - When did you decide on this career?
   - Why do you think you would like this type of job?
   - What do you think determines an individual's progress on this job?
   - How have your previous jobs brought you to this point in your career?
   - Why did you select your college or university?
   - Have you changed you major field of interest? Why?
   - Do you prefer on-the-job training or a formal program?

9. **Educational experience.** Details about your educational background.
   - How has your college experience prepared you for a business career?
   - Why are your grades low?
   - Why did you pick your major?
   - What was your class rank?
   - What has been the progression of your GPA?
   - What extracurricular activities were you involved in?
   - What honors did you earn?
   - What were your favorite classes? Least favorite?
   - What classes did you take in your major?
   - What major projects or papers did you complete?

10. **Miscellaneous details.** Other questions that have to do with specifics about the job and the hiring process.

- For what position are you applying?
- Do you have any objections to a psychological interview or test?
- Does your family mind your being away from home on extensive business trips?
- Are you willing to travel?
- Do you have any serious illness or injury?
- Can we get recommendations from previous employers?
- Are you willing to relocate?

INTERVIEW PROBLEMS

Tough Questions

To give you some extra guidance, here is some advice on a few of the questions that students seem to find most difficult.

Question: *"Tell me about yourself."*

This is usually the toughest one to handle. There is so much you could say and so little time. There are two things you should keep in mind as you formulate your answer: First, what you choose to say will tell the interviewer a great deal about the type of person and professional you are. Second, this is one of the few chances you will have to say anything you want and to sell what you want. Without spending too much time on this question, focus on job-related things about yourself, and use the opportunity to sell yourself, not give your life history. Don't spend time talking about hobbies and high school. Be aggressive enough to point out your strengths but not so much as to sound boastful or pushy. Sell.

Question: *"Where would you like to be in five or ten years?"*

The dilemma here is to show a reasonable amount of ambition without appearing naive or unrealistic. Careful advance research is needed to answer this question well. You need to show that you want to progress and grow professionally. You also need to show that you are somewhat familiar with the typical career path in that industry and field. Do not use job titles; the title that you can attain in a given period of time varies widely by industry. Try an answer like one of these:

- "... would like to have significant managerial responsibility with a staff of six to ten people and profit and loss responsibility."
- "... would like to be in a position with significant decision-making authority and a reasonable amount of autonomy."
- "... would like to feel that I have accomplished something

significant for the company and personally rewarding but still have challenges and room to grow."

- ". . . would like to have responsibility for accounts totaling $1- to $2-million."
- ". . . would like to have progressed through a variety of financial assignments and be ready for significant financial responsibility."

Question: *"What are your major weaknesses?"*

What a dilemma! If you say you have none, you will sound vain and naive. If you reveal a true weakness, you may ruin your chances of employment. The best strategy is to turn a weakness into a strength. Do not risk revealing one of your true shortcomings. For example:

- "When I am working on a project I enjoy, I get so wrapped up in it I forget about other parts of my life."
- "I really demand high-quality work, which sometimes irritates people."
- "I am so analytical that my friends sometimes get impatient."

Notice that in each of the answers, the "weakness" could really help the employer if used for the right job.

Question: *"Why did you leave your former job?"*

The key here is to show your job change as a positive and upward move in terms of professional development. Do not criticize former employers or sound negative. This sounds easy, except that you often leave a job because you didn't like it for some reason. But focus on the positive aspects or results of the change. Tell what you learned from the experience. Examples:

- "I really wanted a more challenging position with more opportunity for promotion."
- "It just was not a good match. I realized I wanted more education and a career in finance."

Question: *"What salary are you looking for?"*

It is particularly important for MBAs to provide a reasonable answer to this question, since they are often accused of being overpriced. Do plenty of research before the interview so you know what the common ranges are for that company, that industry, and a person of your qualifications. Always use a range. See "Setting Salary Benchmarks" on page 247 for more information on calculating an appropriate range.

Question: *"What are your outside interests?"*

This is an easy one to make a mistake on. Outside interests tell the employer that you are more than a bookworm. The tendency is to ramble on extensively about your hobbies and leisure activities because they are so easy to talk about. Muzzle yourself! Offer up a *few* examples to show your well-roundedness. Pick those that are unlikely to raise any objections. Don't talk about so many that the interviewer will wonder when you have time to work.

Overcoming Objections

As you go through many interviews, you are likely to encounter situations where the interviewer does not seem pleased with something about your qualifications or experience. If you are astute, you will sense when you are running into some type of objection. Occasionally an interviewer will tell you straight out, "I don't like . . . ," or, "You aren't. . . ." More often, you can tell by the direction of the probing and subsequent reactions that it's just not going well. Part of being a good salesperson is overcoming objections.

If you are skillful, you can turn objections around during the interview or at least minimize the damage. First, be sure to acknowledge the interviewer's objection (if it's valid). Don't get defensive. Then, show the interviewer that you have enough other strengths to more than compensate for that weakness. Turn the interviewer from the negative thinking to a positive, "can do" attitude. To illustrate, here is a review of some common objections you will encounter:

Objection: *"Your grades are too low."*

There are two good responses to this. First, counter with several examples of your skills, abilities, and accomplishments, and expand on how those can contribute to the company and make up for the low grades. *Don't* try to defend the grades by describing all the unfair grading, rotten professors, or other mitigating circumstances, unless they are very unusual (e.g., death in the family). Second, if you are already an MBA, point out that nobody graduates with less than a 3.0 GPA (usually), and emphasize the competitiveness of the student body. Use this as additional support to the first point.

Objection: *"You don't have any work experience."*

You need to focus the interviewer's attention on everything you have learned instead of what you haven't. Emphasize "real world" types of classroom experience you have, such as cases, projects, and simulations. Also point out any experience in extracurricular activities that you can relate directly to the job. Talk about your success at learning quickly and your desire to learn. Show how you can accomplish things for the company in spite of your lack of work experience.

Objection: *"You don't have enough experience."*
Make the most of the experience that you do have. Expand on your accomplishments and what you have learned, and lead the interviewer into a deeper discussion of your responsibilities on the job. Talk about your commendations and high ratings. If you need additional support, draw on your education, using the approach in the previous paragraph.

Objection: *"You are too experienced."*
There are many variations of this objection, such as:

- "You're overqualified."
- "You're not entry-level material."
- "We can't pay you enough."

This objection is often raised when you change career directions. Frankly, it is one of the most difficult to handle because of tightly structured corporate career ladders and salary steps. Companies fear that once you are in the door, you will be bored, unchallenged, and difficult to manage, or you will leave.

First, emphasize your flexibility and patience. Show the interviewer that, despite your experience, you can be satisfied and happy with the job under discussion. Focus on the benefits of your maturity and experience. Show the interviewer how the job fits into your life plan, and emphasize that you will be content with the career path being offered. Be sure this is genuine, or you're sunk.

Objection: *"Your work record is too spotty."*
Employers get very nervous about candidates who have changed jobs frequently or been unemployed for extended periods. They fear that your commitment to work is low and that you are unlikely to return any dividends from their investment in training you because you will quit.

If you have a legitimate reason, such as economic conditions, children, illness, spouse transferred, or a plant closing, say so; your reason will likely be accepted and the objection eliminated. If not, do not try to hide or bluff your way through the answer. You must convince the employer of your seriousness about your career. Show that you are ready to stay in the job for a while. Focus also on what your variety of experiences can contribute.

Objection: *"We don't need an MBA for this job."*

Employers are trying to get you to justify why you're worth the extra salary it will have to pay for an MBA. Talk about the new skills and abilities you have acquired (be specific) in your MBA. Show them how these will lead to improved performance. Want a real winner? Offer to compromise on starting salary if the company will allow you the opportunity to demonstrate how much better you can perform with an MBA and then agree to give you a substantial raise if you perform well (gutsy move but it works).

Illegal/Unethical Practices

Unfortunately, unethical and illegal practices do happen in the placement/employment process. Most companies do not engage in such practices, but you should nevertheless be aware of them and know your rights as an interviewee. The "Guide to Illegal Interview Questions" on page 232 is an excellent summary of illegal questions that you may encounter. "Ethics and Honesty in MBA Placement" on page 57 is a statement of ethical principles that most recruiters and schools adhere to.

So what should you do if an interviewer asks you an illegal question or engages in unethical practice? On the one hand, you should always try to maintain a positive approach throughout the interview. Give the interviewer the benefit of the doubt. Very few employers intentionally ask illegal questions. The laws governing equal employment opportunity are very complex and change so often that employers have to work hard to stay current. It is particularly difficult for nonpersonnel professionals to stay current. You should never assume an employer has bad intentions just because he or she might inadvertently ask you something illegal. Only in rare instances will you need to directly challenge an interviewer, and the last thing you want is a confrontation.

On the other hand, you are entitled not to answer the question. You have your rights as an interviewee, and the law is designed to protect those rights. There is no reason in today's job market to forgo those rights if you encounter a bad situation.

How can you respond to an illegal question in a positive manner? The key is to understand why the question is asked. Interviewers usually ask questions about race, religion, or sex because they fear the effects certain personal characteristics they associate with stereotypes will have on the company. Most illegal questions relate directly to your ability to perform in the job, your commitment, and whether you will stay with the company. If you understand this, you can address the employer's fear while avoiding answering illegal questions directly. Consider the following illegal questions and the assumptions that often underlie them:

Questions	Assumption/Fear
Will you have children?	She will leave the company, or she won't be committed to the company.
How old are you?	. . . doesn't have enough productive years to recover my training costs.
What nationality are you?	. . . these people are not hard workers.

Although these types of assumptions cannot be condoned, you can use them to defuse a difficult situation. The best answer to an illegal question is to address the employer's real concern:

Question	Answer
Will you have children?	I can assure you that any family plans I have will not interfere with my career.
How old are you?	I am sure that I can be a very productive employee for you.
What nationality are you?	I am a very hard worker and believe that I can contribute to your company.

I recommend this approach as a way to preserve your own integrity as well as your chances for the job. This approach lets the recruiter and you save face, keeps private the information that should be, avoids a confrontation, and addresses the employer's concern. It provides positive responses that assert your rights. Most interviewers will respond to this approach by quickly recognizing their errors.

If this approach does not work, however, you have a tough decision to make. Examine the consequences of answering the question. If the question is really incidental to the process, it may be harmless to answer it and then report the unethical or illegal practice to the interviewer's boss or your placement office. (Placement offices routinely discuss these types of situations with employers and are there to handle them.) There may even be times when you choose to completely ignore the incident because the question is so inconsequential.

If you believe that answering the question will seriously jeopardize your chances of being hired or compromise your ethics, then, by all means, don't answer it. Politely decline to answer and explain your reason. Be sure you know what you are talking about if you do challenge the question. Maintain a positive, friendly tone and empathize with the interviewer by asking if there is some other issue you can address. Do not criticize or belittle the interviewer; let him or her save face even if a mistake has been made.

Finally, if the interviewer does not respond favorably to your positive approach, I'd suggest you simply refuse to answer the question and terminate the interview. If a company is so narrow-minded as to base a hiring decision on other than bona fide occupational qualifications, you will probably not want to work for it.

Guide to Illegal Interview Questions

Preemployment Questions	Lawful	Unlawful
Name	First, Middle, Last	Requirement of prefix Mr., Miss, Ms., Mrs.
	Use of any other names or nicknames necessary for checking previous work experience or education.	Inquiries about names which would indicate national origin.
		Inquiries regarding names changed by marriage, divorce, court order, etc.

(continued)

Source: Virginia Polytechnic Institute and State University Equal Opportunity/ Affirmative Action Office. Reprinted by permission.

Preemployment Questions	Lawful	Unlawful
Address	Applicant's address and length of residence in this city/state.	Questions regarding foreign addresses that would intentionally or unintentionally indicate national origin. Whether applicant owns or rents home or lives in an apartment. Names and relationships of persons with whom applicant resides.
Marital Status	Whether applicant can meet specified work schedules. Whether applicant has any additional responsibilities that would interfere with proper attendance.	Whether applicant is married, single, divorced, separated, engaged, etc. Number and ages of dependent children. All questions related to pregnancy or methods of family planning. Questions regarding child care arrangements.
Height and Weight		Questions regarding height and weight are considered unlawful unless based on a Bona Fide Occupational Qualification (B.F.O.Q.), and such instances are rare.

(continued)

Preemployment Questions	Lawful	Unlawful
Race		Questions regarding race.
		Inquiry into color of eyes, hair.
		Other questions that would indicate race.
Religion	Questions regarding religious denomination or beliefs if based on B.F.O.Q. as in the case of ministers, teachers, or other employees of specific religious organizations. Questions regarding availability for work during specific time periods. (Reasonable accommodations must be made for employees whose religious practices interfere with work schedules.)	Questions regarding religious beliefs if not based on B.F.O.Q. Questions such as "What religious holidays do you observe?" if asked prior to employment.
National Origin	Languages applicant speaks, reads, or writes.	How foreign languages were learned. Ancestry or birthplace of parents or spouse. Associates or other relatives from foreign countries. Birthplace of applicant.

(continued)

Preemployment Questions	Lawful	Unlawful
Citizenship	"Are you a citizen of this country?" "If not a citizen, are you legally eligible to accept work and remain in this country?" Statement that, if hired, applicant must furnish proof of citizenship or appropriate visa.	Whether other members of applicant's family are U.S. citizens. "Of what country are you a citizen?" Require proof of citizenship prior to employment.
Sex		All questions regarding sex of the applicant unless based on B.F.O.Q., such as a men's locker room attendant.
Education	Schools attended Degrees acquired Transcripts, if required of all applicants for similar work.	Questions regarding national, racial, or religious affiliation of schools attended.
Photograph	May be required after hiring if necessary for business purposes.	Requirement that applicant attach photo to application. State that attaching photo is optional.
Experience	Inquiries regarding previous work experience. Foreign countries visited.	

(continued)

Preemployment Questions	Lawful	Unlawful
Criminal Record	"Have you ever been convicted of a crime?" (Information obtained must be used only if it relates to applicant's fitness to perform a particular job. Ex: Person convicted for embezzlement would be a high risk for a position as a cashier in a store.)	"Have you ever been arrested?" (An arrest is merely the detaining of a person to answer a crime and has no effect on fitness to perform a particular job.)
Credit Rating		All questions regarding credit rating, charge accounts, garnishments, or other indebtedness.
Handicap	Questions regarding handicaps voluntarily disclosed by applicant if information is used solely for Affirmative Action.	"Do you have any handicaps or physical defects?"
Relatives	Names and addresses of parents of a minor applicant. Explain conflict of interest rules and ask if these affect applicant.	Names and addresses of applicant's relatives.
References	Names and addresses of persons willing to provide character or professional references for applicant.	Require references from pastor, priest, rabbi, or other religious associates.

(continued)

Preemployment Questions	Lawful	Unlawful
Organizations	Names of professional organizations to which applicant belongs. Offices held in professional organizations.	"List all clubs or organizations to which you belong." Requesting other information about membership in organizations if this information would indicate race, religion, or national origin of applicant.
Emergencies	Names of persons to be notified in case of emergency.	Names of relatives to be notified in case of emergency.
Age	Questions as to whether or not applicant meets minimum/maximum age requirements.	"How old are you?" Birthdate.
Military History	Experience/education in military services that would relate to the job applicant is seeking.	Type of discharge. Military disciplinary record.
Medical Exams	Require medical examinations prior to employment only if required of all applicants and necessary to assess ability to perform job safely and effectively.	Making medical history available to hiring manager.

This chart does not include information on every situation that may arise in the interviewing process. Contact your MBA placement office or other authority if you have concerns not addressed in this chart.

OTHER TYPES OF INTERVIEWS

The most common type of interview is one-on-one: one interviewer and one interviewee in a room alone. Probably 90 percent of your interviews will be of this type. You may also encounter panel or team interviews, which are a little more difficult to handle. Panel interviews are more impersonal, because it is very difficult to establish good rapport with four or five interviewers at one time. You are likely to feel a little intimidated, lonely, and perhaps ganged up on. Just don't expect to have the same rapport you are accustomed to, and don't judge your success in the interview by the lack of rapport. Stay calm; talk to panel members one at a time rather than all together; answer their questions as best you can. It's really no different from a series of four or five single interviews. Team interviews (two interviewers) are not nearly so difficult. You can develop a rapport with two people, and you should not find them to be that much of a problem.

There are a few companies that use stress interviews, where the style is intimidating and belligerent. These are purposely designed to see if you will break under pressure, and they often work. The key is recognizing the style early. Stress interviews are so uncommon that you don't expect to get one, and when you do it takes 5 or 10 minutes to regain your composure, and by then you've already blown it. Your natural reaction is to get agitated and defensive. But you need to recognize what's happening and quickly shift to a different mode. Think of it as a game; your best offense is to pretend it's just a normal interview and ignore the pressure. Afterward, though, you should think carefully about whether you will be comfortable working in the type of environment that necessitates a stress interview.

NEW TRENDS

Today there are tremendous pressures on corporations to reduce costs, including recruiting costs. As a result, companies are beginning to interview candidates by some new techniques that reduce travel costs. All of these new methods reduce direct contact with the employer, making it more difficult for the candidate.

One not-so-new method that is frequently used now is the telephone interview. This type is often used for screening interviews, particularly those that follow up resumes received in the mail, and for co-op and intern positions. The biggest problem is that information flows through only one channel of communication—spoken words. You lose all benefits of observing the interviewer's body language. This forces you to be more precise and articulate in your answers. It can be a bit uncomfortable, but you have to make the best of it. Fortunately, the employers also miss information, so they limit their use of the telephone interview.

The newest approach is video interviewing. This takes two forms: videotaped and interactive. The better form is interactive video (which is usually via satellite or fiber-optic network); each party can see the other as they talk back and forth. Videotaped interviews either use a standard set of questions or require that you prepare a 5- to 10-minute statement.

If you are going to have a video interview, find a way to get on camera and practice. Talking to a video camera can be a very unnerving experience if you aren't used to it: people tend to stiffen up or become very self-conscious. There may be a camera person in the room, which can be distracting, and there will probably be special lights and wiring. Television also exaggerates certain movements and gestures. It really isn't that big of a problem, but it is different and you will probably bungle it a few times if you don't practice. New technologies are emerging that should reduce the difficulties with video interviewing, making it much more practical and friendly. Ultimately, this will benefit both candidates and employers.

Another old but now more frequently used method is contract interviewing. With this approach, a company hires a consultant to do screening interviews. This person may know little about the company but is trained in interviewing and given the criteria by which a company wishes to judge candidates. Typically the consultant is located near a source of applicants (e.g., a university). This method can be considerably cheaper than sending a company representative. It probably won't become very popular at the MBA level, since companies usually take great care in hiring MBAs because of the greater investment and higher level of the position. However, should you encounter contract interviewers, you will likely find them to be quite competent. Your biggest problem is that they may not know much about the company beyond basic information. Also, you cannot be sure that the interviewer's style at all reflects the company's culture. Since it's likely to be just a screening interview though, the experience should be fine and requires no special preparation. Do try to establish direct contact at the company.

YOUR REJECTION ACTION PLAN

So far this chapter has assumed the interviewing process will culminate in your getting an offer. Suppose you don't get one? You'll probably be very disappointed, but by now you've learned how to handle that. However, can you do anything constructive with rejection?

Moping and being depressed helps massage your bruised ego, but it doesn't help you in the long term. Effective MBAs use rejection to learn about themselves and to make improvements.

First, call up the employer who rejected you and ask why. You'll be surprised how many will take time to critique your qualifications and interview skills. Not many people really want to see you fail. Most welcome the chance to help people build their professional career. Pick one with whom you had fairly good rapport and ask for an honest critique. Don't argue or try to change the decision; just listen.

Next, develop an action plan for improvement. Ask yourself:

- What did I do wrong?
- How could I have avoided the mistakes?
- What additional training do I need?
- What did I learn about myself?
- Was I perceived correctly? If not, how can I change that?

Use these lessons to improve your portfolio and land the next job.

THE FINAL
STRETCH

Chapter 12

The Job Offer

The purpose of all your work—and of this book—is getting a job offer. If you have prepared yourself well and the economy is sound, the odds of your getting this far are very good. Let's talk about the offer in more detail.

A job offer usually contains several basic pieces of information:

- job title
- office location
- starting salary
- bonuses
- relocation expense reimbursement
- conditions of employment (reference check, drug test, physical, etc.)

In some companies you may not immediately know to which department you will be assigned, but you will generally be told the type of job and the location. The time allowed for considering an offer varies greatly. Between two and four weeks is the norm. Very large corporations may give several months; smaller organizations or those filling an immediate opening may permit less. There is usually some room to negotiate a deadline that is acceptable to both parties.

You should establish on what terms or range of terms you would accept an offer before you ever receive one. There is nothing wrong with sleeping on an offer or discussing it with friends and family, but there is also no reason to delay unnecessarily. If you've done your homework, you should know about what terms to expect, and you should know whether you liked the sound of the job and the company. If you like the offer, go for it as soon as you can. However, always allow at least 24 hours after your last interview before accepting. It's easy to get excited during the interview and overlook the not-so-nice parts of a company.

You may wish to wait until you receive other offers. It's generally good to have all your alternatives in front of you before you make a decision. So try to negotiate enough time to allow other prospects to come to fruition. But no employer likes to be put off very long. Doing so only tells the employer you really aren't very interested and the company might be better off pursuing other candidates. If you really don't like your other prospects better than the employer from whom you have the offer, don't wait. Don't risk losing a good job just to have a look at other options that may never happen anyway. If you know it's for you, it's all right to accept your first offer.

NEGOTIATING YOUR OFFER

Unfortunately, entry-level salaries for the average MBA are often not negotiable. Salary structures, particularly in large corporations, are fairly rigid and usually allow only minimal leeway. Smaller companies and higher-level positions in large companies usually have more flexibility. For the average MBA, negotiating a substantially better offer is not very realistic, but most companies want to know if their offer is not competitive and will try to improve it within narrow limits.

Suppose that you receive an offer from a company that you really want to work for, and the salary is too low. What do you do? If the offer is substantially low, tell the company. Remember that this is a business deal and you have a right to fair compensation. However, if the difference is not significant, consider that you may have more to lose politically by bargaining than you stand to gain financially. If you do negotiate:

- Be sure that you really want to work for the company. Don't negotiate salary unless you have a legitimate interest in the job.
- Tell the employer honestly that you feel the salary offer is too low.
- Consider negotiating on benefits, moving expenses, and bonuses rather than base salary.
- Note this fact: It is often easier to earn quick raises than to negotiate a higher starting salary.

THE EMPLOYMENT CONTRACT

Now that you have the offer, what kind of promise do you really have from the company? What kind of promise have you made? Can the employer revoke the offer? What happens if you renege on your acceptance? Can the employer lay you off soon after you start work? Can you sue the employer if your offer is revoked? These are all very important questions to which you may not like the answers. I would like to tell you that the employer's offer and your acceptance create a binding contract that guarantees you a job. Unfortunately, the truth is that they do not.

Employment in the United States has long been considered by the courts to be an "at-will" relationship. That is, the employee serves at the will of the employer, who has long had the right under the law to hire and fire at will. The promise of employment in the private sector has been one of indeterminate length subject solely to the preferences of the employer, regardless of performance. Courts have historically been reluctant to force an employment relationship on an employer. Although there has been some change in this position, the predominant position of the courts continues to be one of hire and fire at will, although anti-discrimination and equal opportunity laws now limit an employer's freedom. There has also been some movement to protect employees from wrongful discharges and blatant disregard for promises made.

What this means is that, legally, the job offer and acceptance do not usually constitute a binding, enforceable contract. While the outcome of cases has varied from state to state, the courts' basic position remains employment "at will." Thus, in the absence of an employment contract or very specific commitment, the employer is free to revoke a job offer, or fire you two days after you report to work or whenever it so chooses. A mere promise of employment such as is usually included in most offer letters is not considered to be an employment contract. Generally, neither are statements made by recruiters, such as "opportunities for advancement," "permanent position," or "job security," enough to create a binding contract. The courts seem to look for clear, unequivocal evidence that the employer's intent was to create a binding relationship stronger than the normal at-will relationship. Such situations are rare for newly or recently graduated MBAs.

That does not mean that the employer can run completely roughshod over you. There are protections under the law if you can prove that an employer has intentionally misled you or misrepresented the situation. Some courts have also ruled in favor of students under the legal theory of "detrimental reliance." That is, even if a binding employment contract does not exist, an employer may be liable for damages if a student relies on the job commitment and takes actions that are personally detrimental. Examples might include quitting another job, relocating, or signing a lease for an apartment.

In summary, from a legal perspective it would appear that the job offer/acceptance does not offer the security of a legal contract. Just as you don't know how long your employment will last, your job offer could be subject to revocation at any time. And things do change. Business conditions can take a turn for the worse, plants close, managers change, bankruptcies occur. As a result, job offers do get revoked, and MBAs do get laid off soon after starting work.

Fortunately, there are more considerations to this than just legal ones. For competitive and ethical reasons, most employers do not take advantage of the freedoms allowed by the law. Companies that have a history of reneging on job offers or laying off new hires quickly find that they can no longer attract top applicants. Visits to college campuses yield empty or half-filled schedules; resumes received are frequently from lower-quality applicants who have to take more risk. There are enough high-quality companies hiring that good MBA candidates don't have to take those risks. Thus, most companies work very hard to avoid having to take such drastic action, knowing that it can take up to five years to rebuild their recruiting efforts if they get a bad reputation.

Furthermore, most companies and candidates will agree that reneging on a promise is ethically wrong. Fortunately, the majority of companies and recruiters are ethical and honor the commitments they make, regardless of whether they are legally enforceable. In business, one quickly learns that integrity and reputation are everything. For this reason, there is a very high probability that your job offer will be honored. It's simply good business. But you need to be aware of the exact nature of the commitment you have.

RENEGING ON A JOB OFFER

Suppose that you are comfortably settled in for your final semester of MBA studies, with a "perfect" job offer in hand and accepted. You are making plans for a brief vacation before work, planning ways to spend your new salary, and enjoying a little "senior slump." Then, the phone rings and it's a recruiter with whom you interviewed months ago. Much to your surprise, she offers you a job at $5,000 more per year starting salary. Everything else about the job is as good as the offer you have already accepted. What do you do?

Many a student has been perplexed by such a dilemma. You have no legal obligation to stand by your first acceptance. Legally you can renege and take the second offer. What it boils down to is an ethical issue: should you renege on an acceptance?

There are two answers: the way employers would like things to be and the way the game is played. I hate to see MBAs renege on the acceptance of an offer. It angers employers, reflects badly on you as a professional and as a person, reflects badly on those who may have written or given references for you, and reflects badly on your school. The ethical standard in this country is that we honor commitments; many successful businesspeople tell of opportunities passed up in order to honor commitments. Two of the traits highly desired in business today are integrity and honesty. Customers expect quality and service; bosses expect you to do what you say you will; employees expect you not to betray them. By any ethical standard, reneging on a job offer, by employers or MBA candidates, is wrong.

That's the ideal. But here are a few cold, cruel facts. While most companies will try extremely hard not to revoke a job offer, they will do it. If business conditions worsen considerably, companies may be forced to take drastic measures, including revoking job offers. They may also fire you soon after you report to work. In layoff situations, the least senior people are often the first to go, sometimes with little severance pay. Nobody likes to do it, everybody feels bad about it, and everybody wants to avoid it; but employers will, and legally can, do it.

So if employers do it when it suits their own best interest, shouldn't students? Are employers held to any lower a standard than students? No. It's a tough world. If employers want the freedom to dish it out (which they have), they are going to have to take it too.

I wish I could tell you never to renege on an acceptance, but that's not totally realistic. You will have to decide for yourself what you will do. There is an old saying, though, that everyone can be bought—the only question is at what price. Would you renege on an acceptance if the salary were 10 percent higher? Maybe not. But what about double? You can't help but stop and think about the extras you could buy for yourself with that money or the college education for your kids you could one day provide.

Remember, though, that your integrity is very difficult to rebuild once destroyed. If you consider reneging, don't be too shortsighted. You will make people angry at the company you dump, and your reputation with them will be sullied. Be sure you can afford that. Might you ever want to work for that company in the future? Will you ever have to deal with it as a supplier or customer? Will you be in professional organizations together? Could the company spread a "bad rap" on you? Employers do talk, you know.

If you renege, do so with as much class as you can. Tell the company immediately so it can start recruiting again as soon as possible. Be gracious and appreciative of what the company has done for you. Be forthright and honest about your reasons. But don't expect the company to be happy about it.

SETTING SALARY BENCHMARKS

There is more to a job than just money. However, salary remains an important issue to all of us. It represents many things to many people. It enables us to follow the life-style that we want, to move up and prosper; it represents our worth compared with others'; and it is only one of the many rewards of a job. You can quickly see why determining an exact salary level to seek is not easy.

What you can do is set three benchmarks in deciding what salary to ask for:

- what you would need to pursue the life-style you want
- what your market value is
- the other rewards of the job

In order to set the first benchmark, you should first develop a preliminary budget to obtain a reasonable estimate of your expenses (see "Budgeting Work Sheet" on page 253). You should prepare three budgets: a minimum requirement, a "like to have," and the best case. But you need to develop a base salary range early so you can answer recruiters' questions easily and can get your needs and expectations in line as discussed in "The Facts About MBA Salaries" on page 16.

One difficulty in determining the salary you will need is that the cost of living varies greatly from city to city and from metropolitan to nonmetropolitan areas. A good salary in one area can mean just getting by in another. The American Chamber of Commerce Researchers Association publishes a cost-of-living index for 260 urban areas in the United States on a quarterly basis; the accompanying table shows its index for selected major cities for the fourth quarter 1988. This survey involves extensive research on the price of consumer goods and services for a midmanagement standard of living (taxes not included) as contributed by local chambers of commerce on a voluntary basis. It has been published since 1968. Most of the Fortune 500 companies subscribe to it and use it in their salary planning.

The indexes are based on an average of 100 for all of the urban United States surveyed. Those areas with an index greater than 100 are more expensive than average while those with an index of less than 100 are less expensive than average. You can also use the indexes to compare salary offers between cities. Let's look at Memphis, Tennessee (index = 96.4) and Nassau County, New York (index = 160.3), for example. A $35,000 salary offer in Memphis would require a $58,200 ($35,000 x 160.3/96.4) offer in Nassau County to maintain the same standard of living. Or, done another way, a $45,000 offer in San Diego (index = 127.1) would be equivalent to $32,643 in Baton Rouge, Louisiana (index = 92.2) ($45,000 x 92.2/127.1).

I suggest that you prepare your budget for the "average" city and

ACCRA Cost of Living Indexes

Based on midmanagement standard of living, fourth quarter 1988

Area	Index	Area	Index
Birmingham, AL	99.1	Albuquerque, NM	103.4
Mobile, AL	98.6	Santa Fe, NM	112.2
Montgomery, AL	100.4	Buffalo, NY	102.0
Fairbanks, AK	128.2	Nassau County, NY	160.3
Phoenix, AZ	105.3	Syracuse, NY	93.6
Tucson, AZ	101.3	Charlotte, NC	101.5
Palm Springs, CA	113.3	Greensboro, NC	100.2
Sacramento, CA	108.8	Raleigh, NC	103.0
San Diego, CA	127.1	Cleveland, OH	105.4
Boulder, CO	104.6	Columbus, OH	104.4
Denver, CO	105.3	Toledo, OH	102.1
Hartford, CT	120.6	Oklahoma City, OK	93.4
Wilmington, DE	113.8	Portland, OR	104.1
Jacksonville, FL	99.1	Harrisburg, PA	106.5
Miami, FL	114.6	Philadelphia, PA	128.2
Orlando, FL	99.8	Pittsburgh, PA	104.3
Atlanta, GA	107.6	Charleston, SC	100.7
Champaign-Urbana, IL	104.2	Columbia, SC	97.6
Bloomington, IN	99.2	Chattanooga, TN	91.3
Indianapolis, IN	98.0	Knoxville, TN	97.5
Cedar Rapids, IA	105.1	Memphis, TN	96.4
Wichita, KS	96.5	Nashville, TN	100.0
Lexington, KY	100.4	Dallas, TX	104.1
Louisville, KY	96.3	Houston, TX	102.9
Baton Rouge, LA	92.2	San Antonio, TX	97.6
New Orleans, LA	97.5	Salt Lake City, UT	98.8
Minneapolis, MN	102.5	Richmond, VA	110.5
St. Paul, MN	103.4	Roanoke, VA	99.8
Gulfport, MS	92.8	Seattle, WA	106.7
St. Louis, MO–IL	99.2	Spokane, WA	92.8
Great Falls, MT	96.2	Charleston, WV	97.3
Lincoln, NE	93.3	Green Bay, WI	96.8
Omaha, NE	92.6	Kenosha, WI	106.0
Las Vegas, NV	102.8	Laramie, WY	101.9
Manchester, NH	128.3		

Source: American Chamber of Commerce Researchers Association Cost of Living Index, Fourth Quarter 1988, vol. 21, no. 4.

then adjust your requirements up or down, depending on the city in which a company you are considering is located.

The second benchmark is your market value. There is no such thing as one "market salary" for an MBA. The MBA is such a varied, diverse degree that salary ranges are wide. Starting salaries vary tremendously by geographic location, job function, educational background, industry, and years of work experience. The correct approach is to look *only* at salary data that fit the demographic characteristics of the company and job you are considering *when compared with your qualifications.* Only then will you have your true market value.

There are three good sources of MBA salary data to use in assessing your market value.

1. Your school's MBA placement report
2. *College Placement Council Annual Salary Survey*
3. *Northwestern Lindquist-Endicott Report*

Your school's placement report is by far the most accurate indicator of your market value, since it reports salaries only of students who have qualifications similar to yours and who are going to work for similar companies in your area. Pay very close attention to it.

The *College Placement Council Annual Salary Survey* is available only to member college placement offices and employers, so you will have to visit a college placement office to obtain the data. It is a survey of 164 leading university placement offices nationwide that collect salary data from companies and students. Published quarterly, it is the most widely used and quoted survey. Chapter 1 of this book includes CPC data for 1980–89 and should be all you need in this regard.

The *Northwestern Lindquist-Endicott Report* is available for a $25 fee by writing to:

Northwestern Endicott Report
Placement Center–Scott Hall
Northwestern University
Evanston, IL 60201

The Northwestern University Placement Center has been doing this report for more than forty years. It is a survey of about 250 companies and reports their salary offers to college graduates, including MBAs. Breakdowns are provided by undergraduate degree. It is generally available in January; your college placement office should have a copy.

Your third benchmark is more difficult to assess. Each job will offer you a bundle of rewards and satisfactions. How important salary is relative to the other rewards will vary according to the specific job you are considering and your value structure. We all seek a certain overall level of satisfactions and rewards from our jobs. Each perk, benefit, and accomplishment helps us reach our overall satisfaction goal. Salary is a key piece of that, but you may be willing to forgo some salary for more satisfaction in another area. Similarly, if the job does not contribute much in other areas, your salary demands are likely to be higher.

It's extremely important that you not focus on money alone. There is much more to the total compensation to be had from a job than just money. What you really seek is an *overall* level of satisfaction. Above a certain minimum level of financial security, you may be willing to trade off money for other satisfactions. Remember that money is not the only source of satisfaction. Look closely at *everything* the job has to offer.

You will find that your salary expectations will vary with each job you consider. A $32,000 offer from a company that is located in a place you consider great to live in, that is also near your family, whom you dearly love, and that offers you the type of work that really excites you may be much better than a $41,000 offer for a job in a place you don't like, 500 miles from your family, which requires frequent travel and looks like it will cease to challenge you in three years.

To figure this out, let's continue our example. A very useful thought process when comparing two job offers is to list the advantages that the lower paying job has over the other job. Then imagine someone asking how much you would be willing to pay for each of those advantages. In the example, you might say:

- place I like to live = $4,000/year
- close to my family = $2,000/year
- job I really enjoy = $5,000/year
- small amount of travel = $500/year

The total is $11,500. Add that to the lower salary offer ($32,000 + $11,500) and you get $43,500. Now compare that with the $41,000 offer and you will see that you really are getting more in the lower-paid job. By putting a dollar value on some of the intangible rewards of a job you can more accurately compare the two offers. We all tend to be blinded by dollars sometimes and forget to account for the rewards that don't come in our paycheck.

Taken together, your three benchmarks set the range of salary you should expect and ask for:

- lowest salary—higher of your personal minimum or the market minimum
- highest—the market maximum

- adjustment for the other rewards of the job

For example, suppose Joe has determined that he needs for his life-style:

- minimum $22,000
- would like $26,000
- best $30,000

His market research shows that for a person of his qualifications entering the type of job he is considering, the salary range is:

- low $23,000
- high $28,000

Therefore, his minimum expectation should be the higher of the market minimum ($23,000) and his personal minimum ($22,000), which is $23,000 (why ask for less than the market is willing to pay?). His maximum is the market maximum of $28,000 (you can't expect more than the market is willing to pay). Joe asks for $23,000–$28,000; XYZ company offers him exactly what he wants in the way of a job but only $20,000. However, XYZ will give him a company car and the chance to own part of the business in three years. Joe decides that the other rewards make up for the lower salary and takes the job.

Obviously, your personal needs could be much higher than the market value. In that case, you will have to reevaluate your own expectations or change careers. If the market value is much higher than your personal expectations, congratulate yourself on being prudent, realize that you are worth more than you think, enjoy the fruits of your years of hard work, and go for it!

When and how to discuss salary are matters that require careful judgment. In general, you should not discuss salary during the screening interview unless you are interviewing with an employer who you are not sure understands the MBA job market. Doing so makes it appear that salary is your primary criterion for choosing a job. This connotes immaturity to an employer and usually elicits a negative response. At the same time, you are entitled to have some idea of the salary that the company is likely to offer. Check with your placement counselor and published sources before the initial interview to pursue the question in detail. Usually, you will conclude your on-site interview with the personnel representative of the company. At that time it is appropriate to talk about salary, but always ask about a salary range. Don't attempt to pin the company to a specific starting salary. A good approach would be something like this: "What range of starting salary do new employees with qualifications similar to mine receive in your company?"

Budgeting Work Sheet

	Expenses per Month	Can Get By	Would Like	Great
Essential	Housing			
	Car and/or Transportation			
	Electric			
	Phone			
	Other Utilities			
	Homeowner's Insurance			
	Car Insurance			
	Food			
	Clothing			
	Other			
Nonessential	Entertainment			
	Savings			
	Other			
	Total per Month			
	Total per Year (x 12)			

CONFLICTING DEADLINES FOR ACCEPTING
JOB OFFERS

It is quite common to find yourself with a deadline for accepting a job offer that either conflicts with another offer or is before the time that you will likely receive an offer from another company for which you want to wait. Employers are quite familiar with this problem, and you need not panic; most will gladly extend their acceptance deadline two to four weeks if they have the flexibility. They know you may be considering several employers; although they might wish you would want no other job, most would also not even hire you if you were so naive as to not look at several job alternatives. Although there are circumstances that will force an employer to place a quick, firm deadline on you, most will gladly work with you. Simply call up the recruiter and explain that you need some extra time, and you will likely receive it. A successful approach would be: "I am very interested in the offer you have made me, but I'm afraid I will not be able to complete my job search by the deadline we agreed on. I would like to be able to evaluate all my alternatives. Would you be willing to give me ____ extra weeks in which to make a decision?"

A few cautions:

- Be sure to ask for all the time you need. Do not plan on asking a second time.
- Be fair to the employer. If you really do not want that job and have another offer that you know you would rather take, decline the job without delay.
- Be completely honest with the employer.
- Don't ask for more than a few weeks. Any more shows lack of interest and will indicate you are just stalling.

Chapter 13

Assessing Corporate Culture

There is no question that each business organization has its unique character. A company develops its own personality, values, traditions, attitudes, and behavior. Joining an organization and developing your career are very similar to dating and marrying. Simply put, before you join a company you had better be sure that you are very compatible with it, because you are going to spend an awful lot of your time and energy there. The fit between you and that organization's culture is just as important as the fit between your skills and the work that needs to be done. Without a doubt, most of the problems that MBAs encounter in new jobs stem from a mismatch of cultural values rather than any lack of ability to perform the job adequately. MBAs are typically well trained in how to analyze the relative merit of a company's business and their ability to contribute to the organization. It is difficult, however, to persuade them to look at this important other half of finding a happy career match.

Let me try to convince you. Suppose you and your spouse want to raise beautiful children who enjoy lots of love and attention from both parents. How well will you fit in a company that expects its people to work long hours and weekends? From all of your management classes, suppose you have developed a real appreciation for the value of the human resource in the organization. You want to put into practice some of the participative, people-oriented practices you have learned. Will you be happy in an autocratic organization? On the other hand, suppose money and power are what turn you on. Will you enjoy working at a company where teamwork and frugality are the rule?

There are no absolutes in the employment market. You must recognize that since there are many types of corporate cultures, if you ignore that aspect in evaluating your prospects, you might as well be playing Russian roulette. Unless you are extraordinarily lucky or adaptable, the odds of your being happy are slim.

To assess corporate culture, you must answer two big questions: what do you need to know, and how do you find it out? The what is much easier than the how.

WHAT YOU NEED TO KNOW

The things you need to know are all the *contextual* factors—those things outside the basic content of the job that affect your life in that company. The major items are:

- **Purpose of the organization.** What is the organization trying to achieve? Why does it exist? Does the company have a stated mission?
- **Philosophy.** What is the guiding light of the company? How does the company conduct business? What limits are placed on the strategies used to achieve its goals?
- **Corporate values.** What beliefs or credos exist? Is the company conservative or liberal? What are the values of the people working there?
- **Behavioral expectations and limits.** Does the company tell you how to behave in certain situations? (Most will.) Does it extend these expectations into your personal life? Does the company encourage conformity or tolerate mavericks?
- **Attitudes of employees.** What do the employees talk about? Are they happy and motivated or complacent and lethargic? Are they conservative or liberal? Power hungry or helping-oriented?
- **Work ethic.** How hard do people work? What role does work play in their lives?
- **Dress code.** Is the norm for a man a suit and tie, or casual? Do the women wear dresses or suits?
- **Character of the organization.** Is the organization stodgy and sluggish or vibrant and hustling? Centralized or decentralized? Entrepreneurial or bureaucratic?
- **Success factors.** What is it that makes people succeed in the organization? What are the characteristics of the high-level successful people? How do you climb the ladder?
- **Social norms.** Does the organization require certain types of social obligations and behavior from you? Do you have to belong to certain clubs or socialize in the right places? Are you expected to attend informal gatherings frequently? Do employees socialize together often?
- **Management norms.** How are the employees managed? Are managers autocratic or democratic? How much control is ex-

ercised over people? How would you have to behave to best get along with your boss?

- **Atmosphere.** As you walk through the office, are people relaxed and happy or formal and on edge? Is there an atmosphere of trust or fear?
- **Career progression.** How do people progress through their careers? Is progression largely seniority based or results based? Is movement across functional areas encouraged?
- **Strategic orientation.** Does management have a clearly outlined strategy? Is its thinking short- or long-term?
- **Ethical standards.** Are people concerned about honesty and fairness in business? Is there a sense of broader social responsibility?
- **Political environment.** To what extent is organizational politics a factor in accomplishing tasks (it's always present to some extent)? Do different parts of the organization work together well, or is there a strong sense of "protecting one's turf"? Which is more important: who you know or what you do?
- **Communication.** Do people talk openly and freely, or are discussions guarded? Are communication lines formal, progressing through layers of the organization? Or do you see top management talking regularly with lower levels of the organization? To what extent does management keep employees informed about the company's progress?

The list could be extended. The key is recognizing that you need to understand *all* aspects of the company. Anything about the organization that will affect you on or off the job should be thoroughly investigated.

HOW TO FIND IT OUT

How to find out this information is not nearly as easy. Some of it is difficult and awkward to ask an employer about. Even if you did, the answer might be suspect since the truth about organizational culture is often different from what managers perceive it to be. Most of the questions can be answered conclusively only by being inside the organization. In some cases you can obtain only a general sense of the organizational climate and not specific information to answer your concerns. All of this makes it difficult to size up a good fit. Furthermore, MBAs are often best trained in the analysis of hard facts, not in the somewhat fuzzy analysis of corporate culture.

But just because it's difficult doesn't mean you shouldn't try. Fit is so important to your career that you need to collect as much information as you can, no matter how difficult or incomplete the data. You must be a careful observer when you are interviewing at the company's site. First, get a feel for the environment. Then look carefully at the people. Notice what they talk about and how they act. Look at their dress, and their pace as they move about. Listen carefully to how they talk to each other. Try to take the pulse of the organization. Sense what is happening around you while you are there. Try to imagine yourself working there. Use all your senses to absorb as much information as you can. You will be surprised at how much you can learn.

Some of the information can be collected by direct questions during the interview. This will not insult the company and in fact will win points for your maturity. Some good questions that will tell you about the corporate culture are:

- What is a typical day in your work life like? week? year?
- What is the philosophy of the company?
- How would you describe the values of the company?
- Does the company have a motto?
- What types of people do you think fit best into the company?
- What is the purpose or objective of the company?
- How do you balance your personal and work life here?
- What do you think it takes to succeed here?
- How would you describe the culture of this company?
- How would you describe a typical manager in the company?
- What characteristics do your most promotable people seem to have?
- What do you think is the ethical orientation of the company?
- What is the best way to get along with people in this company? Your superiors?
- What type of career progression do you think is best in this company?
- What types of communication does management use to keep employees informed?
- What is the company's strategy?

If you have particular concerns, don't be afraid to ask about them. For example, suppose you have two young children who need you at home often. Ask the interviewer how the company might react to that. True, such a question could put the company off. But, if it does, do you really want to work there?

IS IT RIGHT FOR YOU?

The bottom line, of course, is fit, which only serves to emphasize the importance of a good self-assessment process. (If you don't know yourself, you'll never know if you fit.) After learning all you can about the culture, ask yourself:

- How well will I fit?
- Will I be happy?
- Did I feel comfortable on the site visit?
- Will I grow in the directions I want to?
- Are these my kind of people?
- Can I imagine myself working there?
- If I have to make compromises, can I accept them?
- What are the rewards for the compromises I have to make?
- Is this my kind of organization?
- Does it do business the way I like to?
- Is the environment the type in which I can be most successful?
- Are my values consistent with the company's?
- Does my life-style (or the one I want) fit the expectations of the organization?

If you can answer these questions in a way that is satisfactory to you, then go for it. If not, it is completely legitimate to turn down a job because of a poor fit with the culture, even if the content of the job is perfect for you. Many MBAs struggle with a decision of this type. All the objective analysis may suggest a job is good, but the culture just doesn't feel right. Fit is such a strong determinant of success that you need not worry at all about using it as a reason for not going to work for a company. It's fine to pay the price of being mismatched to gain needed experience or to position yourself for another move, but very few people can achieve long-term success without a strong fit with the company's culture. If you choose to make compromises, be aware that you are and know that you will probably be wanting to move again soon.

Chapter 14

Decisions, Decisions

You've worked hard, planned, and taken advantage of every opportunity; and, lo and behold, you have a job offer—in fact, perhaps several of them! If you are like most people, none of the offers are perfect; but none of them are clearly bad either. You are left with a tough—but fun—process of deciding which is the best of the bunch. This chapter will help you make that decision.

A USEFUL DECISION MODEL

The decision model presented in this chapter is a simple one that is designed to help you gain perspective on your job alternatives. Although it uses some quantitative techniques, the process is not precise. It is a structured thought process designed to help you sort out the pros and cons of your alternatives. A work sheet is included at the end of the next section to help you.

The model does not make judgments about what's right and wrong for you. *That is your decision.* You determine what values to include, you rank them, you decide what alternatives to include, and you evaluate each alternative on each criterion. Only you can decide what is best for you. There are no normative criteria by which to judge a job; this model allows you to choose the best job for *you*. The steps are:

1. **List your decision criteria.** Make a list of all the things that are important to you in a job (you should have done this in the chapter on self-assessment). Be sure to include tangible things, such as money, benefits, and geographic location, as well as the intangibles, such as values, feelings, and people. Don't be hesitant to include anything that is important to you.
2. **Rank your decision criteria.** Go through your list and rank the decision criteria in order of importance. Assign "1" to the most important. If you cannot decide between two criteria, assign them the same ranking, but think hard before you do it. A major part of this model is the process of deciding what really is important to you.

3. **Decide what is essential.** Look again at your criteria list and decide what is absolutely *essential* for you to have in a job. (That is, you must have that characteristic in the job that you take; a job without it would not be acceptable.)
4. **List your alternatives.** Across the top of the page, list each of your job options in a separate column.
5. **Evaluate each alternative.** Evaluate each job by each of your decision criteria. Do so by assigning it a rating from 1 to 10, with 1 being high.
6. **Evaluate essential criteria.** Look at those criteria you have indicated are essential. Check to see that you have rated each job no lower than "3" on each of those criteria. If you have, it probably means that that job does not meet that criterion very well; so that job must be eliminated as an alternative. If you find that you are eliminating all of your alternatives, or most of them, you may want to reevaluate whether those decision criteria are truly essential. If they are, and your alternatives do not meet them, then you need to look for other jobs.
7. **Calculate an overall ranking score.** For each job alternative, multiply the priority you assigned to each decision criterion by the rating you assigned for that job alternative and sum through all criteria for each given alternative. You should end up with one number under "Ranking Score" for each alternative.
8. **Compare and rank those alternatives.** Look at the ranking score for each of your job alternatives. The lower the score, the more desirable the job is for you. Use those ranking scores to assign a ranking to the alternatives. Then look at the relative difference between the scores. If the difference is small, then the alternatives are essentially ranked the same. If the difference is large, your decision is easy. Also, pay attention to which criteria a job alternative is weak in.
9. **Calculate a "high priority" ranking score.** Calculate another ranking score but this time do so only for the decision criteria you ranked 1–5 in priority. Check to see if the overall ranking is still the same. If not, you may have an alternative that scores very high in your most important criteria but low in other areas. This step will warn you of an alternative that has some very good and very bad parts as opposed to moderate ratings throughout.

HOW TO USE THE MODEL

Unfortunately, most people rarely find the perfect job, particularly directly out of school. The good news is that if you work hard, you can have several opportunities to choose from; the bad news is that none of them may be exactly right, though many of them will be close. You must be prepared to make compromises. Many students become frustrated and confused when trying to make a decision, because they have not prioritized their decision criteria.

Perhaps the greatest advantage of this model is that it forces you to explicitly decide the criteria by which you will evaluate jobs and to decide what is really important to you. You should spend the most time with that part of this process. Be sure you list everything that is important to you, no matter how small or seemingly insignificant. Think carefully about what really makes a difference to you. Rating the alternatives is a subjective process. Even though you are working with numbers, they are only a reflection of your subjective judgment about the relative value of an alternative. Don't assign priorities the way you think you *should,* but rather the way you really feel about them. No one has to see this but you; no one has to live with the job you choose but you.

It is tough to realize that no job will satisfy all of our wishes completely. Too often job hunters label everything they want as essential. This only leads to frustration. Most people will have only three to five essential criteria. If you have worked hard at your career planning and placement process you should have job alternatives that meet your essential criteria because you evaluated very early what was important to you (see "Self-Assessment" on page 95). However, if you have taken a trial-and-error approach to your job search, it is not uncommon to find at this point that none of your job alternatives are really right for you. If so, you need to think very carefully about the compromises you are about to make and whether you need to look for other jobs.

The results derived from the use of this model are a ranking score and a relative ranking of your alternatives. The range of the ranking scores depends on the number of criteria you have. The table below gives you some ranges of overall ranking scores that will be considered low (= most preferable), midrange, and high for three different numbers of decision criteria.

Number of decision criteria	Low	Mid	High
10	50–160	160–275	275–375
15	120–360	360–600	600–840
20	210–630	630–1,050	1,050–1,470

For the "top-five score" the evaluation of the ranges is independent of the number of decision criteria (as long as you have at least five) and would be:

Low	Mid	High
15–45	45–75	75–105

To reiterate, the lower the ranking scores, the better.

When you have all the numbers calculated, you need to evaluate them and use them to make a decision. Check the following items:

- Are the essential criteria rated 3 or better? Eliminate any alternative that is rated below 3 after rechecking your ratings.
- Check the absolute level of the ranking scores against the preceding table. Evaluate them as:

    low range—excellent prospect
    midrange—good potential, but there may be some
        problems
    high range—probably not a good prospect; eliminate
        these if possible

    A difference in evaluation between the overall and top five ranking scores usually means a "good news/bad news" situation. Be wary of any alternative that does not fall in the low range for your top five decision criteria.

- Check the relative differences and rank your alternatives. Small differences between the overall scores are insignificant and indicate the same rank. If the difference between the scores is large, your decision will be easy. Usually, at least one alternative will fall out.
- Check the individual ratings for your top two job alternatives (if the overall scores are close) to make your final decision. Assess where the individual differences are and pick what feels best.

An example work sheet for Joan Cox is shown below. Joan has three job alternatives and has ranked the decision criteria as shown. She has decided that her top three criteria are essential for her to have in any job. Let's evaluate her alternatives.

- All three essential criteria have been rated as 3 or higher on all alternatives, so we do not eliminate any on that basis.
- The absolute level of the overall ranking scores falls in the midrange, indicating good alternatives but some potential problem areas in the long term.
- The "top five scores" are in the low range, indicating that the alternatives all score well on the highest-priority criteria.
- The relative comparison of the overall scores shows that alternatives 1 and 2 are essentially tied although 2 is slightly better. Alternative 3 is significantly worse. We rule out 3 and say it's a toss-up between 1 and 2.
- The relative comparison of the "top five score," though, shows that all three alternatives are essentially tied. This indicates

Decision-making Work Sheet: Joan Cox

a Decision Criteria	b Priority	c Essential	d Alt. 1	e Alt. 2	f Alt. 3
Like people	9		5	3	3
Challenging work	2	Y	2	1	2
Growth potential	3	Y	3	2	3
What I want to do	1	Y	3	1	2
High salary	4		2	3	2
Good benefits	5		1	1	1
Good location	6		1	3	7
Secure position	12		2	2	6
Growth company	10		4	3	1
Good training	8		2	2	2
Mgmt. potential	7		4	3	1
High visibility	11		2	4	6
Prestigious	13		4	3	6
Ranking Score			262	245	346
Rank			1	1	3
Top 5 Score			29	26	24
Top 5 Rank			1	1	1

Your Decision-making Work Sheet ———————

a Decision Criteria	*b* Priority	*c* Essential	*d* Alt. 1	*e* Alt. 2	*f* Alt. 3
Like people					
Challenging work					
Growth potential					
What I want to do					
High salary					
Good benefits					
Good location					
Secure position					
Growth company					
Good training					
Mgmt. potential					
High visibility					
Prestigious					
Ranking Score					
Rank					
Top 5 Score					
Top 5 Rank					

that alternative 3 has problems in the low-priority criteria but is fine on the top-priority criteria. It probably has good short-run potential, but real problems long-term.

- Joan eliminates alternative 3 and chooses alternative 2, since it has a little stronger ranking by most criteria. This model confirmed her own subjective evaluation and showed her why she was so confused about alternative 3 (it was good news and bad news).

A blank work sheet for your use follows the example.

Throughout this process, keep in mind that this model is just a framework for your analysis. Do not trust it alone in making a decision, but use it along with your feelings and intuition. It will lead you through a structured thought process by clarifying what criteria are important to you, helping you to rate your alternatives on your important criteria, and providing perspective on how your alternatives compare. If you are confronted by several good, but not perfect, job alternatives, this model is an extremely useful tool to help and guide you but not to tell you the answer.

TESTING YOUR INTUITION

After all the objective analysis, the final test is your "gut feeling," your intuitive sense of whether the job is right. Inside each of you is a guiding voice called your intuition. Learning to trust it is difficult, since its advice doesn't always seem logical or rational. Have you ever started to do something and stopped because something just didn't feel right? Or conversely, when you are making a decision, have you had one alternative that just sits right with you? Or, maybe you have made a major change in your life (like getting your MBA) because you just knew it was the right thing to do?

Well, all of those were your intuition at work. Many career guidance writers ignore it because it cannot be scientifically explained very well. But it is a valuable addition to the objective, analytical tools already presented. Unfortunately, your inner voice can be drowned out by the "shoulds" and "ought-tos" you have absorbed along the way. If you can tune in to your inner voice, pushing aside all the extraneous thoughts, I think you will find a trustworthy guide for your job decisions.

I have observed many happy and contented job seekers graduate and go on to successful careers; they all seemed to act more or less the same when they made their "good" decisions. From these observations, I suggest you ask yourself the questions that follow as a final check on what your inner voice may be telling you.

- Are you excited and impatient to get started?

- Does your "gut" feel good?
- Do you wish you were finished with school now so you could get started right away?

I learned this, at least, by my experiment; that if one advances confidently in the direction of his dreams, and endeavors to live the life which he has imagined, he will meet with a success unexpected in common hours. He will put some things behind, will pass an invisible boundary; new, universal, and more liberal laws will begin to establish themselves around and within him; or the old laws be expanded, and interpreted in his favor in a more liberal sense, and he will live with the license of a higher order of beings. In proportion as he simplifies his life, the laws of the universe will appear less complex, and solitude will not be solitude, nor poverty poverty, nor weakness weakness. If you have built castles in the air, your work need not be lost; that is where they should be. Now put the foundations under them. . . .

Why should we be in such desperate haste to succeed and in such desperate enterprises? If a man does not keep pace with his companions, perhaps it is because he hears a different drummer. Let him step to the music which he hears, however measured or far away. It is not important that he should mature as soon as an apple tree or an oak. Shall he turn his spring into summer? If the condition of things which we were made for is not yet, what were any reality which we can substitute? . . .

—Henry David Thoreau

- Do you feel a sense of inner peace and relaxation about your decision?
- Does it feel comfortable, as good a fit as your favorite lounging clothes?

- Do you have a smile on your face and a bounce in your walk when you think about it?
- Do you think you can succeed?
- Does it feel like a dream coming true?
- Do you find it hard to believe your good luck?
- Are you already planning how to spend the money?
- Do significant others think it's "just right" for you?
- Is it too good to be true?
- Are you afraid something will happen to take it away from you?

If you can answer yes to most of these questions, then you can bet you've made the right choice. If the answer is no to many of the questions, then you may have a problem. More than likely, you have taken, or are about to take, a job that doesn't really fit you. I suggest you reconsider. I have seen students take jobs that they know are wrong long-term just to get some experience or get a start with a particular company. That's fine as long as you consciously understand the sacrifices you are making. But, if you can't answer yes to these questions and are not *consciously* taking a poorly fitting job for a particular reason, you should definitely reconsider your choice.

TIPS ON WHAT TO LOOK FOR IN A CORPORATE JOB

Since many students look for careers in medium-sized to large corporations, this section has been included to offer advice on some of the more desirable characteristics for long-term success in jobs in these corporations. These tips are for the MBA who is looking for a relatively fast track to management careers in a corporate environment (remember, any career objective is okay). Look for jobs that have many of the following characteristics:

- **High Visibility.** Look for jobs that give you an opportunity to interact with high-level executives or where your work will be seen frequently by them so that the people with the power to promote you will see you. It is easy to get buried in a large organization.
- **Major Responsibilities.** Look for jobs that give you the chance to truly contribute to the organization. People who make a difference are usually rewarded.
- **High Growth.** Look for parts of the company that are experiencing high growth. Although there are significant contributions to be made in properly managed, mature industries, the betting person's place to be is in high-growth segments of a company's business. In those businesses, new positions are

created quickly, and you can be sucked up the career ladder as the business booms.

- **Selective Training Programs.** Although they're becoming more rare, training programs that target a small number of selective hires each year typically give you the exposure and the chance to move up the organization quickly. Jump on them if you can.
- **Job Movement.** To move into and up through management ranks, an employee needs to have exposure to a variety of job functions in the company. Look for career paths that offer good mobility.
- **Managers You Get Along With.** Although the idea is subject to much debate, many people succeed in large corporations by knowing the right people and having a mentor or "champion" in higher places. If your personality is not compatible with those of the managers you can observe before you take the job, the odds of their taking you under their wing are small. Look for people with whom you will fit well.
- **Good Resume Material.** Many students find themselves changing jobs three to seven years after they leave school. Look for jobs that will be good jumping-off places to other jobs should the potential you believe is there not come through. Cover yourself so that you will have strong experience on your resume should you need to make the "new-graduate job change."
- **Opportunity to Succeed.** Look for positions where you can have successes early in your career. Although you will not be able to avoid risks, a few successes early in your career build your confidence and the company's confidence in you and will likely open doors to significant future growth. If you opt for the high-risk position early, be prepared to leave the job if it doesn't work out. If you are perceived as a loser early in your career, you may never recover in that company.

Chapter 15

Going to Work

Congratulations! If you have applied yourself diligently to the career planning and placement process described in this book, the chances are very good that you have accepted a job in which you will be happy. You are about to embark on a brand-new phase of your life. As an MBA, you have excellent prospects for a challenging and successful future. You should be proud of the hard work that has brought you this far and of the success you are now enjoying.

Like all changes and transitions in life, moving ahead from school to work requires adjustments and growth. While transition is exciting, even exhilarating, it can also be stressful and confusing. Change is a natural part of life and is destructive only when not managed properly. The purpose of this chapter is to help you anticipate some of the major changes that may occur and to help manage the transition so that it is a positive one for you as you face new challenges both professionally and personally.

PROFESSIONAL CHALLENGES

Part of your excitement at this point is probably due to the anticipation of a brand-new chapter of your professional life (for some of you) or starting your professional career (for others). In either case, you are about to enter a new organization and a new role as an MBA professional; both require some adaptation. Your biggest challenge will be adjusting to the organization you are about to join. All organizations have their own culture, norms, and values. It is a mistake to view a business organization as only individuals performing tasks. There is a collective spirit that exists apart from the individual employees, although it is shaped by them. Perhaps the best way to conceptualize this is to think of the organization as a person that you must come to know. Just as you must get to know the individuals you will work with, and all of their individual characteristics, you must also get to know the organization.

The organizational climate and culture have developed over many years in some companies and exert a very strong influence on the way their employees function. To ignore the "rules" and norms of the company would be a major mistake. Your "acculturation" to the company will take place throughout your first year and beyond and will happen in many subtle ways; no one will hand you an instruction manual. Your challenge is to absorb that culture and adapt to it.

God, give us grace to accept with serenity the things that cannot be changed, courage to change the things which should be changed, and the wisdom to distinguish the one from the other.

—Reinhold Niebuhr
"The Serenity Prayer"

Your other major professional challenge is to adjust to your new role as a professional, and, more specifically, to your role as an MBA professional. Your student days are over. When you walk through the doors to go to work, you are a professional. You will be expected to look and act like one (see page 210). Most important, you will be expected to perform like one (within the limits of your experience). Peers and bosses will expect you to contribute to the organization, to produce within deadlines, and to assume significant responsibility. People will begin to depend on you and respect you and your opinions and judgments. You will be given the opportunity to accomplish things and to fail. As an MBA, you will be expected to be able to perform better than your undergraduate peers, to be able to contribute more quickly, and to assume greater responsibility due to your extra training, age, and maturity. Furthermore, since you will likely be paid a high starting salary, there will be pressure on you to produce results to justify that salary. Your role and the expectations placed upon you will be vastly different from what you experienced during your time in MBA school. It may take some time for you to learn what these expectations are and to begin to think of yourself as a professional.

Most new employees expect far too much from their first job. The most successful ones manage their expectations and arrive at a realistic perspective. Don't expect a lot of glamour and excitement at first. It will take some time to reach the level you want and to be able to make the contributions you want to. Your new colleagues will respect you and accept you more quickly if you develop realistic expectations about your new career.

It is clear that your first year in a business organization is a pivotal one. Many eyes will be watching you; the work you do, the way you handle yourself, and the impressions you make in that year will go a long way toward building your reputation in that company. Do well, and you can get a fast start to your career; do poorly or even averagely, and it may take years to recover. That said, let me give you some tips on what to do during the first year so you can adapt smoothly and build a good reputation.

- **Wait and see.** Go in with open eyes and ears and a muzzled mouth. You need to understand the organization's own way of doing business before you start bringing in your personal style. Don't shirk away from contributing or stifle all your individualism, but fit in, learn the culture, and earn the respect and comradeship of your colleagues before you attempt to make any major changes. Companies usually don't appreciate brash, rookie outsiders trying to tell them they should do things differently. They are particularly wary of MBAs, who have a reputation for doing just that. You will have your chance, but take it slow.
- **Prove your competence early.** Nothing will gain you the respect of your peers as quickly as good solid performance. Work particularly hard your first year so you will become known as an industrious, solid performer who can be counted on to contribute. Don't look at your first year as just a training period. It's amazing how many doors can open for you early in your career when you show that you have the maturity and ability to hit the ground running.
- **Learn the politics.** Pay careful attention to who holds the power in the organization, to who the leaders are (they may not be the same), and to the "rules" for communicating. Learn how the bureaucracy works, who needs to be copied on which memos, what the bosses' pet peeves are, and so forth. Getting ahead is not just a matter of performance. It is also getting along with and influencing the people in the organization.
- **Get to know the people.** Spend time socializing with the people in the organization. Nobody likes a cold, unfriendly person. Talk with your coworkers, have lunch with them, and join them for happy hour so that you will be accepted personally as well as professionally. A word of caution: don't overdo it during work hours.
- **Work well with your boss.** The relationship you establish with your boss is a critical one. You are there to make your boss's life easier and to help accomplish his or her goals. Get to know

your boss and what he or she wants. Build a strong relationship. Help your boss, and your boss will usually help you get ahead.

- **Look for a senior sponsor.** This is controversial advice. Some recommend that you find a mentor or sponsor to pull you up through the organization. Others say this is very risky since your future is secure only as long as your mentor is in good favor. It is dangerous to align yourself too closely with a mentor. However, seek out a more senior member of the organization who is willing to help you learn the job and the company. Look for somebody who has lots of experience and is willing to share it. You will be miles ahead if you can learn from that person's mistakes rather than making all of them yourself.

- **Be open and learn.** Look, listen, and ask questions. Open your senses and your mind to what's happening around you. Observe your colleagues. You have lots to learn, from where to get paper clips to what clothes to wear to how the boss likes the work done. The only way you'll ever learn is to open up. Just because you have left school does not mean the learning is over.

- **Know what's expected of you.** Find out early what the company expects of you. Ask your immediate supervisor exactly what you will be evaluated on during your first year. Then, make plans to meet or preferably exceed those expectations. Try very hard not to fall short your first year.

PERSONAL CHALLENGES

This period of your life will present many personal adjustments for you in addition to the professional adaptations just outlined. Your first challenge is to recognize this and allow yourself time to adjust to it.

Many of you expect to feel only excitement and happiness about leaving school and starting work. It can come as quite a surprise when you experience very mixed feelings during the change. You may feel:

- sad that you are leaving school, your friends, and your home
- apprehensive about the new responsibilities, a new city, the change
- uncertain as to whether you can do the job
- excited about the challenge
- unsure whether you made the right decision
- happy that you will have some money

- confused by all your feelings
- exhilarated by your future prospects
- proud of what you have accomplished

It's perfectly normal for you to experience a range of emotions, both positive and negative. Don't worry about them. And don't expect them to stop after you make the change. Throughout your first year there will be many highs and lows. Common feelings are:

- a surge of confidence when you find you can do the job
- being overwhelmed at all you have to learn and do
- confusion at the complexities of the business world
- joy at all the fun you are having and the new friends you meet
- insecurity as you prove yourself
- pride in your accomplishments
- disappointment at the routine and less glamorous parts of your job
- loneliness and isolation if you're in a new city

It's a different world out there, and it requires some adjusting, even if you have worked before. I can't tell you exactly what you will experience. On balance, it will be fun and exciting. But the day-to-day ups and downs may surprise you. Remember, they're perfectly normal.

The demands of graduate school have taught you much about organizing your life and budgeting your time, but you still had much more flexibility and control over your time while in school. On the job you will be expected to be in the office at least five days a week from 8 to 5. Most MBAs find that they will work additional hours at home and sometimes on weekends; commuting can add another 1–4 hours to that workday. Life in the working world is much more structured and routine than it is in graduate school; most students feel a large loss of personal time. In addition, your new work responsibilities may put more demands on you to meet deadlines tighter than you have been used to—those in graduate school are usually planned well in advance. Time management at work and at home will become increasingly important.

On the positive side, students usually feel relieved that they no longer are burdened by the seven-day-a-week grind of school. Although you will miss the long breaks you enjoyed as a student, you will probably not miss working on papers all weekend or studying for exams late into the night. It is often nice to be able to leave your work at the office and not have it intrude on your home life so much.

Stress management will also become important to you. Most students discover that the high expectations, constant short deadlines, fast pace, and profit pressure of the business world take some adjustment. You may feel overwhelmed by the responsibilities thrust upon you and the ever-present but uneven push to produce results. Unfortunately, the business world does not always run in an orderly and smooth fashion. You will grow accustomed to requests from your manager at 4:45 to write an important memo immediately and pleas from customers who need service now. It can be quite a fast-paced life, and time is money in business.

Stress can have very powerful and harmful effects if not managed properly. It has been identified as a key contributor to many major health problems, including heart disease and high blood pressure. It can sap you of energy and enthusiasm and decrease your productivity and happiness at work and at home. Teaching you all the various stress reduction techniques is beyond the scope of this book, but you should realize that your new job may be quite stressful and that there are a number of techniques you can learn to help you manage that stress. The key is to manage your response to stress. Most people find that exercise and a life-style that balances work with relaxation help. Make plans now so stress does not become a destructive force in your life.

Part of the stress of a new job stems from moving to a new community. Not only is the move itself stressful, but you then have to adjust to a new area, learning the traffic patterns, finding a bank, locating new doctors, and finding new stores to shop in. While all this is exciting, the little things can add up to a sense of loss of familiar surroundings. In addition, you may have left your friends behind and feel isolated until you meet new ones. This is particularly challenging for single people.

The transition from college to work can be a particularly stressful time for married couples and families. The move may disrupt your children's schooling and separate them from their friends. Your new job will place lots of demands on your time and emotional energy, so you may see your family less and have less to give them when you do. The transition is particularly challenging if both husband and wife are starting new jobs. The uncertainty and loneliness of dealing with new people and perhaps a new city can be hard on everyone and are especially hard on children. You should structure family time to keep the communication lines open and to spend time together regularly. It's important that everyone feel the family's love during the transition.

So what can you do to cope with this tumultuous first year? Try some of these strategies:

- **Be patient with yourself.** You have much to learn and many changes to adjust to. Give yourself time; don't expect too much too soon.

- **Pace yourself.** Don't try to do too much at once. There will be many new things to do and see, and you can't do them all at once.
- **Allow time for yourself.** Be sure you have some time for fun, play, hobbies, family, or whatever makes you feel good and lets you relax.
- **Get advice from others.** Let other people help you make the transition. Friends, family, and colleagues can be tremendous sources of support and advice.
- **Energize yourself.** Do the things that keep you at your peak energy level, such as eating well and getting lots of rest, and treat yourself kindly.
- **Make time for friends and family.** Allow time for friends, family, or other significant people in your life. Find ways to stay in touch with those you leave behind and ways to meet new friends. The warmth and support of those close to you will be important.

SPECIAL
INFORMATION

Chapter 16

Interpersonal Communications and Relationships

By this point it should be crystal clear to you why the ability to communicate is so important. Think about the many tasks you have been given already in this book. You have learned about selling yourself, screening interviews, hiring interviews, information interviews, and friendworking, all of which require you to interact effectively with other people. The chapter presents a few basics of interpersonal relationships and some practical tips to help you in your job search.

A BASIC COMMUNICATIONS MODEL

Here is a very basic communications model that I learned in a freshman communications course:

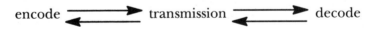

This model says that there are three steps to any communication. First, the person speaking must translate his or her thoughts, feelings, and intentions into some sort of message that conveys those thoughts, feelings, and intentions to the other person: that is encoding. Then, the speaker must actually deliver or transmit the message to the other person, using words, gestures, and body language: that is transmission. Finally, the receiver must translate the message into the thoughts, feelings, and intentions of the speaker: that is decoding. When the recipient replies to the original speaker, the process is reversed. Failure can obviously occur at any of the three steps.

This model is simple enough to use every day. When I miscommunicate with someone (or am particularly concerned that my message get across), I think about this three-step process and try to discover which step went wrong (or which step is particularly liable to cause trouble).

I could fill an entire chapter with examples of how this process works and how it can break down. The key point is that effective communicators learn to pay attention to all three steps. They are in touch with their own thoughts and feelings so that what they have to communicate is clear; they develop the skills to translate their thoughts and feelings into strong messages; and they learn to read other people so they can transmit their messages in a manner that others are most likely to interpret correctly.

Did you tackle that trouble that came your way
With a resolute heart and cheerful?
Or hide your face from the light of day
With a craven soul and fearful?

. . . .

The harder you're thrown, why the higher you bounce;
Be proud of your blackened eye!
It isn't the fact that you're licked that counts;
It's how did you fight and why?

And though you be done to death, what then?
If you battled the best you could;
If you played your part in the world of men,
Why, the Critic will call it good.

—Edmund Vance Cooke
From "How Did You Die?"

When you look at this model carefully, you can see all the places it can break down through nobody's fault. Cultural and regional differences, environmental and situational factors, moods, and simple mistakes can easily confuse communications. It seems that the number one reason for miscommunication is a failure to understand the complexities of "encoding ⟶ transmission ⟶ decoding." Far too many people *assume* that if they are feeling or thinking something, it is obvious in their communication. As a result, any negative reaction they get from someone else is the other person's fault for not understanding. Good communicators work to make sure all three phases of interpersonal communication are in sync before drawing any conclusions about the other person's thoughts, feelings, or intentions. You are responsible for your thoughts, feelings, and intentions and the method you use to transmit your message. You are not responsible for the other person's reaction (since it is out of your control), although you are responsible for trying to transmit your message in a manner that is most likely to be interpreted the way you want it to be, given what you know about the other person at the time.

Good communicators learn to use *verbal* and *nonverbal* communication channels. Verbal communication consists of the words we use when we speak. Nonverbal communication is all of the other elements of communication, such as facial gestures, body language, tone of voice, eye contact, and posture. It is estimated that anywhere from 60 to 80 percent of communication is nonverbal. Think about a very common question we hear all the time: "How are you today?" If a person asks you that as you pass in the hall, uses a monotone, and makes only brief eye contact, you know that no answer is needed—it's just a greeting. Now, suppose a person says, "How are you today?" stops, turns toward you, adopts a relaxed posture, and smiles at you. That is a person who is really interested in knowing and wants to engage you in conversation. You can clearly see the impact that your nonverbal communication has on the message you transmit.

That leads to a few basic principles that you must bear in mind to avoid miscommunication:

- Just because your intentions are obvious to you, they are not necessarily obvious to the other person.
- Just because you *think* you communicate clearly, it doesn't mean the other person understands.
- Don't assume anything.
- Take responsibility for the entire content of your communication, verbal and nonverbal.
- Develop good communication skills so your messages are as clear as possible.

GOOD INTERPERSONAL COMMUNICATIONS

Over the years I've watched many people who seem to communicate easily and to get along well with others. I've often asked myself, "What is it that makes them so effective?" I've concluded that it's a set of things:

- unconditional positive regard for people

- an interest in other people
- empathy
- articulateness
- expressiveness
- active listening
- attentiveness

Unconditional positive regard, interest, and *empathy* are all part of the encoding stage. "Unconditional positive regard" is a term that Carl Rogers coined in his theories on counseling. In *On Becoming a Person* he defined it as:

> . . . a warm caring for the [person]—a caring which is not possessive, which demands no personal gratification. It is an atmosphere which simply demonstrates "I care"; not "I care if you behave thus so.". . . It involves an acceptance of and a caring for the person as a separate person, with permission for him to have his own feelings and experiences, and to find his own meanings in them.

It's a nonjudgmental attitude of accepting people as they are and respecting them just because they are people. When you meet people like this, you don't feel that you have to prove yourself or earn their respect and positive feelings. They are just there and give to you freely. When you meet a recruiter with this attitude (there are many), you will walk away feeling respected and important, even if you aren't the person for the job.

Coupled with that should be a sincere interest in people. To be effective, you should be genuinely interested in what other people think and feel. If you're not, others will sense that they are only stroking your ego or a tool to accomplish whatever you're after. Many of the employers you encounter will be genuinely interested in your success even if they can't hire you.

Finally, if you are to know how to encode your message, you have to have a certain degree of empathy. Empathy is the capacity for participating in another's feelings or ideas. It is the ability to see the world through another person's eyes, to remove yourself from your own feelings and imaginatively experience the world as another person does. You can never completely do this, but good communicators can always imagine how another person might be experiencing the world and encode their message in a way that is sensitive to that person. If you walk through life with blinders on, seeing things only from your own frame of reference, you will often miscommunicate. Everybody experiences life a little differently, and, if you are to communicate effectively, you have to grow to appreciate these differences.

The second stage of the model requires you to be *articulate* and *expressive*. Articulateness is simply the ability to put into words whatever you are thinking or feeling.

For most MBAs, this is not much of a problem in business situations, though you may find it difficult to talk about yourself in interviews. You have to have enough mastery of the English language to convey ideas and impressions precisely.

But articulateness is not enough: you also need to be expressive. Expressiveness, as used here, means the ability to use nonverbal as well as verbal communication and the willingness to share thoughts and feelings. It's amazing how much nonverbal elements can add to communication. They make words come alive and convey your true emotions. In addition, you can't possibly be an interesting and effective communicator unless you freely share and express what's on your mind and in your heart. You have to share some of your thoughts and ideas to establish any reasonable degree of communication, and you must convey your enthusiasm and warmth as a person to be effective.

Finally, stage three has two parts: *listening* and *attentiveness*. Listening is so important and so poorly done that there is a separate section on it below. Simply put, how can you ever decode anything if you don't listen carefully? Part of good listening and good communicating is attentiveness to what the other person is saying. You cannot really listen if you are distracted by other thoughts and don't see and hear all the communication. Attentiveness means using all your senses to "tune in" to the other person.

All of these need to be wrapped in an environment of *open communication*. Too often in today's world people communicate by playing games. Nothing destroys relationships more than deception. The best relationships, business or personal, are built on an assumption that the parties will communicate openly and honestly. This means anger and displeasure as well as happiness and pleasure. It means asking questions when you aren't sure what the other person thinks or feels. It means stating your thoughts and feelings honestly and assertively. It means that you know that everything that is happening between you is "on the table."

ESTABLISHING RAPPORT

Establishing rapport is the first step in a successful conversation. Think of it as opening a channel for an easy flow of communication. It is that warm, comfortable feeling you establish with a person that lets you talk easily and encourages a dialogue. It makes the difference between the pleasant, "Oh, my, is it over already?" type of discussions and the stumbling-for-words, squirming-in-your-seat type.

Establishing rapport is highly dependent on the individuals involved. While it is a very difficult thing to teach, there are some basic principles that will make it easier for you to establish rapport.

Smile. Everybody likes friendly people; their smiles project warmth and encourage conversation.

Exchange pleasantries. A period of small talk and pleasantries helps break the ice and relax both parties. Don't expect to get right down to business.

Find a common interest. Look for some shared interest with the person. In an interview, coming from the same town as the interviewer, or having the same major, or even the weather outside is enough to give some small sense of affinity.

Be friendly. Project a genuine warmth and approachability that is inviting to the other person.

Open your face. People often tighten their face when they are nervous or anxious. The result is a scowling, frowning appearance that discourages rapport. Relax your face. Open your mouth and eyes wide for 15 seconds to release the tension before the interview; you'll look much more approachable.

Open your body. Similarly, crossed arms, hands in pockets or clasped tightly in front, and turning away from the person project a "stay away" message. Face the other person, free your hands by your side, and let your body language express your friendliness.

Offer an expressive handshake. Use your handshake to say, "I really am glad to meet you." Don't shake the person's arm off, but put some feeling into it.

Make eye contact. How can you warm to someone who won't look at you?

MAKING GOOD CONVERSATION

Throughout your job search and your career, you will find yourself in situations where you will want to make conversation with people you don't know at all or only superficially. Mastering the art of "cocktail party conversation" is a real necessity for your career. It's easy to converse with people you know well or whom you would like to know well on a personal basis. But how do you make good conversation with those you don't know well and probably never will know well or have any desire to? Here are some tips:

Find common ground. Look for something that you might have in common. The weather, the hotel you are in, and the menu in the restaurant are always good starting places.

Ask questions. As long as you don't get too personal, ask for some detail about the other person. Standard questions like "Where are you from?" "What do you do?" and "Do you have any kids" can get the ball rolling.

Get others to talk about themselves. It's an old trick to find something other people really like and get them talking about it. People love to talk about themselves if you just get them to open up. They also feel good about you if you have shown lots of interest in them and their life.

Volunteer yourself. Offer some information about yourself to give the other person something to talk to you about. For example, mention a hobby or big event in your life or a big piece of news. Don't wait to be asked, just say it.

Talk about current events. They are always great conversation starters. However, stay away from politics and religion; they are often sensitive topics and can lead to heated discussions.

Don't argue or disagree. Keep your ego in your pocket. In casual conversation, disagreements have no place, no matter how friendly they seem.

You should realize that almost everyone is at least a little uncomfortable making conversation. Anything you do to carry the conversation, no matter how awkward you may feel, will be greatly appreciated by the other person. Remember, if you are feeling uncomfortable about the situation, that the odds are very good the other person is too. Good conversationalists don't worry much about being embarrassed. They simply talk about events, the weather, other people, and themselves.

LISTENING

Most people think of listening as a natural, instinctual behavior, but it is not. Hearing, the physical reception of sound, is a natural body function, but listening, which is paying attention to what one hears, is an acquired skill. The problem is that it is very easy to hear something without really listening to it. Most of us prefer to talk and are often guilty of "listening with one ear."

Experienced interviewees learn to listen attentively to the interviewer and are more effective because they are able to respond to the heart of the question. They waste little time, provide direct answers, and establish good rapport with the interviewer by doing so. In more casual situations, good listeners make people feel important because they rarely ignore anything that is said.

Some tips for good listening:

Be prepared to listen. Remind yourself to be an active listener. Decide to follow these methods.

Stop talking. A conversation is a dialogue. Close your mouth long enough to give the other person a chance to speak. You can't listen and talk at the same time.

Don't rehearse. Many people rehearse their next statement or answer at the same time they are listening. While doing so, they may "tune out" some of what is said. Listen closely to everything that is said before you formulate your response.

Shut out distractions. Focus your attention completely on listening. Learn to ignore distracting noises or other interference.

Don't interrupt. *Never* break in as the other person is talking. Always let the other person finish.

Clarify. Ask for clarification if you don't understand the exact meaning of a statement or a question.

Hear the entire message. Pay attention to the content, the non-verbals, and the tone. All the pieces work together to give you the complete message.

Reflect. Restate the question as you heard it, particularly for critical points or questions. It helps you and the other person be sure you understand each other.

Don't react emotionally. Watch for your emotional "hot buttons"—that is, certain words, ideas, or phrases that will cause you to react emotionally. Don't become defensive.

Don't form premature judgments. Just collect the information while listening. The analysis and judgment can wait until later.

FIXING PROBLEMS

When all of that has been said, you may ask, "How do I become a good communicator if I'm not one now?" To a large extent, the only way to ever get good at this is to face your fears, put yourself in situations with other people, and practice doing it. That's why most MBA programs today include a lot of class presentations, group work, and class participation. You simply have to do it to become comfortable with it. With a little practice, I think you will discover you are better at it than you think and that it's not so bad. It helps if you know some people who are good conversationalists. They take the pressure of carrying the conversation off you, and you can observe them to learn how they do it.

Toastmasters International runs the best formal program I know of to help you gain confidence in your oral communication skills. It is an international organization of speaking clubs that has a chapter in almost every city (or you can start one). The program combines a series of structured speaking exercises and peer critique with group support for your difficulties and is a lot of fun and highly effective. The confidence and skills learned seem to carry over into all types of interpersonal communication, and I am so convinced of its merit that I have made it a standard "fix" when I counsel students who have problems communicating.

Toastmasters International can be contacted at P.O. Box 10400, Santa Ana, CA 92711 (714-542-6793).

Chapter 17

Letter Writing

Throughout your job search you will have occasion to write a variety of letters including cover letters, interview follow-up letters, acceptance letters, letters declining an offer, etc. These letters can be just as important as your resume or what you say in an interview. When you consider how little information an employer has about you (relatively speaking) before you are hired, you can understand why. Letter writing is another piece of the strong communication skills MBAs need to present. The letters you write tell the employer something about your ability to communicate, your sense of professionalism, and your professional maturity. Writing business letters, though, is quite different from writing personal letters, papers, reports, and other academic items. You will need to approach your job hunting letters with a very different style and understand some guidelines for each type of letter to be effective. Don't overlook this important part of your job search.

HOW TO WRITE A BUSINESS LETTER

One of the worst mistakes most job hunters make is to write long, flowery letters. Businesspeople prefer short, direct letters that do not waste their time. Malcolm Forbes has given the best advice I have ever seen on how to write a business letter, and I quote it here in his own words:

A good business letter can get you a job interview.

Get you off the hook.

Or get you money.

It's totally asinine to blow your chances of getting *whatever* you want—with a business letter that turns people off instead of turning them on.

The best place to learn to write is in school. If you're still there, pick your teachers' brains.

If not, big deal. I learned to ride a motorcycle at 50 and fly balloons at 52. It's never too late to learn.

Over 10,000 business letters come across my desk every year. They seem to fall into three categories: stultifying if not stupid, mundane (most of them), and first rate (rare). Here's the approach I've found that separates the winners from the losers (most of it's just good common sense)—it starts *before* you write your letter:

- **Know what you want.**

  If you don't, write it down—in one sentence. "I want to get an interview within the next two weeks." That simple. List the major points you want to get across—it'll keep you on course.

  If you're answering a letter, check the points that need answering and keep the letter in front of you while you write. This way you won't forget anything—*that* would cause another round of letters.

  And for goodness' sake, answer promptly if you're going to answer at all. Don't sit on a letter—*that* invites the person on the other end to sit on whatever you want from *him*.

- **Plunge right in.**

  Call him by name—not "Dear Sir, Madam, or Ms." "Dear Mr. Chrisanthopoulos"—and be sure to spell it right. That'll get him (thus, you) off to a good start.

  (Usually, you can get his name just by phoning his company—or from a business directory in your nearest library.)

  Tell what your letter is about in the first paragraph. One or two sentences. Don't keep your reader guessing or he might file your letter away—even before he finishes it.

  In the round file.

  If you're answering a letter, refer to the date it was written. So the reader won't waste time hunting for it.

  People who read business letters are as human as thee and me. Reading a letter shouldn't be a chore—*reward* the reader for the time he gives you.

- **Write so he'll enjoy it.**

  Write the entire letter from his point of view—what's in it for *him?* Beat him to the draw—surprise him by answering the questions and objections he might have.

  Be positive—he'll be more receptive to what you have to say.

  Be nice. Contrary to the cliche, genuinely nice guys most often finish first or very near it. I admit it's not easy when you've got a gripe. To be agreeable while disagreeing—that's an art.

Be natural—write the way you talk. Imagine him sitting in front of you—what would you say to him?

Business jargon too often is cold, stiff, unnatural.

Suppose I came up to you and said, "I acknowledge the receipt of your letter and I beg to thank you." You'd think, "Huh? You're putting me on."

The acid test—read your letter *out loud* when you're done. You might get a shock—but you'll know for sure if it sounds natural.

Don't be cute or flippant. The reader won't take you seriously. This doesn't mean you've got to be dull. You prefer your letter to knock 'em dead rather than bore 'em to death.

Three points to remember.

Have a sense of humor. That's refreshing *anywhere*—a nice surprise in a business letter.

Be specific. If I tell you there's a new fuel that could save gasoline, you might not believe me. But suppose I tell you this:

"Gasohol—10% alcohol, 90% gasoline—works as well as straight gasoline. Since you can make alcohol from grain or corn stalks, wood or wood waste, coal—even garbage, it's worth some real follow-through."

Now you've got something to sink your teeth into.

Lean heavier on nouns and verbs, lighter on adjectives. Use the active voice instead of the passive. Your writing will have more guts.

Which of these is stronger? Active voice: "I kicked out my money manager." Or, passive voice: "My money manager was kicked out by me." (By the way, neither is true. My son, Malcolm Jr., manages most Forbes money—he's a brilliant moneyman.)

- **Give it the best you've got.**

When you don't want something enough to make *the* effort, making *an* effort is a waste.

Make your letter look appetizing—or you'll strike out before you even get to bat. Type it—on good-quality 8-1/2" x 11" stationery. Keep it neat. And use paragraphing that makes it easier to read.

Keep your letter short—to one page, if possible. Keep your paragraphs short. After all, who's going to benefit if your letter is quick and easy to read?

You.

For emphasis, *underline* important words. And sometimes indent sentences as well as paragraphs.

> "Like this?
>
> See how well it works?
>
> (But save it for something special.)"

Make it perfect. No typos, no misspellings, no factual errors. If you're sloppy and let mistakes slip by, the person reading your letter will think you don't know better or don't care. Do you?

Be crystal clear. You won't get what you're after if your reader doesn't get the message.

Use good English. If you're still in school, take all the English and writing courses you can. The way you write and speak can really help—or *hurt.*

If you're not in school (even if you are), get the little 71-page gem by Strunk & White, *Elements of Style.* It's in paperback. It's fun to read and loaded with tips on good English and good writing.

Don't put on airs. Pretense invariably impresses only the pretender.

Don't exaggerate. Even once. Your reader will suspect everything else you write.

Distinguish opinions from facts. Your opinions may be the best in the world. But they're not gospel. You owe it to your reader to let him know which is which. He'll appreciate it and he'll admire you. The dumbest people I know are those who Know It All.

Be honest. It'll get you further in the long run. If you're not, you won't rest easy until you're found out. (The latter, not speaking from experience.)

Edit ruthlessly. Somebody has said that words are a lot like inflated money—the more of them that you use, the less each one of them is worth. Right on. Go through your entire letter just as many times as it takes. Search out and Annihilate all unnecessary words, and sentences—even entire *paragraphs.*

- **Sum it up and get out.**

  The last paragraph should tell the reader exactly what you want *him* to do—or what *you're* going to do. Short and sweet. "May I have an appointment? Next Monday, the 16th, I'll call your secretary to see when it'll be most convenient for you."

  Close with something simple like, "Sincerely." And for heaven's sake sign legibly. The biggest ego trip I know is a completely illegible signature.

Good luck.

I hope you get what you're after.

Sincerely,

Malcolm S. Forbes

COVER LETTERS

Most people will at some time in their job search have to write a cover letter to send with their resume for a "cold call" to a prospective employer or in response to an advertisement. The purpose of your cover letter is to persuade the reader to read your resume. In it, you should state your purpose for writing, entice the reader to read your resume, and state the specific action you would like to have take place.

As a general guideline, your cover letter should consist of three paragraphs, each of which addresses one of your three objectives. The first paragraph in most cases should be a statement that you are writing because you are seeking employment in a certain area. If you have been referred by someone, this is the place to mention it. Also, this is a great place to say why you are writing to *that* company. Two or three sentences are usually adequate for this opening paragraph.

The second paragraph, your "sell" paragraph, should tell the employer why you will be good for the company. It should make the employer want to read your resume and the rest of the letter. It is the most important part of the letter and the part most likely to determine its success. Focus only on what you can do for the employer, not how great you think the company is. Highlight your most important qualifications for that company, show the match between your interests and skills and the needs of the company, and show how your background is related to the career objective you are pursuing. If you anticipate any negative reaction on the employer's part to anything on your resume, address it head-on in this paragraph.

In your third paragraph you usually will want to request an

interview with the company. Be sure to put all of the burden and responsibility for follow-up on yourself, not on the employer. Give the employer several weeks to review your resume and say that *you* will make contact then. Be very specific as to what you would like to happen and how you will follow up.

Your cover letter is as important as your resume and deserves the same time and attention. It too is designed to sell, except that it is designed to sell the employer on reading your resume, not to win an interview. Don't try to make it do more than is possible. Let the resume win the interview; let your cover letter win a reading of your resume. Use basic business letter–writing principles and be sure to focus on what you can do for the prospective employer. Two sample cover letters are included here to help you.

INTERVIEW FOLLOW-UP LETTERS

Interview follow-up letters are easy to write, so there's no reason not to send them. Their purpose is to thank the interviewer, keep your name in front of the employer, reiterate your enthusiasm and interest in the company and job, and clarify or add to the discussions held during the interview.

Thanking the employer is the major purpose of the letter, which need not be long and should not be too formal. Write a warm, friendly (though not too friendly) letter to express your appreciation for the time the interviewer spent with you. It need not be very long or elaborate. The fact that you took the time to do it and your sincerity are all you need.

The follow-up letter is also a golden opportunity to tie up any loose ends left from the interview. If you stumbled over a question, use this letter to make sure the interviewer understands. For example:

> I'm not sure I was perfectly clear about my responsibilities at ABC Corporation, so I would like to explain further. . . .

Or, you may wish to include additional important information that you overlooked or forgot because you were nervous:

> I neglected to mention to you that I was involved in a research project three years ago that. . . .

If you encountered any objections to your qualifications or the interviewer exposed a weakness, the letter can be used to reduce the damage:

> While I realize that my education does not fit your requirements exactly, I can assure you that my interest in your company and its research program will more than compensate.

Cover Letter 1 ———————————————

Mr. Maxwell Barker
Hunt Industries, Inc.
New York, NY 10031

Dear Mr. Barker,

I am completing my MBA at Harvard Business School this June and am looking for a job as a financial analyst. Tom Smith, who is a member of our College Advisory Council, suggested that I write to you and enclose the attached resume when I told him of my interest in Hunt Industries.

As you can see from my resume, I have had extensive educational experience in finance, including an undergraduate and a graduate degree, and extensive finance course work. From what I have read about your company, I think my strong computer skills coupled with my finance training would enable me to make a strong contribution in your current productivity drive through automation. In addition, my position in student government has given me the leadership skills I think I need to grow with your company.

I would like to have the chance to meet with you to discuss my qualifications further. I will be in New York the week of March 20 and I would like to request an interview. I will call you in two weeks to see if we can arrange a time. Thank you.

Best regards,

Brenda Jones

Enclosure

Cover Letter 2

Mr. Shane Black
TRW Corporation
Detroit, MI 48220

Dear Mr. Black,

I have recently become aware of TRW's new acquisitions in aerospace and defense and am interested in your career opportunities in those subsidiaries. I am currently completing my MBA in production and operations management at Fuqua School of Business and expect to finish in March; a resume is enclosed for your review.

I think that my combination of skills, experience, and education would make me a valuable part of your team. As you can see from my resume, I spent three years with ABC Corporation in the defense division after earning my undergraduate degree in engineering. From that, I have a good understanding of the defense business and government contracting. My MBA has now given me the business skills I need to pursue a career in manufacturing. Please note in my resume the descriptions of the special projects I completed; they should enable me to contribute very quickly in TRW.

I would like to request an interview with you when you visit Duke in October. I will call you next week to see if we can schedule it. Thank you for your time and I hope to see you next month.

Sincerely,

Bob Stockton

Enclosure

An expression of enthusiasm and interest is a must. (After all, if you aren't enthusiastic and interested, why write at all?) Unfortunately, most follow-up letters fail at this point. Fluff and bull will get you nowhere. Keep your follow-up letter honest, sincere, and believable. Contrast these two statements and consider why the second is more believable:

Bad: There is no question in my mind that your company is the world leader in this field and the company with which I would like to spend my career. It would be an honor to work for your company.

Good: I sincerely enjoyed the discussion we had about your chemical marketing division. While I have only begun to learn of your career opportunities, I am excited about the potential in your company.

Follow-Up Letter 1

Ms. Lynette Carter
Liberty National Corporation
Charlotte, NC 28220

Dear Ms. Carter,

Thank you for the time you spent with me while you were on campus last Thursday. I thoroughly enjoyed our interview and am quite eager to visit your plant. I was particularly excited about the new market development department we discussed; that seems to be a perfect match for me.

I hope to hear from you soon. Thank you again for your interest in me.

Sincerely,

Beth Eckston

JOB OFFER/ACCEPTANCE LETTERS

Both job offer and acceptance letters should be written and considered *as if* they were a contract (even though they are legally not). Their primary purpose is to detail the exact terms and conditions of your employment offer so that both you and the company

Follow-Up Letter 2

Ms. Cindy Stuart
Arthur Smith & Co.
New York, NY 10024

Dear Ms. Stuart,

Thank you for such a productive interview last week. I am excited about the opportunities and particularly appreciate the thoroughness with which you presented them.

While reflecting on the interview, I remembered a paper that I wrote on the simulation techniques you are using. I am enclosing a copy for your review so that you can see the research I have done in this area.

I hope I'll get the chance to discuss this more with you at your office. From what I know, I think that I can contribute to Arthur Smith's success. Thank you again.

Best regards,

John Thomas

Enclosure

---

are clear about what has been agreed to. Both letters are likely to be somewhat formal.

The offer letter should include at least your position title and starting salary. In most cases, it will also include the site location at which you will be working and the starting date. Additional terms and conditions of employment such as a physical exam and licensing certifications should also be in the letter. There is nothing wrong with asking for all agreements and understandings about your employment to be put in writing. Written confirmations prevent misunderstandings in business and are not an indication of mistrust. When in doubt, ask for it in writing.

Your acceptance letter should state exactly what you understand to be the terms of the offer that you are accepting. Do not respond with "I accept your offer as outlined in your letter of May 7, 1989," or "I accept your offer of employment." Be perfectly clear: "I accept your offer of employment as an account executive in the Raleigh, NC, branch office at a starting salary of $28,000 per year." The easiest approach is to copy the exact wording from the offer letter.

Job Acceptance Letter

Mrs. Rene Yardley
KPMG Peat Marwick Main
Philadelphia, PA 19015

Dear Mrs. Yardley,

I am happy to accept your offer of employment in the Philadelphia office of Peat Marwick as a consultant with a starting salary of $25,000/year. I understand that I must pass a physical before beginning work and that you will pay all my moving costs. As we discussed, I plan to start work on August 1.

I want to thank you for all of your time and efforts on my behalf. I am thrilled with my new position and am looking forward to the projects I will be assigned. Have a nice summer, and see you in August.

Sincerely,

Susan Long

You should also use your acceptance letter to express your enthusiasm for your new job. The acceptance of an offer is the end of the recruiting process, and since you have won the job, you may think you don't need to impress the company. However, this is also the beginning of your career with the company. You can build goodwill before you arrive for work by expressing your excitement about your new job. It's always a plus when the employer becomes excited about your arrival. Start building good relationships with your acceptance letter.

DECLINING AN OFFER LETTER

Your letter declining an offer should begin the same way as an acceptance letter, except of course it says, "I do not accept. . . ." Too often though, that is all it says. When you receive a job offer, a company is likely to have invested considerable time, effort, and energy in talking to you and recruiting you. It has probably paid for you to visit its headquarters or plant, entertained you, and treated you very well. Employers will be disappointed when you decline an offer, even though they always expect a percentage to do so. But if they receive a short, cold, curt letter saying nothing but, "Thanks, but no thanks," they are likely to feel somewhat used. In business you never know when you may meet someone again, perhaps as a client, or boss, or supplier. So don't burn your bridges. Although it may seem at the moment that you will never have contact with employer X again, you may in fact apply for a job at Company Y only to discover that the recruiter you were so cold to at Company X is now the personnel manager at Company Y.

Take the time to thank the employer for the efforts made on your behalf. Say that you noticed and appreciated what the company did for you, and make sure you part on good terms.

Letter Declining an Offer

Mr. T. G. Hill
ACME Corporation
Atlanta, GA 30379

Dear Mr. Hill,

I am sorry to inform you that I am declining your offer of employment as a market analyst in your Atlanta office in order to accept another position that I think will be better for me at this time.

I would like to thank you for your offer, and for the exceptional courtesy and helpfulness of all the people with whom I came into contact at ACME Corporation. It made the interview process a real pleasure.

Best of luck in the future, and thank you again for your offer.

Best regards,

Mark Jones

Chapter 18

Special Issues for MBAs in Career Planning

When counseling MBAs, I am frequently asked to address issues like overtime, two-career couples, finding a job in a specific city, overcoming a bad experience in a previous job, and selecting a good career counselor. If any of these are important to you, then you need the special advice that follows.

OVERTIME

As a professional, you will be expected to work overtime if it is needed to get the job done. To gain the rewards of a professional career, you give up punching a time clock and limiting yourself to 40 hours per week. Depending on the company, industry, job level, and your ambitions, you will find a variety of standards for overtime. I know companies where the real up-and-comers routinely work 70–80 hours per week, whereas in others 45–55 is the rule. Generally, the amount of overtime you work will increase as you take on increasing responsibility and your pay goes up. Fast-track employees usually find themselves working many extra hours. As discussed earlier, *you* have to decide how you want to balance your life.

Most students want to know how much overtime will be expected of them before they accept a job, which makes sense. The key is to avoid giving the impression that you want to punch a time clock and are unwilling to do what it takes to get the job done and contribute to the company when you ask questions designed to protect your own life goals. Never address overtime in the initial interview. It is always best to pursue this issue during the on-site interview and to do so indirectly. Some excellent questions that will give you a pretty good idea of the overtime involved are:

- What is a typical workweek like?
- What is a typical year in this job like?
- What seasonal fluctuations can you expect?
- What is a typical day like?

The interviewer's response will likely include references to any heavy demands, overtime, bad times, and easy times that you may encounter on the job. Don't make it obvious that you are very concerned about overtime, and don't directly ask how much overtime you have to work. The implication of that question is that you don't want to work any. By all means, though, do find out what the demands of the job are going to be on you (and your family if you have one). As a last resort, the best direct approach is to ask a fellow alumnus(a) or friend who works in the company and with whom you feel comfortable asking an off-the-record question.

TWO-CAREER COUPLES

Two-career couples face particular problems because they must find two jobs in the same location at the same time. Starting and maintaining two aggressive careers is a big challenge that requires special consideration. Most of the difficulty occurs when two people link their job searches too tightly. Too many couples set out to find *two perfect* jobs at the same time. That's nearly impossible. Most often one person ends up delaying his or her job search a little while to get one career off the ground. One of you needs to be prepared to make that sacrifice.

One big mistake that most two-career couples make in a job search is making one employer responsible for the jobs of both people. This usually happens indirectly and can be as simple as making statements in an interview such as: "I'd really be interested in talking with your company, but of course my husband has to find a job also."

Red flags begin appearing everywhere for the employer. By forcing your spouse into the situation, you create in the employer's mind much doubt as to whether it would be realistic to hire you. The fear is that the company must find a job for your spouse or it will lose you. Since your spouse is at that point unknown, the company may ignore you. In addition, it is hard enough to find a match between one person and a company, let alone two people. Unless you are an absolute superstar (which you shouldn't assume), the consequences may be disastrous.

Each person should begin the job search separately. Remote locations of certain companies may be eliminated early because of the lack of other employment opportunities, but the best solution is to try all possibilities: you never know what will happen during the job search. Obviously, if you have to choose where to devote your time, devote it to the company or location where the spouse is most likely to find a job. But early in your job search it is simply foolish to eliminate opportunities.

At some point, one person will have to take the lead. After some months of churning the waters and developing opportunities, one partner is likely to begin to develop more promising leads than the other. As soon as that happens, the other can begin to narrow the search to the specific geographic area in which the first partner has a good prospect. It is important to realize that such short-term sacrifices are the norm for two-career couples and not let a power struggle develop. Finding two good opportunities simultaneously is highly unlikely, and the second partner can often achieve his or her job objectives by being patient for a short time.

RESTRICTED GEOGRAPHY

For one reason or another, students often choose or are forced to restrict their job search to a specific geographical area. The on-campus job search strategies become relatively useless if you restrict your job search to a specific city. There will likely be very few companies on campus from any particular city, and you will be forced to lean heavily on mail campaigns, friendworking, classified ads, and possibly employment agencies. Try the following:

- Visit the area in question several times. You need to be able to offer the employer a chance to meet you at your own expense. Plan a mail campaign about one or two months before you visit the city, and include in your cover letter a statement such as "I will be visiting Atlanta during my spring break of March 22–25 and would like to meet with you to discuss my qualifications further. I will call you the first week of March to arrange a time." Unless you have extraordinarily strong qualifications, you are unlikely to generate a large response to any long-distance job search unless you are willing to make the trip yourself.
- Use employment agencies. Their greatest strength is that they provide strong coverage of specific geographic areas. Investigate this strategy thoroughly.
- Subscribe to a newspaper in the area in which you are seeking employment. Although many jobs will not be advertised, some positions will be. You will gain a perspective on the starting salaries in positions that are available in the market.
- Do not place a "situations wanted" ad in the paper. Such ads

are not very successful, and they usually connote desperation.
- Beat the pavement. It may be necessary. There is some slight advantage to personally delivering your resume to the personnel office. Often the little extra initiative demonstrated and the mental image you leave behind may be enough at least to get you an interview.

In short, recognize that restricting the geographical location to which you will move severely limits the job opportunities you will likely have. Remember to be flexible in other parts of your objective if you're forced into one specific location.

OVERCOMING NEGATIVE JOB EXPERIENCES

Unfortunately, not all job experiences are good ones. Many professionals have found themselves in jobs in which they were unhappy. Poor fit, tyrannical bosses, unkept promises, etc., all contribute to bad job experiences. Others have been fired or forced to resign because of mistakes, poor performance, or poor judgment. As is only human, the result is often feelings of bitterness, anger, or failure.

The problem is not that these feelings exist but that they often linger too long and prevent you from projecting the positive atti-

---

When things go wrong, as they sometimes will,
When the road you're trudging seems all uphill,
When the funds are low and the debts are high
And you want to smile, but you have to sigh,
When care is pressing you down a bit,
Rest! if you must—but never quit.

. . . .

Success is failure turned inside out—
The silver tint of the clouds of doubt—
And you never can tell how close you are,
It may be near when it seems afar;
So stick to the fight when you're hardest hit—
It's when things seem worst that YOU MUSTN'T QUIT.

—Anonymous
From "You Mustn't Quit"

---

tude you need to land a new job. Employers will not hire an unhappy, negative person. Quite simply, people with a negative attitude tend to be malcontents, have lower productivity, and depress the morale of an organization. Employers fear that you will take your angers out on them. Frankly, their fears are entirely justified.

It is imperative that you overcome your negative experiences and leave them behind, carrying with you only the lessons you learned. You can bet that you will not find a good job if you remain cynical, bitter, and angry. Too many bright and motivated MBAs return to school because of a negative or disappointing job experience and fail because they stay angry. The symptoms may include:

- sharp, angry answers to questions about previous employers
- lots of negative, blaming statements
- absence of smiles and laughter
- low, monotonous, controlled voice
- lethargy (they drag themselves around)
- loud, aggressive behavior
- unwillingness to seriously pursue another job

Some or all of these symptoms may appear either as a general behavior pattern or only in response to certain questions about prior work experience.

For your own good health as well as for your job search, your task is to do two things: overcome the negative, bitter, and angry feelings in order to project and live with a positive attitude; and learn how to deal with interview questions about that job experience.

Overcoming the negative feelings is not an easy process. To put them in perspective, consider the following steps:

1. Talk to friends, family, or a counselor about your feelings of anger, failure, guilt, etc. Repressed feelings are like a rumbling volcano. It requires considerable energy to control them, and no matter how good you think you are at doing it, they are likely to pop out in less direct ways. Find a way to clear the air.
2. Do not take all the responsibility upon yourself. The odds are that both you and your previous employer contributed to a less than satisfactory situation. Be fair to yourself and accept responsibility only for what you truly deserve.
3. Accept your mistakes and failures and stop punishing yourself. Even if you did make mistakes, there is nothing to be gained by self-punishment. It is OK to make mistakes. If you talk to very successful businesspeople, you will find that most have made serious blunders somewhere in their careers. Ac-

cept yours as being natural, inevitable, and human. You aren't perfect, so forgive yourself.

4. Let go of your guilty feelings. You probably don't have much to feel guilty about. Stop assuming that your own inadequacies caused the negative experience. Even if you did not perform as you should have, guilt serves only to punish you and changes nothing.

5. Change your experience into a positive one by focusing on the lessons you learned. Usually there is a wealth of new information about yourself to be learned from a negative experience. At least you now know what to avoid. Analyze *objectively* the reasons things didn't work out, and use that information to make a good choice next time. Consider that bad experience as just a step, albeit a painful one, in your development. Be thankful you now know some things to avoid.

6. Get on with your life. It's bad enough that that experience affected your life so much when it happened, so don't let it continue. It will continue to torture you only *if you let it.* Discuss it, analyze it, cry over it, and then leave it behind. Applaud yourself for the courage to do something about it. Try writing down all your horrible feelings and thoughts about the experience and then burn them or bury them to symbolically eliminate them from your life.

Once you have developed a positive attitude, handling the interview questions is easy. The keys are:

- Don't blame anybody, particularly previous employers.
- Don't express any anger or bitterness, either in words or otherwise.
- Focus on why that experience will make you a better employee in the future.

There is no need to discuss all the details, except in rare instances. In many cases, there is no need to even discuss the negative aspects. It is perfectly OK to say that you had a job you didn't like, as long as it is expressed positively. For example, compare the following statements about the same job:

| **negative:** | "I hated the job. My boss was terrible, and the company never planned well." |
| **positive:** | "The job was not a good fit for me. I learned that the quality of the management team and good corporate planning are very important to me." |

negative: "They dead-ended me. I never got any of the good jobs, so I never had any visibility or advancement."

positive: "I was not advancing at the pace I wanted to. I learned that assignments you receive greatly contribute to your success in an organization, so I am very concerned about my starting assignment."

Notice that the negative approach uses lots of "you" type statements pointing the finger at the company. The tone is sour and somewhat bitter; the message is an angry one. The positive approach focuses on how that experience is contributing to the person making a better job decision today, and therefore becoming a better employee. Both positive statements openly admit that you were disappointed with the job, but the focus is on the *positive results* of a negative experience.

CHOOSING A CAREER COUNSELOR

Fortunately, there are many well-trained and competent career advisers available to you. You should look for advisers whose main interest is in helping *you* determine *your* values and guiding you to a decision that is best for you as an individual. Some advisers attempt to sell you on *their* approach to life and a career. Parents and friends are often anxious to help you by showing you the professions that work so well for them. Well-intentioned faculty members may present their discipline as the perfect one for you because they love it so much. The problem is that in their zeal to help you they end up trying to force you to fit their mold rather than helping you construct your own.

"But wait a minute," you say. "I need to find out about the experience of other people." You are right. The experience of others is very valuable. People who have worked in a profession or who have close contact with a certain field can give you valuable insights. But there is a huge difference between telling you how they experienced it and telling you that it would be the best experience for you.

Look for advisers who avoid dogmatic statements like "It's best to . . . ," "You should . . . ," or "The best career is. . . ." Look for nonjudgmental people, people who are anxious to share their own personal experiences and opinions, but who recognize them as subjective ones. Avoid people who are trying to push something on you. Remember that they do not know you. Even if you do not know yourself thoroughly, you still know more than they do. Also remember it is difficult for many people to leave their own values and interests aside to view your options through your eyes.

Use advisers to collect valuable information, to reality-test your own conclusions, and to help structure your thoughts. Look for advisers who ask you lots of open-ended questions designed to help them understand you better before they begin to give you their opinions. People who do not understand you can hardly offer good opinions. The best ones will give you the pros and cons, talk about the risks and rewards of a choice, and probe to see if you have collected all the information you should. Then they let you make the decision.

Your MBA placement office is probably your best source of qualified career counselors. Usually, they know the MBA job market and employers well and are trained to help you. Faculty members can also help, but you must be careful since they tend to be so specialized that they may champion their own discipline too much. There are also private career counseling organizations available, particularly in major metropolitan areas. They can be quite expensive and vary in quality, but they can also be extremely helpful. Because of the large number of services available to you on campus, you are unlikely to need their services except in special circumstances.

Finally, don't forget all the other valuable advisers in your life. Despite the caveats issued earlier, friends, faculty, parents, and professional contacts are very valuable advisers in your career planning and placement process. As long as you are careful to integrate only that advice which reflects your own personal values and are not swayed by their opinions or pressured by their desires, you should plan to talk to everyone that you can. The more experience that you can obtain the benefit of, whether it is your own or someone else's, the better off you will be. Many of the people close to you have known you for a long time and are likely to provide valuable insights in your self-assessment process. Many can offer you the wisdom of years of experience, and most have made mistakes that they can help you avoid. So talk and listen to everyone that you can, and accept their advice judiciously.

Chapter 19

Special MBA Populations

You saw in an earlier chapter how heterogeneous the MBA population is. While some like to think of all MBAs as the same, there are really a wide variety of backgrounds and objectives within the MBA population. This chapter discusses the special job search problems and issues facing some of the most common subgroups and offers special advice for each.

INTERNATIONAL MBAs

The percentage of foreign MBA students enrolled in U.S. programs continues to increase. The globalization of world markets, the impact of the U.S. economy on the world economy, and the general excellence of U.S. business schools are all contributing factors. However, foreign MBA students on F-1 or J-1 visas who wish to stay and work in the United States face a very difficult task.

F-1 visas allow foreign students to enter the United States and stay as long as they are enrolled as full-time students. After finishing full-time studies, students are allowed to stay for approximately one year to obtain "practical training." At that time, they must leave the country. J-1 visas are similar except that they allow students to come to the United States in an exchange program but allow no work period.

If a foreign MBA student wants to stay in the country, that person must obtain a job. Then, the hiring *employer* must sponsor the person in his or her application for a permanent visa by certifying to the U.S. Department of Labor that it could not hire a U.S. citizen to fill the job and therefore the foreigner should be allowed to stay permanently. In this way the U.S. government keeps foreigners from taking jobs away from Americans.

For foreign MBAs, it is extremely difficult to get such sponsorship, because a company would have to lie to convince the Labor Department. As discussed earlier there is probably an oversupply of MBA graduates in this country. Even though the quality may vary, that is not usually an acceptable argument to the Labor Department. Furthermore, Labor Department officials have indicated in conversations that they may question whether an MBA is even needed to do the job. That is, they may force the company to hire an undergraduate and provide further training. The result is that today it is expensive, time-consuming, and usually futile for a company to sponsor a foreign MBA except in the most unusual circumstances. Most companies have responded by refusing even to attempt it. It is not that they don't like foreigners or don't want to hire them; it's just that they don't have to go through all the hassle and expense because there are other MBAs available.

The response I often get to this is "But I'll just work for my one year." MBA employers won't even consider it. It costs a great deal of money to train an employee, and the first year on the job an employee rarely contributes anything close to what he or she costs the company in salary and benefits. No self-respecting businessperson is going to hire you and lose money just so you can get a little experience.

The one year of work stipulation is designed to allow U.S. companies to train employees for their operations overseas. And that, in fact, is one big job market for foreign MBAs. There are a number of U.S. employers with operations overseas that like to hire U.S.-trained, foreign-born MBAs to work in those overseas subsidiaries. The reason is that it is much cheaper to hire a foreign national than to relocate a U.S. employee to a foreign country. Plus, Americans often aren't as effective because of cultural differences. Since just about all of the Fortune 500 companies have operations in other countries, they are all prospects. Be warned, though, that many of them leave the hiring to their managers overseas and may refer you directly to the overseas site.

If you want to stay in the United States, you have to find a position where your nationality and cultural background give you a unique advantage over an American MBA. Then and only then can you compete effectively. It is generally futile to compete head-to-head with a U.S. MBA where the job requires no international experience. Good prospects might include:

- export/import firms
- diplomatic service (although you may not be guaranteed a U.S. posting)
- banks with a large foreign business
- international departments of large corporations
- international trade

- international consulting firms
- international marketing positions

You are most likely to succeed if you look for jobs in large internationally oriented trade centers such as New York; Washington, D.C.; Miami; or Los Angeles. You might also consider a PhD in business, since there is a large shortage of business faculty at the university level, and so permanent visas are easier to come by.

There are some special situations where a U.S. company can make a strong case that a U.S.-born MBA could not do the job. Japanese and Korean industry is such a competitor of U.S. business today that U.S. companies are hungry for a better understanding of firms in those countries and how to compete with them. Thus, Japanese and Korean MBAs are highly sought. Certain undergraduate disciplines such as electrical engineering and computer science are fairly scarce among MBAs. A foreign MBA with those credentials might be hired. If you have work experience with a major foreign competitor of a U.S. firm, the firm might be willing to fight the Department of Labor. In all of the above cases, note that there really is no exception to the law. The foreign MBA must have some unique competitive advantage over a U.S. MBA and market that advantage effectively.

International MBAs can find jobs in the United States, but they should be warned that it takes lots of time, a special marketing strategy, and—frankly—a bit of luck.

TECHNICAL MBAs

Technical MBAs are those with a science, engineering, or computer science undergraduate degree. These candidates are among the hottest products in the MBA job market today. If you are such a person, you're in luck. If you plan your career properly and prepare yourself well, you should have a successful and profitable job search.

The demand is high for technical MBAs and according to employers is currently exceeding the supply. American industry has for a long time had brilliant technical and business minds. Unfortunately, the two often struggle to communicate effectively. Accountants and engineers, for example, often have a hard time understanding one another. Enter the technical MBA. Trained in both business and a technical discipline, the technical MBA serves as a bridge and an interpreter, enabling the two groups to work well together.

Your technical background can be a tremendous asset to you or a tremendous liability, depending on your job objective. If you are seeking a position that demands both your technical and business skills, you can expect higher salaries and multiple offers. These are usually the bridging positions I referred to. Employers see added value in purchasing both sets of skills and are willing to pay for it. It is for these types of positions that workers are in short supply. As long as you seek a position where your technical degree complements your MBA (and vice versa), you will have a competitive advantage in the marketplace versus an MBA with a liberal arts or business background.

Just the opposite is true if you abandon your technical background. If you decide to become a financial analyst or investment banker, for example, you may find yourself at a competitive disadvantage. If your technical background is of no particular advantage in a job for which you are applying, you will have only two years of business training to market whereas a business undergraduate can claim six. Employers will justifiably not pay you a premium salary in these cases, and you may find it difficult to compete. That's not to say you shouldn't try. If your career compass is pointing you in a different direction, if you aren't happy in your technical career and know it's not for you, then it's better to make the switch. But if you enjoy the technical career but want a little different mix between technical and business, then you will be in the best competitive position.

The mix you prefer between technical and business tasks will be your biggest decision. At one end of the spectrum you have jobs that are about three-fourths technical, one-fourth business. Examples include engineering, computer science, and research and development management; technical consulting; and technical support. In these positions you are still largely a technical person but need business skills to manage people and interface with customers. At the middle of the continuum are the half technical, half business jobs. In these jobs you wear a technical hat one minute and a business hat the next. Examples include marketing of technical products, systems engineer for a high-tech company, technical liaison roles on marketing teams, and internal consultant. At the other end of the continuum are positions where you are primarily a businessperson but use your knowledge of the technical world to make you more effective. Examples include project management, manufacturing management (plant manager career path), and financial and business analysis (sometimes). Of course these examples are generalizations and may or may not hold true in different organizations. The key point is that you will have to decide what balance you want in your professional life.

Why do technical people get MBAs? Most new technical MBAs

report a frustration with purely technical work. They want a different kind of challenge, a different type of task. They talk about wanting more contact with people, more responsibility. They want to be part of the decision-making process, and they want to be part of the leadership team. For them, the purely technical work simply isn't consistent with their interests and skills.

In addition, they see greater opportunities for advancement and salary increases with MBAs. There has long been a problem in American business of a career plateau for technical people in the twelve to eighteen years after school and $50,000–$60,000 salary range. While many companies have developed dual career ladders (professional and managerial), there are many that have not. Many technical people see that they must switch to management to get the rewards they want. While MBA and technical starting salaries are sometimes more or less the same, MBAs advance faster after the first eight or ten years. Even more important, there is no upper limit since MBAs have the credentials to rise all the way to the top more easily.

In the long term, the most important thing is to choose the career that fits you best. But, if it fits, choose a career path where your MBA and technical training work together and you will see your salary and marketability soar.

NO WORK EXPERIENCE

One of the most frequent questions I get from prospective MBA students is "Do I need work experience before I get my MBA?" It is widely reported that one must have at least a year or two of work experience to get a good job after MBA school. While there is some truth to that, it is largely misrepresented.

What you really need to compete effectively in the MBA job market is maturity. It is imperative that you demonstrate you understand what the working world is all about, a certain amount of real-world savvy, a mature understanding of what you want out of life, and what you can reasonably expect to get from the job. Anything less and you will find the job search very difficult. It turns out that the easiest way to obtain that maturity is to go to work for a while. Working for a living has a funny way of pounding most of the callowness out of a person very quickly. Furthermore, it is rare to see someone who has worked for a year or two who has not attained enough maturity to compete effectively. Thus it is very convenient for employers and schools to "require" some work experience. It is not the specific skills you have obtained that are so important as the professional growth.

Just because work experience is the most convenient and surest way to grow professionally does not mean it is necessary. In fact, there are some very good opportunities for MBAs with little or no work experience and some excellent strategies to help you attain the necessary professional maturity. Many large companies prefer to hire MBAs with no experience and then train and acculturate them in their own system. They prefer to start from scratch rather than undo bad habits; Arthur Andersen & Co. and IBM are two prominent examples. Some companies like Air Products & Chemicals and CSX have well-designed training programs just for inexperienced MBAs.

The problem is many of your competing MBAs will have work experience. There is no mistaking that they have an extra air of confidence about them, a presence in the interview that comes from the extra maturity and savvy that they have. You can compete but you have to work hard to attain some of the same maturity while in school. Some successful strategies are shown below. Note that they all focus on getting your "hands on" and immersing you in experiential, real-world activities. You can compete quite effectively, in fact, but only if you put forth the effort to add maturity to your portfolio and target those companies that accept MBAs with no experience. An immature, naive, and inexperienced MBA will really struggle.

- **Co-op/Internships.** Still the quickest and easiest way. Do it for free, if necessary, to get the experience.
- **Experiential-Type Classes.** Look for case courses or courses that use lots of experiential-type projects. Focus electives on application-oriented courses rather than theoretical.
- **Consulting.** Volunteer to assist professors with consulting projects.
- **Computer Skills.** Can give you good employable assets so you can be productive early and give you time to mature.
- **Course Projects.** Do projects instead of research papers whenever you can. They'll give you good real-world experience and something tangible to sell to employers.
- **Career Planning.** Lack of direction and unrealistic career goals emphasize your immaturity and inexperience.
- **Job Search Training.** Even more vital since shyness and a sloppy resume only add to an impression of immaturity.

CAREER CHANGERS

Career changers are those persons who have qualifications and usually experience in a field unrelated to business and are using the MBA to change to a different career path. Their challenge lies in handling the unrelated experience. Several problems may arise:

- You will be uncompetitive because you lack as much relevant training.
- You will be perceived as lacking commitment because you're making a change.
- You have gone too far to learn a new career.

Unfortunately, many employers overlook the value of other types of training when combined with an MBA. While most of them would profess to be broad-minded and appreciative of more creative career paths, in practice they are much less so. When they compare you side by side with people more extensively trained in related fields, you may lose out. It's sometimes tough for employers to view a person who, for example, taught school for five years and has a marketing MBA as equal to one who has an undergraduate degree *and* an MBA in marketing, even if they really are equal.

It is absolutely critical for career changers to aggressively promote their transferable skills, since they may not be as apparent. You will need to be proactive, learning to anticipate objections and head them off, even if they aren't verbalized (which happens). Look for ways to construct your resume and answer interview questions that constantly lead the employer to the value of your unrelated experience.

Career changers must master the concept of transferable skills. Just because your previous title, career, company, industry, etc., don't seem related to business doesn't mean you didn't learn a lot of things that can be used in your new business. It's your responsibility though to market those skills; if you don't, many employers will quickly overlook them. Go back to the chapter on self-assessment and focus hard on your transferable skills. Reread "Marketing Yourself" to be sure you can aggressively market yourself. Also, you must consider using a combination resume with the skills section coming first to highlight the transferable skills. The MBA is a terrific degree for a career changer, but you may have to work a little harder to land the first job.

WOMEN AND MINORITIES

The business world desperately needs well-qualified women and minority members to rise into management. Equal opportunity and affirmative action are major issues for employers today as they work to change what was largely a white male world. Racial and sexual bias has not completely disappeared from the job market, but there is a very strong demand for female and minority MBAs. You shouldn't feel bad about exploiting that either. Nobody is going to give you a job just because of your race or sex, but it can help you get your foot in the door.

The major challenge you face of course is discrimination. The people hiring MBAs tend to be fairly sophisticated, more highly educated employers and are therefore less likely to let prejudices affect their hiring. The problems have sometimes arisen with smaller, more parochial firms. Large corporations generally have a much better record.

You need to be looking carefully at your prospects to learn what their real commitment is to equal opportunity. It is fair to ask directly:

- How strong is your commitment to affirmative action?
- As a woman (or a black, a Hispanic, etc.), what are my chances for promotion to management?
- How many black (or female, etc.) first-level, midlevel, and senior managers do you have?
- What are you doing to increase that?
- What impediments will there be to my advancement?

You will get good answers to these questions, particularly from personnel people. To be sure of an organization's commitment, pay close attention when you are on your hiring interview. Are any important people female or members of minorities? Who are the "shining stars"? Do senior people treat you as an equal? midlevel people? junior people? Are there frequent references to exclusionary groups like men's clubs or predominantly white clubs? Look for concrete evidence and behavior that say the company really does what it professes to do.

Suppose you encounter discrimination during the job search? Don't put up with it. There are tactful ways to handle inadvertent or insignificant lapses in interviews, but you needn't tolerate deliberate discrimination. There are too many good MBA employers in the market. If you've worked hard to develop the qualifications, you don't have to compromise.

Another big challenge is to find a network of friends to help you in your job search. Many of the older "old-boy" networking channels have not been as accessible to women and minorities. In response, a large number of women's and minority professional organizations have been formed to create new networks. They should be quite helpful in your job search. Most cities have women's and minority business groups where you can make contacts. National organizations (see the appendix, "Career Resources") sponsor national meetings and publications to address your particular concerns and also sponsor local chapters. Many minority organizations sponsor job fairs with strong employer attendance.

The man who wants a garden fair,
Or small or very big,
With flowers growing here and there,
Must bend his back and dig.

The things are mighty few on earth
That wishes can attain.
Whate'er we want of any worth
We've got to work to gain.

It matters not what goal you seek
Its secret here reposes:
You've got to dig from week to week
To get Results of Roses.

—Edgar A. Guest
"Results and Roses"

I'm pleased to say that my female and minority students have always had equal (or better) access to the good jobs with good salaries. At least early in their career they seem to get equally good assignments and are promoted equally. Thus, I am optimistic that you won't encounter problems in the MBA job market, at least as you are starting out.

Chapter 20

Preemployment Drug Testing

The abuse of drugs by American workers has reached epidemic proportions. Its cost to American business in terms of worker health, safety, and productivity is tremendous. Alcohol and drug abusers are absent from work 2.5 times as often as other workers, and their average productivity is 25–33 percent lower. One drug policy adviser says that drug abuse costs U.S. employers an average of $500–$1000 per employee per year. Drug abuse also contributes to strained relations between workers, domestic and financial difficulties for employees, theft of company and coworker property to support drug habits, and drug dealing at work. Estimates made in 1986 and 1987 indicated that there were as many as 5,000 first-time users each day and that 17 percent of all U.S. workers had used illegal substances while on the job.

As a result, many employers have implemented drug testing programs. These include random testing of employees and—of special interest to those reading this book—preemployment testing of potential new hires. While there may be some philosophical misgivings about the way American business is attacking the problem, drug testing is here to stay. According to a 1986 College Placement Council preemployment drug survey, 28 percent of its member employers were at the time conducting preemployment drug tests and another 19 percent planned to implement them during the next eighteen months. Thus, at present, close to half of the major employers in the United States, many of whom hire MBAs, will be testing new employees for drug use before they start work.

Furthermore, there is currently no legal prohibition against such testing programs in the private sector. The law basically says that the private employer is entitled to a drug-free workplace and may hire and fire at will. The courts have essentially upheld the use of drug tests to ensure a drug-free workplace. A surprising fact to most students is that the constitutional rights to due process, privacy, and freedom from unreasonable searches apply only to acts of the government, not those of private employers. The major limitation to such programs comes from the discrimination and handicap laws that require that such programs have no disparate impact on protected groups, such as blacks, Hispanics, women, and handicapped people. Employers are bound by civil law responsibilities not to be negligent, or to libel or slander. However, these statutes govern how the employer conducts the tests and uses the results, not whether the tests can be conducted.

In the public sector, the laws are more strict. The Constitution provides for the protection of citizens from unnecessary or excessive intrusions by the government. Legal challenges to drug testing by the public sector have been based largely on claims that such testing invades a person's privacy, constitutes an unreasonable search, and deprives a person of due process. However, the courts have not agreed with these challenges where drug testing is being conducted for good business reasons. They have consistently ruled that a person's right to privacy does not apply to the use of illegal substances. Because of the high cost of drug use in the workplace and the safety hazards it creates, the courts have ruled that most testing is not an unreasonable search. Finally, where the testing programs are conducted fairly and equitably, the courts have ruled that the government is not depriving a person of due process.

While there are some concerns about drug testing programs, there is also much broad concern and support for stopping the use of drugs in America, including their use in the workplace. As a result of the huge costs and threats to public safety from the use of drugs by American workers, drug testing, including preemployment drug testing, is probably here to stay. So you must understand what drug testing is, how it is usually conducted, and how to be sure you are treated fairly. This is a very complex issue with many unresolved legal issues, but let's take a look at some basic guidelines.

A DRUG TESTING PRIMER

Drug testing is conducted by verbal, written, and polygraph questioning and by blood, urine, saliva, or hair sample tests. Most of it is done by a urine test, which is usually included as part of your preemployment physical. The company is not obligated to tell you that a drug test will be performed, nor does it have to tell you the details of the results. While many will discuss it with you, some will simply tell you that you failed the physical.

Most drug testing is performed in outside laboratories. There is a complex set of procedures (called evidentiary procedures) used in handling your urine sample that help ensure that it does not become mixed up with another person's or contaminated. These procedures have been required by the courts in any litigation concerning tests.

The most uncomfortable part of the process (if you don't use drugs) may be giving the sample. Believe it or not, there is a major problem with people trying to smuggle in uncontaminated urine instead of using their own or contaminating their own urine sample so that the test readings are false. Consequently, you will be under some observation during the testing. The most unobtrusive method I have heard of involves passing your sample through a small door in the bathroom as soon as you urinate and having it temperature-tested to be sure it is at body temperature. In some companies, a technician of the same sex may join you in the bathroom to directly observe you urinate. In others, they simply leave the door open so they can indirectly observe you. Still others allow complete privacy.

There are two types of drug test: the screening test and the confirmatory test. The screening test is relatively cheap ($18–$25) and quick and can test for up to fourteen drugs. It is the first test performed on all samples. Unfortunately, it also has a false-positive error rate reported to be as high as 20 percent, although its false-negative error rate is very low. The confirmatory test is much more expensive ($50–$70), takes longer, and can test for only one drug at a time. This test uses a gas chromatograph–mass spectrometer, which is the most accurate instrument available, and it is very reliable.

False-positive readings from screening tests are a significant issue for job candidates. Screening tests are just what their name implies: an inexpensive method to screen out non–drug users with little chance of missing a drug user. Thus, if it fails, it usually fails with a false-positive (incorrectly reporting drug use). The manufacturers of the tests, while claiming a very high accuracy rate, caution that the results should be backed up by a confirmatory test.

The reasons for false-positives are many and varied. There is no licensing at the current time for testing laboratories, and, therefore, the quality of their work varies tremendously. Even in the good laboratories, inexperienced technicians can contaminate test results. The conditions under which samples are taken are critical for good results. It has been reported that eating a large amount of poppy seeds on hamburger buns can be detected as marijuana by a screening test. Passive inhalation of marijuana smoke can sometimes be detected. Some herbal teas have a minute amount of cocaine that has little effect on the user but can be detected on a screening test. Some over-the-counter drugs contain small amounts of substances, such as phenobarbitol, that are legal but more frequently abused. Finally, certain prescription drugs that you could be using may be screened for since they are often abused.

The problem is not that the *screening* test fails. It is not intended to be more than an economical first step. The problem arises when some employers fail to confirm the results with the gas chromatograph–mass spectrometer test, which is not fooled by things such as poppy seeds and herbal teas. In a well-run testing program, the screening test is performed first and all positive samples are checked using a confirmatory test. However, there is no legal requirement to do this, and some companies choose not to incur the extra expense (usually only in the preemployment case).

The laboratory can test for almost any drug the company requests, but it tests only for those specific ones the company wants it to. There is no such thing as a "standard test." It is basically an economic decision on the part of employers as to how many drugs they want to screen for. The drugs most commonly tested for are cocaine, marijuana, opiates, amphetamines, barbiturates, Valium, Darvon, and Methadone.

The tests currently in use test for the *use*, not the abuse, of the drug. There are no accepted "intoxication" or "impairment" levels such as the standard for alcohol. Companies can choose the level at which the test is considered positive, but these levels are very low and have no relation to impairment. Furthermore, the testable residues of drugs can stay in the body for up to several weeks, unlike alcohol, which is metabolized out of the body in a few hours.

In September 1986, President Reagan signed an executive order directing every federal agency to evaluate the applicability of a drug testing program and directed the Department of Health and Human Services to develop guidelines for drug testing by federal agencies. These guidelines, issued in February 1987, represent a model for all testing programs and are regarded as quite strict. Some highlights:

- Agencies *must* test for marijuana and cocaine and may test for opiates, amphetamines, and phencyclidine (PCP). With reasonable suspicion, they may test for any drug in Schedule I or II of the Controlled Substances Act (essentially all controlled substances).
- The regulations require a secure and proper chain of custody, handling, and transportation in the specimen collection process.

- Collection procedures must provide for individual privacy, but agencies must also take steps to ensure that urine specimens are not adulterated or diluted.
- The regulations call for bluing agents in the toilets so attempted dilutions of the sample are obvious. Also, no unnecessary outer garments (coats, jackets, etc.) that might conceal substances used to tamper with the specimen are allowed to be worn into the testing area. Persons should not have access to faucets, soap dispensers, or cleaning agents.
- An observer of the same sex must accompany the individual into the restroom but shall remain outside the stall.
- Immediately after the collection, the collection personnel shall measure the temperature of the urine and inspect it to ensure it has not been tampered with.
- Both screening and confirmatory tests are required (if the screening test is positive).
- Results are reported to the medical review officer only.
- Drug testing labs are required to have elaborate quality assurance programs.
- Retesting is called for if there is any doubt as to the validity of the first test.
- Individuals with confirmed positive drug tests are to be referred to an employee assistance program.

Employers handle a positive preemployment drug test in different ways. Some will simply tell you that you failed your physical and your offer is withdrawn; they may say you failed your drug test but not provide details. More progressive companies will give you a chance to explain the results and may still hire you if they judge the drug use to be harmless. In that case, you may be subjected to random testing on the job to confirm that you have stopped using drugs. It should be emphasized that in the private sector it is the employers' choice as to how they handle a positive result. They are under no obligation to hire you or give you a second chance.

DEALING WITH PREEMPLOYMENT DRUG TESTING

There is only one way to be sure you won't have problems with preemployment drug testing—*don't use drugs*. It is not the intent of this chapter to encourage drug use or to protect drug users in any way. As stated earlier, you cannot avoid drug testing but you can protect your reputation. Unfortunately, however, some companies and laboratories do not run their programs properly and you could be denied employment. To assist you, I have prepared the following advice for different situations you may encounter.

1. You receive a job offer and there is no mention of drug testing. Ask:

- Will you conduct a preemployment drug test?
- Proceed to No. 2 below and ask those questions if the answer is yes.

2. You receive a job offer and are told that you will be subjected to a preemployment drug test. Ask:

- Is the offer contingent on a negative drug test?
- Will a confirmatory test be performed if the screening test is positive?
- Is the laboratory reliable?
- Will a proper chain of custody procedures be followed so there will be no mix-ups?
- Will the test results be discussed with me?

There is an obvious risk here that you will imply that you are a drug user simply by asking these questions. If you are not, preface your questions with a statement such as "I am not a drug user and am not concerned about passing a well-run drug test. However, I am aware that there are some quality differences in testing programs that can affect the outcome of the test, possibly falsely incriminating me. Therefore, I'd like to ask you a few questions about your preemployment drug testing."

If you make it clear that you are not trying to evade the test or beat the system, no employer should mind answering your questions. Most recruiters are well aware of the problems, particularly if they are trained in personnel.

When the test is done, be sure to report to the nurse or technician all prescription and over-the-counter drugs you have used in the past month; they may cause a false-positive reading.

3. You have a positive drug test that is incorrect:

If you know for sure that the test result is a false positive, then you should press your case with the employer. Employers are not eager to lose a good recruit (nor do they want a drug user), and most will want to be sure a fair decision is made. Also, most understand how the test could be incorrect and should be receptive to that possibility.

Insist that you are not a drug user. Do not threaten or insult the employer, but be firm in your assertion that you are innocent. Resist the urge to be defensive and angry. Ask the employer:

- For a detailed explanation of testing procedures. Look for the possibility that your sample could have been switched with someone else's.

- Whether a confirmatory test was performed. If it was not, insist that one be done, pointing out the high false-positive error rate for screening tests used alone.
- For a retest if there is evidence that the test was faulty.

4. *Your drug test is positive and you have used drugs:*
You are basically at the mercy of the company. If you are a strong candidate and have used drugs only occasionally, *some* companies will consider hiring you anyway. They may require some sort of rehabilitation program and follow-up testing to be sure you honor a promise to quit using drugs. If your reputation and credentials are strong, you may be able to make a case for ignoring the drug test. However, beware that most companies have a hard and fast rule against hiring anyone with a positive drug test and they will not bend; your offer will be automatically revoked. Some companies will allow you to reapply after a waiting period of six months to one year.

If you are a regular drug user, you are out of luck. My advice is simply to quit using drugs; find a rehabilitation program if necessary. It is highly likely that most companies will be testing employees, as well as candidates, for drug use within the next few years. Your only real solution is to stop using drugs.

It appears you have no legal right to refuse the drug test *if* you want to work for an employer that requires one, particularly if there is a health or safety reason for requiring it. There have been some court cases that have led most attorneys to remind employers that, while the law allows them to perform the tests, it also requires them to use the information in such a way as not to harm the individual. These cases have found employers guilty of libel and defamation when the test results were not handled in appropriate confidentiality and secrecy. Also, one employer was found guilty because it fired an employee without using a confirmatory test.

These cases offer some reassurance to candidates. While you must take the test (if you want to work for that employer), employers do have the responsibility to take care with the process and with the results. From the very sketchy case law that has emerged and attorneys' recommendations as to what may happen in future cases, I believe you have these rights:

- The sample-taking procedure should be conducted with dignity and with no undue or unnecessary physical contact or invasion of privacy.
- You are entitled to have a confirmatory test if the screening test is positive.

- You should be told if a drug test will be performed, particularly if you specifically ask the question.
- You have a right to ask questions about the testing process to protect your rights.
- Typically, there are only a few people, such as the company physician and someone in personnel, who need to know the test results. Your prospective boss usually needs to know only that you failed the physical. Only those who truly need to know should have access to the results of the test.
- You are entitled to know exactly why you are denied employment if it happens after a drug test.
- You are entitled to know whether the laboratory is regarded as reliable.

Chapter 21

Co-ops and Internships

Co-op (short for cooperative education) and internship programs offer the best way for you to make sure that your career objective is the right one and to gain marketable work experience. Such programs are particularly valuable for students who do not have much practical experience to guide them. They have long been a mainstay in engineering curriculums but are often grossly underutilized by business students.

Both of these programs provide short-term, full-time professional employment, often during the summer. Co-op programs have traditionally been alternating periods of work and school. They are usually coordinated through the university and provide some type of college credit. Internships are less formal arrangements, usually for one specified period of time, made directly between the employer and student with only minimal, if any, connection to the university. Because MBA programs are usually only one to two years long, alternating periods of work and school are often impractical, and the net effect for MBAs is that there is little difference between co-ops and internships. The form chosen for the program is a matter of convenience for the student, the university, and the employer. Both types provide excellent professional experience.

What can a co-op or intern position do for you? Many things; it can:

- provide work experience that you can market to employers
- enable you to try out your career objective
- let you get your foot in the door of a company that could end up offering you a permanent job
- pay you good money to defray the cost of your education
- supplement your classroom learning

In today's MBA job market, the best jobs are going to candidates who have some relevant professional work experience, from an internship or a permanent job, in addition to an MBA. Students with no work experience have the difficult task of developing themselves thoroughly in all other areas to compensate, and even then they are at a disadvantage.

Employers look very favorably upon co-op and intern experience. Students who have worked for two to four quarters can compete quite successfully with other MBAs who have had full-time experience before returning to obtain their degree. Since most companies devote considerable energy to providing a good experience for the student, obtaining a co-op or intern position is a top priority for students who have no professional work experience and a key step to finding a good job after the MBA.

Equally important is what the work experience can contribute to your career planning. No matter how well you research a career option by talking to people and digging for all the information you can, there is nothing like actually doing a job to really learn whether you like it. Your research is critical, but you are still only reading someone else's experience and opinions; you really must live it for yourself. A co-op or intern position allows you to do that. It is a unique opportunity to experience a professional career option without making a lengthy commitment. What more could you want?

While you are employed as an intern, most companies will be carefully evaluating you for a permanent position. Just as it is a unique opportunity for you to experience them without making a commitment, it is a chance for them to see how well you perform without making a commitment to you. The percentage of intern and co-op students who later receive a permanent job offer from the company with whom they intern is very high. While there's no guarantee, the odds are good that you will receive an offer if you perform well. At a minimum, you will gain valuable contacts inside that company who may be useful to you later in your job search.

Salary levels are usually quite good. You will typically be paid more than a student with an undergraduate degree to account for your additional education but less than a graduating MBA. You will make more than from any part-time summer job you could obtain, so it's a superb way to earn money to finance your education. Typical salaries range from $1,500 to $2,500 per month.

You will also be able to use the knowledge and practical experience you gain on the job to make your classroom experiences mean more to you. The theory that you can learn in the classroom without knowing how the learning is applied in the real world is rather hollow. If you lack work experience, you'll find your MBA experience to be so much more valuable after you return to school.

Co-op positions and internships are a no-lose proposition for both the company and you. Employers are able to take a risk-free look at you, usually complete some projects that have been waiting for extra help, and get an early start on recruiting you for possible future employment. You are able to gain valuable business experience and test out your career objective while being paid well and usually having some fun. It's a fine deal for both parties.

Every MBA student without significant professional experience should seriously consider a co-op or intern position. For students with more extensive professional experience, the answer is not so clear-cut. If your previous work experience is *directly related* to your post-MBA career objective, an internship is unlikely to do anything for you but give you a well-paying summer job and an entree to a specific company. If you have your heart set on a specific employer and are able to obtain a short-term position with that employer, go for it. Otherwise, you may be better off going to summer school and finishing your degree earlier.

For students who are changing fields, the internship is not quite as important as for the inexperienced student, but close to it. These students will be recognized as competent professionals in the MBA job market but will still suffer from a lack of relevant experience. The internship retains its value in this case for testing out a career objective and for gaining marketable experience.

FINDING A POSITION

Internships and co-op positions are obtained in much the same way as full-time positions. Although many companies offer intern programs, the competition is intense: not everyone will be able to find a position. Therefore, you should start early and plan on an aggressive job search.

The recruiting season for full-time positions typically runs from September 1 to June 1, but the co-op and intern recruiting season begins about January 1. Most positions are available for the summer months (although there are others). If you are a full-time student, you should not be away from campus during your final year in the MBA program. The on-campus interviewing process is so valuable to you that you must not miss it. Plan on taking a position sometime during your first year in the MBA program or the summer between your first and second year.

You should plan on conducting a complete job search for a co-op or intern position just as you would for a permanent position, using all of the same strategies, resources, and sources. University placement offices and co-op offices are your best sources, since such positions are rarely advertised by employment agencies or through classified ads. Direct mail campaigns, when targeted, can be effective—often more so than for a permanent job since employers don't expend as much effort recruiting on campus for internships. Unfortunately, there are not many resources to tell you whether a company has a co-op or intern program. Often, you must write blindly. But friendworking is a very effective method.

The interesting thing about internships is that they are often created for a specific candidate. Although some companies have ongoing programs, most also have the flexibility to structure a position if they see a candidate that they want badly enough. Therefore, it is not wasted effort to approach companies that do not publicize an intern program. If your credentials are good enough and you can build your case well, they may just create a position for you.

There are a few differences in the search process:

- It is perfectly acceptable to be less specifically directed at this point. Employers recognize that you have not completed your education and therefore may not yet know exactly what you want to do. The objective written on your resume can be as simple as "Co-op/intern position in finance." In the interview you will be more free to discuss alternative objectives without being penalized.
- The entire screening and employment process is generally a little easier and a little less rigorous for co-op or intern positions. Since companies are not making a commitment for more than three to six months, they typically do not devote the time and energy that they do for the permanent hires. Although they still seek well-qualified candidates, they are willing to take more chances.
- Often there is no on-site interview. On-campus interviews or telephone screenings may be adequate for a hiring decision. On-site visits generally occur only when candidate and employer are located near each other.
- Employers also often devote less energy to replying to letters and following up with candidates for co-op and intern positions. Do not be surprised if you are not treated with as much attention during your recruiting for intern positions as you will be for permanent ones.

WHAT TO EXPECT ON THE JOB

While a co-op or intern position can be a very rewarding experience, it also has its unique frustrations. Since you will be employed with the company for only a short period of time, you will not be able to contribute much in the normal flow of operations. The training time alone will consume much of your work experience.

You may find yourself feeling left out of many activities. Most employers will be sure that you have important work assignments, but you may still have a sense of being out of the mainstream of the organization and wishing you had a bigger role in the work. This is no comment on your capabilities but simply a recognition of your short tenure and training time.

Most companies will provide you with several weeks' orientation and training to expose you to all facets of their business. Keep in mind that one of their purposes in having you there is to sell you on the company. Conceptually, the co-op or intern position is as much a recruiting tool as it is a source of part-time professional help for them. Expect to be treated very well and to be introduced to a large number of people. Frequent tours through different departments at plant sites are quite common.

It is very easy for some companies to forget about co-op and intern students because of their short tenure. A co-op/intern program can be very difficult for them to manage. Since many of the positions are summer ones, managers often find themselves without sufficient time to structure a good intern experience because they are short-staffed at vacation time. It is all too easy for them to give co-op students menial tasks, because it is too time-consuming to do otherwise. There is no company that does this intentionally; yet it does happen. Speak up should you find yourself in that position. If you ask to talk to your supervisor, you can virtually guarantee that he or she will thank you for bringing the subject up and will make changes.

Other co-op/interns may find themselves facing extraordinarily high expectations, because some companies see hiring co-op/interns as an easy way to cover for summer vacations. In their zeal to provide real-life experiences for the students, they may throw you into difficult assignments without adequate training and background. My advice is the same: ask for a conference with your supervisor and discuss the matter. Most will quickly restructure your assignments to be more realistic. Overall, the internship is usually a very valuable experience, but be prepared to deal with some of these frustrations.

RETURNING TO SCHOOL

When students return to school after a co-op or intern assignment, they usually have one of three reactions:

- "I loved it."
- "I enjoyed it, but it's very different from what I expected."
- "No way. That's not for me."

If you love what you do during your intern assignment, there's no problem. You did your research well, made a good decision, and have confirmed it with practical experience. You're on your way to a successful search for a full-time position.

A lukewarm reaction is very common. Most students find that the working world and the job they chose are not quite what they thought they would be. Their expectations are often too high, particularly if they have had no professional work experience. Somehow, when you are in school, the world of work looks so exciting and invigorating. However, once you get there, you discover that it also has its down days, its drudgery, its bad parts. Usually, the rewards you expect are there, but you learn the bad news with the good news.

As a result, you may feel somewhat disillusioned and let down when you return to school. Although it is not easy to face disappointment, you will be taught a valuable lesson: disappointment and disillusion can be translated into more realistic expectations about your career. One of the reasons employers like to hire someone with some professional work experience is that those with work experience know what it means to go to work, to work 8 or 10 hours a day, and to face some of the less challenging parts of a job. New permanent employees always go through a period of surprise and disappointment when their overglamorized expectations about jobs are not met. An internship helps shorten that period.

Take an honest inventory. Sit down and list the pros and cons of your experience. If you feel disappointed, ask yourself if the rewards you expected were really there. Then check your list of disappointments with a counselor or someone who has worked professionally for some years. Many students will find that there really were many good parts to their job and that the bad things they experienced were really just some of the realities of going to work—a letdown when unrealistic expectations weren't met.

Returning from an unhappy co-op or intern experience is tough. Your hopes and expectations were high when you left school. You expected big challenges and successes. When it doesn't pan out that way you may return to school feeling like a failure.

Nobody likes to have an unpleasant experience, so I will not pretend that an unhappy co-op or intern experience is an easy thing to tolerate. However, there is value in it. I am always thankful when students return from a co-op or intern experience to tell me they do not like a career option, rather than waiting six months after I have placed them in a similar permanent job to tell me the same thing. They have discovered what they don't like while they still have time to correct it.

So you should use your disappointment as the opportunity for a good learning experience. You have ample time to redo some research, review your self-assessment, and redefine your career objective before you make a commitment to a company full-time. One of the purposes of a co-op or intern experience is to test your career objective and redefine it if it's wrong. Many people find themselves trapped in full-time jobs that they wish they had never taken. I applaud the student who has enough initiative to try out a career objective, even if it turns out that the objective was wrong. Those students who can use that negative experience to develop a more appropriate career objective are often extremely successful in their full-time job search, because they have learned so much about themselves.

Appendix:
Career Resources

This appendix is arranged in two parts. The first covers specific career areas of interest to the MBA, ranging from accounting through real estate and insurance and various miscellaneous fields. The second part, beginning with general information and ending with the subject of life planning, lists resources that may be of use to the MBA in mapping and pursuing a career. Among the listings in this second part are resources of special relevance to women and members of minority groups; others concern job opportunities in particular states and countries. The appendix is not intended to be an exhaustive list of all resources of interest to MBAs. Rather, it presents those resources that I have used with my students and, in the process, have found to be quite valuable. You, too, should profit from them.

Accounting

Books
Corey, John L. *Getting Acquainted with Accounting.* Boston: Houghton Mifflin, 1977.

Emerson, James C. *Careers in Public Accounting.* Redmond, Wash.: The Big Eight Review, 1986.

Gamblin, Trevor. *Beyond the Conventions of Accounting.* London: Macmillan Press, 1978.

Higgins, John J. *Interviewing for a Career in Accounting.* Rochester, Minn.: Hampton Press, 1981.

Lodge, Arthur. *Opportunities in Accounting.* Louisville, Ky.: Vocational Guidance Manuals, 1977.

Muller, Peter. *Fast Track to the Top Jobs in Accounting.* New York: Putnam Publishing Group, 1984.

Windal, F. W., and R. N. Corley. *Accounting Professional: Ethics, Responsibility, and Liability.* Englewood Cliffs, N.J.: Prentice Hall, 1980.

Directory
Accounting Firms and Practitioners. New York: American Institute of CPA's.

Professional Associations

American Accounting Association. 5717 Bessie Drive, Sarasota, FL 33583.

American Institute of Certified Public Accountants. 1211 Avenue of the Americas, New York, NY 10036-8775.

Association of Government Accountants. Suite 100, 727 South 23rd Street, Arlington, VA 22202.

EDP Auditors Association. Suite 106, 455 Kehoe Boulevard, Carol Stream, IL 60188.

Institute of Internal Auditors. 249 Maitland Avenue, Box 1119, Altamonte Springs, FL 32701.

Institute of Management Accounting. 10 Paragon Drive, Montvale, NJ 07645.

National Association of Accountants. 10 Paragon Drive, Montvale, NJ 07645.

National Association of Minority CPA Firms. 1424 K Street, NW, Box 661, Washington, DC 20044.

National Society of Public Accountants. 1010 North Fairfax Street, Alexandria, VA 22314.

Society of Insurance Accountants. Route 3, Box 166, Crozet, VA 22932.

Tax Executives Institute. Suite 1300, 1300 North 17th Street, Arlington VA 22209.

Advertising

Books

Cohen, Dorothy M. *Advertising.* Glenview, Ill.: Scott Foresman, 1988.

Cummings, Bart. *The Benevolent Dictators: Interviews with Advertising Greats.* Chicago: Crain Books, 1984.

Gardner, Herbert S., Jr. *The Advertising Agency Business.* Chicago: Crain Books, 1980.

Katz, Judith A. *Ad Game, The Complete Guide to Careers in Advertising.* New York: Barnes and Noble Books, 1984.

Kirkpatrick, Frank. *How to Get the Right Job in Advertising.* Chicago: Contemporary Books, 1984.

Management of the New Product Function: A Guidebook. New York: Association of National Advertisers, 1980.

Ogilvy, David. *Confessions of an Advertising Man.* New York: Atheneum Publishers, 1981.

O'Toole, John. *The Trouble with Advertising.* New York: Times Books, 1985.

Paetro, Maxine. *How to Put Your Book Together and Get a Job in Advertising.* New York: Hawthorne Books, 1980.

Pattis, S. William. *Opportunities in Advertising*. Skokie, Ill.: National Textbook Co., 1985.

Pessemier, Edgar A. *Product Management: Strategy and Organization*. New York: John Wiley and Sons, 1982.

Winters, Karen Cole. *Your Career in Advertising*. New York: Arco-Rosen, 1980.

Zimmerman, Caroline. *How to Break into the Media Profession*. Garden City, N.Y.: Doubleday, 1981.

Directories

Advertising Arts and Crafts. New York: Lee and Kirby.

Standard Directory of Advertisers. Wilmette, Ill.: National Register Publishing Co.

Standard Directory of Advertising Agencies. Wilmette, Ill.: National Register Publishing Co.

Professional Associations

Advertising Association: Business/Professional. 205 East 42nd Street, New York, NY 10017.

American Association of Advertising Agencies. 666 Third Avenue, New York, NY 10017.

Association of National Advertisers. 155 East 44th Street, New York, NY 10017.

International Federation of Advertising Agencies. Suite 1115, 1605 Main Street, Sarasota, FL 33577.

Consulting

Books

Association of Consulting Management Engineers. *Selected References on Management Consulting*. New York: Association of Consulting Management Engineers, 1975.

Bermont, Herbert I. *How to Become a Successful Consultant in Your Own Field*. Washington: Bermont Books, 1978.

Concannon, Larry, and Argrette Raffini. *Management Consulting*. Boston: Harvard University Management Consulting Club, 1985.

Fuchs, Jerome H. *Management Consultants in Action*. New York: Hawthorne Books, 1975.

Gallessich, June. *The Profession and Practice of Consulting: A Handbook for Consultants*. San Francisco: Jossey-Bass Inc., 1982.

Goodstein, Leonard A. *Consulting with Human Services Systems*. Reading, Mass.: Addison-Wesley, 1978.

Holtz, Herman. *How to Succeed as an Independent Consultant*. New York: John Wiley and Sons, 1983.

Institute of Management Consultants Yearbook. London: Sterling Professional Publications Inc., 1981.

Kelley, Robert E. *Consulting—The Complete Guide to a Profitable Career.* New York: Charles Scribner's Sons, 1981.

Lippitt, Gordon, and Ronald Lippitt. *The Consulting Process in Action.* La Jolla, Calif.: University Associates, 1978.

Directories

Consultants and Consulting Organization Directory. 6th ed. Detroit: Gale Research Co., 1968.

Directory of Consultants in Computer Systems. 3d ed. Woodbridge, Conn.: Research Publications, 1985.

New Consultants. Detroit: Gale Research Co.

Wasserman, Paul, and Janis McLean, eds. *Who's Who in Consulting.* Detroit: Gale Research Co.

Professional Associations

Association of Consulting Management Engineers. 230 Park Avenue, New York, NY 10169.

Association of Management Consultants. 500 North Michigan Avenue, Chicago, IL 60611.

Institute of Certified Professional Business Consultants. Suite 400, 600 South Federal Street, Chicago, IL 60605.

Institute of Management Consultants. Suite 810–811, 19 West 44th Street, New York, NY 10036.

Corporate Finance and Financial Services

Books

Bank Administration Institute. *A Benchmark Position Description Guide for Banks.* Rolling Meadows, Ill.: Bank Administration Institute, 1983.

Fein, Cheri. *Getting into Money: A Career Guide.* New York: Ballantine Books, 1988.

Ferris, Paul. *Gentlemen of Fortune: The World's Merchant and Investment Bankers.* London: Weidenfeld and Nicolson, 1984.

Fry, Ronald. *Business and Finance.* Hawthorne, N.J.: Career Press, 1985.

Garbade, Kenneth D. *Securities Markets.* New York: McGraw-Hill, 1984.

Harvard Business School Finance Club. *Careers in Finance.* Boston: Harvard Undergraduate School of Business Administration, 1982.

Hussey, David E. *Corporate Planning: Theory and Practice.* New York: Pergamon Press, 1982.

Mainstream Access Inc. *The Banking Job Finder.* Englewood Cliffs, N.J.: Prentice Hall, 1981.

Miller, Eugene. *Your Future in Securities.* New York: Richard Rosen Press, 1974.

O'Toole, Edward. *Opportunities in the Securities Industry.* Lincolnwood, Ill.: VGM Career Books, 1981.

Pezullo, Mary Ann. *Marketing for Bankers.* Washington: American Banking Association, 1982.

Phalon, Richard. *The Takeover Barons of Wall Street.* New York: G. P. Putnam's Sons, 1981.

Prashker, Marti, and S. Valiunas. *Money Jobs: Training Programs Run by Banking, Accounting, Insurance and Brokerage Firms—And How to Get Them.* New York: Crown, 1984.

Richardson, Linda. *Bankers in the Selling Role.* New York: John Wiley and Sons, 1984.

Rosen, Lawrence R. *Go Where the Money Is: A Guide to Understanding and Entering the Securities Business.* Homewood, Ill.: Dow Jones–Irwin, 1974.

Thompson, Thomas W. *Banking Tomorrow: Managing Markets Through Planning.* Richmond, Va.: Robert F. Dome Inc., 1981.

Wright, Don. *Banking: A Dynamic Business.* Dallas: Don Wright Associates Inc., 1980.

Directories

The Banker's Blue Book—International Directory of Banks and Bankers. Chicago: Rand McNally, 1987.

Banker's Who's Who. New Delhi: Business Publications International.

The Corporate Finance Sourcebook. New York: K. Zehring Publishing Co.

Dicks, G. R. *Sources of World Financial and Banking Information.* Westport, Conn.: Greenwood Press, 1981.

Dileep, Rao. *Handbook of Business Finance and Capital Sources.* Minneapolis: Interfinance Corp., 1985.

Directory of Corporate Financing. New York: IDD Inc., 1982.

The Money Market Directory of Pension Funds and Their Investment Managers. Charlottesville, Va.: Money Market Directories Inc., 1982.

Moody's Bank and Finance Manual. New York: Dun and Bradstreet.

Mutual Fund Directory. New York: Investment Dealers Digest.

Rand McNally International Banker's Directory. Chicago: Rand McNally.

Reinhart, Leon. *The Practice of Planning: Strategic, Administrative and Operational.* New York: Van Nostrand Reinhold, 1981.

Security Dealers of North America. New York: Standard and Poors.

Spectrum 2: Investment Company Portfolios. Silver Spring, Md.: Computer Direction Advisors Inc.

Who's Who in Venture Capital. 2d ed. New York: John Wiley and Sons, 1986.

Professional Associations

American Banking Association. 1120 Connecticut Avenue, NW, Washington, DC 20036.

American Finance Association. Graduate School of Business Administration, New York University, 100 Trinity Place, New York, NY 10006.

American Financial Services Association. 4th Floor, 1101 14th Street, NW, Washington, DC 20005.

Financial Management Association. College of Business Administration, University of South Florida, 4202 Fowler Avenue, Tampa, FL 33620.

Healthcare Financial Management Association. Suite 500, 1900 Spring Road, Oak Brook, IL 60521.

Institute of Certified Financial Planners. Suite 320, 2 Denver Highlands, 10065 East Harvard Avenue, Denver, CO 80231.

Institute of Chartered Financial Analysts. Box 3668, Charlottesville, VA 22903.

Institute of Cost Analysis. 7111 Marlan Drive, Alexandria, VA 22307.

International Association for Financial Planning. Suite 800, 2 Concourse Parkway, Atlanta, GA 30328.

National Association for Bank Cost Analysis and Management Accounting. Box 27448, San Francisco, CA 94127.

Securities Industry Association. 35th Floor, 120 Broadway, New York, NY 10271.

Society of Financial Examiners. 1100 Raleigh Building, Box 2598, Raleigh, NC 27602.

Entrepreneurship

Books

Batz, Gordon. *Entrepreneurship for the Eighties.* Reston, Va.: Reston Publishing Co., 1981.

Baumback, Clifford M. *How to Organize and Operate a Small Business.* Englewood Cliffs, N.J.: Prentice Hall, 1973.

Dible, Donald. *Winning the Money Game.* Santa Clara, Calif.: Entrepreneur Press, 1975.

Klatt, Lawrence. *Small Business Management: Essentials of Entrepreneurship.* Belmont, Calif.: Wadsworth, 1973.

Mancuso, Joseph. *Have You Got What It Takes? How to Tell if You Should Start Your Own Business.* Englewood Cliffs, N.J.: Prentice Hall, 1982.

Pedolsky, Andrea, and Diane Sciattara. *Small Business Source Book.* Detroit: Gale Research Co., 1984.

Seglin, Jeffrey L. *America's New Breed of Entrepreneurs.* Washington: Acropolis Books, 1985.

Silver, A. David. *Entrepreneurial Megabucks: The Hundred Greatest Entrepreneurs of the Last Twenty-five Years.* New York: John Wiley and Sons, 1985.

Silver, A. David. *Up Front Financing: The Entrepreneur's Guide.* New York: John Wiley and Sons, 1982.

Swayne, C., and William Tucker. *The Effective Entrepreneur.* Morristown, N.J.: General Learning Press, 1973.

Professional Associations

American Entrepreneurs Association. 2392 Morse Avenue, Irvine, CA 92714.

Association of Collegiate Entrepreneurs. Center for Entrepreneurship, Box 147, Wichita State University, Wichita, KS 67208.

Center for Entrepreneurial Management. Penthouse Suite, 180 Varick Street, New York, NY 10014.

Human Resources Management

Books

Armstrong, Michael, and John Lorengen. *Handbook to Personnel Management Practice.* Englewood Cliffs, N.J.: Prentice Hall, 1982.

Cayer, Joseph N. *Managing Human Resources: An Introduction to Public Personnel Administration.* New York: St. Martin's Press Inc., 1980.

French, Wendell, John Dittrich, and Robert Zawacki. *The Personnel Management Process.* Boston: Houghton Mifflin, 1982.

New Training Organizations. Detroit: Gale Research Co., 1987.

Norman, O. Gene. *Personnel Management: A Selected Bibliography.* Monticello, Ill.: Vance Bibliographies, 1980.

Traynor, William J. *Opportunities in Personnel Management.* Skokie, Ill.: National Textbook Co., 1978.

Directories

National Association of Personnel Consultants Membership Directory. Alexandria, Va.: National Association of Personnel Consultants, 1982.

Wasserman, Paul, and Janis McLean, eds. *Training and Development Organizations Directory.* 3d ed. Detroit: Gale Research Co., 1978.

Professional Associations

American Association for Counseling and Development. 5999 Stevenson Avenue, Alexandria, VA 22304.

American Society for Healthcare Human Resources Administration. 840 North Lake Shore Drive, Chicago, IL 60611.

American Society for Personnel Administration. 606 North Washington Street, Alexandria, VA 22314-1914.

American Society for Training and Development. 1630 Duke Street, Box 1443, Alexandria, VA 22313.

Association of Human Resources System Professionals. 9th Floor, 100 South Ellsworth, San Mateo, CA 94401.

Employment Management Association. 1100 Raleigh Building, Raleigh, NC 27601.

Human Resources Planning Society. Box 2553, Grand Central Station, New York, NY 10163.

International Personnel Management Association. 1617 Duke Street, Alexandria, VA 22314.

National Association of Personnel Consultants. 1432 Duke Street, Alexandria, VA 22314.

Management

Books

Cleveland, Harlan. *The Future Executive: A Guide for Tomorrow's Managers.* New York: Harper and Row, 1972.

Geneen, Harold. *Managing.* Garden City, N.Y.: Doubleday, 1984.

Harvey, Reed A. *Managerial Need Satisfaction in the Retailing Environment.* New York: National Retail Merchants Association, 1981.

Mintzberg, Henry. *The Nature of Managerial Work.* New York: Harper and Row, 1973.

Moski, Bruno A. *The Human Side of Production Management.* Englewood Cliffs, N.J.: Prentice Hall, 1979.

Pleninger, Andrew. *How to Survive and Market Yourself in Management.* New York: AMACOM, 1977.

Directory

American Management Association. *Directory of Management Education Programs.* New York: AMACOM, 1978.

Professional Associations

Administrative Management Society. 2360 Maryland Road, Willow Grove, PA 19090.

American Institute of Management. 45 Willard Street, Quincy, MA 02169.

American Management Association. 135 West 50th Street, New York, NY 10020.

American Society for Public Administration. Suite 500, 1120 G Street, NW, Washington, DC 20005.

International Management Association. 135 West 50th Street, New York, NY 10020.

National Management Association. 2210 Arbor Boulevard, Dayton, OH 45439.

Professional Services Business Management Association. 1213 Prince Street, Alexandria, VA 22314.

Management Information Systems

Books

Alter, Steven. *Decision Support Systems: Current Practice and Challenges.* Reading, Mass.: Addison-Wesley, 1980.

Donald, Archie. *Management Information and Systems.* Pergamon Press, New York: 1979.

French, Jack. *Up the EDP Pyramid.* New York: John Wiley and Sons, 1982.

Greene, Laura. *Careers in the Computer Industry.* New York: Franklin Watts, 1983.

Mainstream Access Inc. *The Data Processing/Information Technology Job Finder.* Englewood Cliffs, N.J.: Prentice Hall, 1981.

Marrs, Texe W. *Careers and Computers: The High Tech Job Guide.* New York: Monarch Press, 1984.

Muller, Peter. *The Fast Track to the Top Jobs in Computer Careers.* New York: G. P. Putnam's Sons, 1983.

Peterson's Engineering, Science, and Computer Jobs 1990. Princeton, N.J.: Peterson's Guides, 1989.

Rowan, T. G. *Managing with Computers.* London: Heinemann, 1982.

Weintraub, Joseph. *Exploring Careers in the Computer Field.* New York: Rosen Publishing Group, 1983.

Williams, Frederick. *The Executive's Guide to Information Technology.* New York: John Wiley and Sons, 1983.

Winkler, Connie. *The Computer Careers Handbook.* New York: Arco, 1983.

Professional Associations

American Federation of Information Processing Societies. 1899 Preston White Drive, Reston, VA 22091.

Association for Systems Management. 24587 Bagley Road, Cleveland, OH 44138.

Association of Information Systems Professionals. 1015 New York Road, Willow Grove, PA 19090.

Data Processing Management Association. 505 Busse Highway, Park Ridge, IL 60068.

Society for Information Management. Suite 600, 111 East Wacker Drive, Chicago, IL 60601.

Manufacturing

Books

Modern Materials Management. New York: Elsevier North Holland Inc., 1977.

Pacifico, Carl, and Daniel Witwer. *Practical Industrial Management.* New York: John Wiley and Sons, 1981.

Ulery, John D. *Job Descriptions in Manufacturing Industries.* New York: AMACOM, 1981.

Vernon, Ivan R. *Modern Aspects of Manufacturing Management.* Dearborn, Mich.: Society of Manufacturing Engineers, 1981.

Zenz, Gary J. *Purchasing and the Management of Materials.* New York: John Wiley and Sons, 1981.

Directories

Kelly's Manufacturer's and Merchant's Directory. New York: Kelly's Directories.

Thomas Register of American Manufacturers. New York: Thomas Publishing Co.

Professional Associations

American Association of Industrial Management. Suite 324, Stearns Building, 293 Bridge Street, Springfield, MA 01103.

American Institute of Industrial Engineers. 25 Technology Park, Norcross, GA 30071.

Association for Manufacturing Excellence. 380 West Palatine Road, Wheeling, IL 60090.

National Association of Industrial Technology. 204A Sill Hall, Eastern Michigan University, Ypsilanti, MI 48197.

National Association of Manufacturers. Suite 1500, 1331 Pennsylvania Avenue, NW, Washington, DC 20004.

Marketing

Books

Adler, Lee, and Charles S. Mayer. *Readings in Managing the Market-*

ing Research Function. Chicago: American Marketing Association, 1980.

Birnes, William. *Selling at the Top: The Hundred Best Companies to Sell for in America Today*. New York: Harper and Row, 1985.

Cleary, David Powers. *Great American Brands: The Success Formulas that Make Them Famous*. New York: Fairchild Publications, 1981.

Direct Marketing Market Place. Hewlett Harbor, N.Y.: Hilary House Publishers, 1980.

Haas, Kenneth. *Opportunities in Sales and Marketing*. Skokie, Ill.: National Textbook Co., 1980.

Hopkins, David S. *The Chief Marketing Executive: A Profile*. New York: Conference Board Inc., 1971.

International Marketing and Purchasing. London: Macmillan, 1981.

Lewis, William, and Hal Cornelius. *Career Guide for Sales and Marketing*. New York: Monarch Press, 1983.

Orent, Norman A. *Your Future in Marketing*. New York: Richard Rosen Press, 1978.

Pessemier, Edgar A. *Product Management: Strategy and Organization*. New York: John Wiley and Sons, 1982.

Rodgers, Buck, and Robert L. Shook. *The IBM Way: Insights into the World's Most Successful Marketing Organization*. New York: Harper and Row, 1986.

Rosenthal, David W. *Careers in Marketing*. Englewood Cliffs, N.J.: Prentice Hall, 1984.

Shook, Robert L. *Ten Greatest Salespersons—What They Say About Selling*. New York: Harper and Row, 1978.

Shook, Robert L., and Herbert M. Shook. *How to Be the Complete Professional Salesman*. New York: Frederick Fell Publishers Inc., 1984.

Sperling, Joann. *Job Descriptions in Marketing*. New York: AMACOM, 1983.

Susser, Samuel S. *The Truth About Selling*. New York: Paul S. Eriksson, 1973.

Wilinsky, Harriet. *Careers and Opportunities in Retailing*. New York: E. P. Dutton, 1970.

Directories

Bradford's Directory of Marketing Research Agencies. Fairfax, Va.: Bradford Directories.

Bradford's Directory of Marketing Research and Management Consultants. Fairfax, Va.: Bradford Directories.

Directory of Department Stores. New York: Business Guides Inc., 1983.

Directory of Marketing Services and AMA Roster. Chicago: American Marketing Association.

Fry, Ron. *Marketing Career Directory.* Orange, Calif.: Career Publishing Inc., 1987.

Professional Associations

American Marketing Association. Suite 200, 250 South Wacker Drive, Chicago, IL 60606.

American Purchasing Society. 580 59th Street, Box 543, Lisle, IL 60532.

American Retail Executives Association. 100 West 31st Street, New York, NY 10001.

American Retail Federation. 1616 H Street, NW, Washington, DC 20006.

Marketing Research Association. Suite 600, 111 East Wacker Drive, Chicago, IL 60601.

National Association of Purchasing Management. 2055 East Centennial Circle, Tempe, AZ 85282.

National Purchasing Institute. Suite D, 201 West Belt Line Road, Cedar Hill, TX 75104.

National Retail Merchants Association. 100 West 31st Street, New York, NY 10001.

Sales and Marketing Executive International. Suite 446, Statler Office Tower, Cleveland, OH 44115.

Public Relations

Books

Blumethal, L. Roy. *The Practice of Public Relations.* New York: Macmillan, 1972.

Buckholz, Rogene A. *Business Environment and Public Policy Implications.* Englewood Cliffs, N.J.: Prentice Hall, 1982.

Deen, Robert. *Opportunities in Business Communications.* Lincolnwood, Ill.: VGM Career Horizons, 1987.

Ewen, Stuart. *Channels of Desire: Mass Images and the Shaping of American Consciousness.* New York: McGraw-Hill, 1983.

Henkin, Shepard. *Opportunities in Public Relations.* Skokie, Ill.: National Textbook Co., 1977.

Henry, Kenneth. *Defenders and Shapers of the Corporate Image.* New Haven: College University Press, 1972.

Mainstream Access Inc. *The Public Relations Job Finder.* Englewood Cliffs, N.J.: Prentice Hall, 1981.

Monaghan, Patrick. *Public Relations Careers in Business and the Community.* New York: Fairchild Publications, 1972.

Rotman, Morris B. *Opportunities in Public Relations.* Lincolnwood, Ill.: National Textbook Co., 1983.

Rotman, Morris B. *The Public Relations Job Finder—Opportunities in Public Relations.* Englewood Cliffs, N.J.: Prentice Hall, 1983.
Weiner, Richard. *Professional's Guide to Public Relations Services.* Englewood Cliffs, N.J.: Prentice Hall, 1975.
Weinstein, Bob. *Your Career in Public Relations.* New York: Arco, 1983.

Directories
Hollis Press and Public Relations Annual. Sunbury-on-Thames, England: Hollis Directories.
The National Directory of Corporate Public Affairs 1986. Washington: Columbia Books, 1986.
O'Dwyer's Directory of Public Relations Firms. New York: J. R. O'Dwyer Co., 1983.

Professional Associations
Bank Marketing Association. 309 West Washington Street, Chicago, IL 60606.
Marketing Communications Executive International. 2130 Delancey Place, Philadelphia, PA 19103.
National Council for Community Relations. Box 69, 5401 West 20th Street, Greeley, CO 80632.
Public Relations Society of America. 3rd Floor, 33 Irving Place, New York, NY 10003.

Real Estate and Insurance

Books
Allan, Richard, and Thomas E. Wolfe. *Real Estate Almanac.* New York: John Wiley and Sons, 1980.
Bloom, G. F., A. M. Weimer, and J. D. Fisher. *Real Estate.* New York: John Wiley and Sons, 1978.
Bloomgarden, Barry. *Your Future in Insurance Careers.* New York: Richard Rosen Press, 1978.
Durst, Seymour B., and Walter H. Stern. *Your Future in Real Estate.* New York: Arco-Rosen, 1976.
Evans, Mariwyn. *Opportunities in Real Estate.* Skokie, Ill.: National Textbook Co., 1983.
Lieberman, David M. *Your Introduction to Real Estate.* New York: Van Nostrand Reinhold, 1979.
Mainstream Access Inc. *The Insurance Job Finder.* Englewood Cliffs, N.J.: Prentice Hall, 1982.
Mainstream Access Inc. *The Real Estate Job Finder.* Englewood Cliffs, N.J.: Prentice Hall, 1981.
Pivar, William H. *The Real Estate Career Guide.* New York: Arco, 1981.

Directory

Industrial/Commercial Real Estate Manager's Directory. Woburn, Mass.: Barry Inc., 1980.

Professional Associations

American Real Estate and Urban Economic Association. College of Business Administration, University of South Carolina, Columbia, SC 29208.

Association of Real Estate Management. 430 North Michigan Avenue, Chicago, IL 60611.

National Association of Realtors. 430 North Michigan Avenue, Chicago, IL 60611.

Miscellaneous Fields

Books

Anderson, Henry W. *The Modern Food Service Industry: An Introductory Guide.* Dubuque, Iowa: William C. Brown Co., 1973.

Benton, Warren. *Execucomp.* New York: John Wiley and Sons, 1983.

Bolz, Robert. *Career Paths in Electrical Engineering.* New York: Institute of Electrical and Electronics Engineers.

Charp, S., and I. J. Hines. *Telecommunications Fundamentals.* Newton Square, N.J.: Network Services Inc., 1985.

Coser, Lewis, Charles Kadushin, and Walter Powell. *Books: The Culture and Commerce of Publishing.* New York: Basic Books, 1982.

Crum, Derkinderen. *Project Set Strategies.* Boston: M. Nijhoff, 1979.

Demmon, Elwood L. *Opportunities in Forestry Careers.* Louisville, Ky.: Vocational Guidance Manuals, 1975.

Dubman, Sheila, Ellen Andrews, and Mary Lewis Hansen. *Exploring Visual Arts and Crafts Careers.* Cambridge: Technical Education Research Centers Inc., 1976.

Fifteen Members of the Fashion Group. *Your Future in the World of American Fashion.* New York: Richard Rosen Press, 1979.

Henkin, Shepard. *Opportunities in Hotel and Motel Management.* Lincolnwood, Ill.: VGM Career Horizons, 1985.

Industrial Research Laboratories of the United States. New York: R. R. Bowker, 1982.

Jensen, Clayne, and Jay Naylor. *Opportunities in Recreation and Leisure.* Lincolnwood, Ill.: VGM Career Horizons, 1983.

Lewin, Leonard. *Telecommunications: An Interdisciplinary Text.* Norwood, Mass.: Artech House Inc., 1984.

Lundberg, D., and Jule Wilkinson. *The Tourist Business.* Boston: Cahners Books International, 1976.

Morrison, Robert H. *The Greedy Bastard's Business Manual.* Phoenix: Morrison, Butterfield, and Boyce Publishing Co., 1981.

Saunders, James H. *Careers in Industrial Research and Development.* New York: Marcel Dekker Inc., 1974.

Snook, Donald I. *Opportunities in Hospital Administration.* Skokie, Ill.: VGM Career Horizons, 1982.

Zimmerman, Caroline. *How to Break into the Media Profession.* Garden City, N.Y.: Doubleday, 1981.

Directory
Research Centers Directory. Detroit: Gale Research Co.

General Information

Books
Baldridge, Letitia. *Letitia Baldridge's Complete Guide to Executive Manners.* New York: Rawson Associates, 1985.

Broneman, Carol, and Robert Lear. *The Corporate Ph.D.* New York: Facts on File, 1985.

Cox, Allan. *The Cox Report on the American Corporation.* New York: Delacorte Press, 1982.

Dictionary of Occupational Titles. Washington: U.S. Department of Labor, 1977.

Dun and Bradstreet's Reference Book. New York: Dun and Bradstreet, 1985.

Dun's Business Ranking. New York: Dun and Bradstreet, 1984.

Encyclopedia of Careers and Vocational Choice. Chicago: J. G. Ferguson Publishing Co., 1981.

Gale, L., and Barry Gale. *The National Career Directory.* New York: Arco, 1982.

Hoppock, Robert. *Occupational Information.* New York: McGraw-Hill, 1976.

How to Find Information About Companies: The Corporate Intelligence Source Book. 3d ed. Washington: The Researchers Ltd., 1983.

Jobst, Katherine, ed. *1987 Internships: 35,000 On-the-Job Training Opportunities for College Students and Adults.* Manassas, Va.: Impact Publications, 1986.

Levering, Robert, Milton Moskowitz, and Michael Katz. *The One Hundred Best-Managed Companies in America.* Reading, Mass.: Addison-Wesley, 1984.

McAdams, Terry W. *Careers in the Non-Profit Sector: Doing Well by Doing Good.* Washington: Taft Group, 1986.

Moody's Industrial Manual. New York: Dun and Bradstreet, 1984.

Moskowitz, Milton, Michael Katz, and Robert Levering. *Everybody's Business: An Almanac—The Irreverent Guide to Corporate America.* New York: Harper and Row, 1980.

Occupational Outlook Handbook. Washington: U.S. Bureau of Labor Statistics, 1988.

Plunkett, Jack. *The Almanac of American Employers: A Guide to America's 500 Most Successful Large Corporations*. New York: Contemporary Books Inc., 1985.

Reference Book of Corporate Management. New York: Dun and Bradstreet, 1985.

Standard and Poor's Corporate Records. New York: Standard and Poor's, 1985.

Toropov, Brandon, ed. *The National Job Bank: A Comprehensive Guide to Major Employers in the United States*. Boston: Bob Adams, 1986.

Wasserman, Paul. *Encyclopedia of Business Information Sources*. Detroit: Gale Research Co., 1983.

Directories

The Billion Dollar Directory. New York: Dun and Bradstreet, 1982.

Braddock's Federal–State–Local Government Directory. Washington: Braddock's Publishing Inc., 1984.

Career Guide to Professional Associations. Cranston, R.I.: The Carroll Press.

Daniells, Lorna M. *Business Information Sources*. Berkeley: University of California Press, 1986.

Directory of Corporate Affiliations. Skokie, Ill.: National Register Publishing Co.

Directory of Executive Recruiters. Fitzwilliam, N.H.: Consultants News, 1986.

Katz, Michael, Robert Levering, and Milton Moskowitz. *The 100 Best Companies to Work for in America*. Reading, Mass: Addison-Wesley, 1985.

Levine, Michael. *How to Reach Anyone Who's Anyone*. Los Angeles: Price Stern Sloan Inc., 1984.

Million Dollar Directory. New York: Dun and Bradstreet, 1985.

Mintz, Morton. *America Inc.: Who Owns Whom*. New York: America Inc., 1972.

Moody's Industrial Manual. New York: Dun and Bradstreet, 1985.

The National Directory of Internships. Raleigh, N.C.: The National Society for Internships and Experiential Education, 1987.

National Trade and Professional Association Directory. Washington: Columbia Books, 1984.

Peterson's Business and Management Jobs 1990. Princeton, N.J.: Peterson's Guides, 1989.

Standard and Poor's Register of Corporations, Directors and Executives. New York: Standard and Poor's.

The United States Government Manual. Washington: Office of the
Federal Register, 1988.
Washington Representatives. Washington: Columbia Books.
Who Owns Whom. New York: Dun and Bradstreet, 1984.
Wright, John W. *The American Almanac of Jobs and Salaries.* New
York: Avon Books, 1984.

Professional Association
National Business League. 4324 Georgia Avenue, NW, Washington,
DC 20011.

Career Planning and Placement

Books
Bolles, Richard. *What Color Is Your Parachute?* Berkeley: Ten Speed
Press, 1988.
Darling, Jan. *Outclassing the Competition: The Up and Comer's Guide to
Social Survival.* Norfolk, Va.: Career Management Concepts Inc.,
1985.
Dauw, Dean C. *Up Your Career.* Prospect Heights, Ill.: Waveland
Press, 1977.
Fast, Julia. *The Body Language of Sex, Power, and Aggression.* Philadel-
phia, Pa.: M. Evans and Co., 1977.
Germann, Richard, and Peter Arnold. *Bernard Haldane Associates'
Job and Career Building.* New York: Harper and Row, 1980.
Lathrop, Richard. *Who's Hiring Who.* Berkeley: Ten Speed Press,
1977.
Malloy, John T. *New Dress for Success.* New York: Warner Books,
1988.
Mencke, Reed, and Ronald L. Hummel. *Career Planning for the 80's.*
Monterey: Brooks/Cole Publishing Co., 1984.
Noer, David. *How to Beat the Employment Game.* Berkeley: Ten Speed
Press, 1978.
Powell, Randall C. *Career Planning Today.* Dubuque, Iowa: Kendall/
Hunt Publishing Co., 1981.
Schwartz, Laura. *How to Get a Glamour Job.* New York: New York
Times Book Co., 1977.
Thain, Richard J. *The Manager: Career Alternatives for the College Edu-
cated.* Bethlehem, Pa.: College Placement Council, 1978.

Directories
Career Employment Opportunities Directory. Santa Monica: Ready Ref-
erence Press.
Career Guide to Professional Associations. Cranston, R.I.: The Carroll
Press, 1976.

College Placement Council Annual. Bethlehem, Pa.: College Placement Council, 1989.

Directory of Career Training and Development Programs. Santa Monica: Ready Reference Press, 1981.

Rockcastle, Madeline T. *Where to Start.* Ithaca, N.Y.: Cornell University Career Center, 1981.

Professional Associations

American Association for Career Education. P.O. Box 40720, Washington, DC 20016.

College Placement Council. P.O. Box 2263, Bethlehem, PA 18001.

National Association of Career Development Consultants. 405 Hilltop Road, Paoli, PA 19301.

National Career Development Association. 5999 Stevenson Avenue, Alexandria, VA 22304.

Career Resources for MBAS

Books

Adams, Bob, *Careers and the MBA.* Brighton, Mass.: Bob Adams Inc., 1988.

Clawson, James G., and David Ward. *The MBA's Guide to Self-Assessment and Career Development.* Englewood Cliffs, N.J.: Prentice Hall, 1986.

Harvard Graduate School of Business Administration. *Careers and the MBA—1985.* Boston: Harvard Student Publications Board, 1985.

Heygi, Albert. *Should You Get an MBA.* Englewood Cliffs, N.J.: Prentice Hall, 1982.

O'Brien, Mark. *The MBA Answer Book: A Career Guide for the Person Who Means Business.* Englewood Cliffs, N.J.: Prentice Hall, 1984.

Salzman, Marian, and Nancy Marx. *MBA Jobs! An Insider's Guide to the Companies That Hire MBAs.* New York: AMACOM, 1986.

Directory

MBA Employment Guide/Association of MBA Executives. New York: Association of MBA Executives, 1986.

Professional Associations

Association of MBA Executives. AMBA Center, 227 Commerce Street, East Haven, CT 06512.

Graduate Management Admissions Council. Suite 1060, 11601 Wilshire Boulevard, Los Angeles, CA 90025.

National Association of JD/MBA Professionals. c/o AE Capital, 19th Floor, 745 Fifth Avenue, New York, NY 10151.

Career Resources for Minorities

Books
The Black Resource Guide. Washington: R. B. Johnson, 1984.
Career Resources for Women and Minorities. Santa Monica: Ready Reference Press.

Directories
Cole, Katherine W. *Minority Organizations: A National Directory.* Garrett Park, Md.: Garrett Park Press, 1978.
The Creative Black Book. New York: Friendly Publications, 1982.

Professional Associations
American Indian Science and Engineering Society. Suite 1220, 1310 College Avenue, Boulder, CO 80302.
National Association of Black Accountants. Suite 107, 300 I Street, NE, Washington, DC 20002.
National Association of Black Women Entrepreneurs. Box 1375, Detroit, MI 48231.
National Association of Negro Business and Professional Women's Clubs. 1806 New Hampshire Avenue, NW, Washington, DC 20009.
National Association of Urban Bankers. 111 East Wacker Drive, Chicago, IL 60601.
National Business League. 4324 Georgia Avenue, NW, Washington, DC 20011.

Career Resources for Women

Books
Career Resources for Women and Minorities. Santa Monica: Ready Reference Press.
Crain, Sharie. *Taking Stock: A Woman's Guide to Corporate Success.* Chicago: Regnery, 1977.
Harrigan, Betty Lehan. *Games Mother Never Taught You.* New York: Warner Books, 1977.
Hennig, Margaret, and Anne Jardin. *The Managerial Woman.* Garden City, N.Y.: Anchor Press, 1981.
Kleiman, Carol. *Women's Networks.* New York: Ballantine Books, 1981.
Moresca, Carmela C. *Careers in Marketing: A Woman's Guide.* Englewood Cliffs, N.J.: Prentice Hall, 1983.
Phelps, Ann T. *New Career Opportunities for Women: A Selected Annotated Bibliography.* New York: Human Sciences Press, 1977.
Place, Irene, and Sylvia Plummer. *Women in Management.* Skokie, Ill.: National Textbook Co., 1980.

Smith, Dian G. *Women in Finance.* Skokie, Ill.: VGM Career Horizons, 1981.

Welch, Mary. *Networking: The Great New Way for Women to Get Ahead.* New York: Harcourt Brace Jovanovich, 1980.

Professional Associations

American Business Women's Association. 9100 Ward Parkway, Box 8728, Kansas City, MO 64114.

American Society of Professional and Executive Women. 1511 Walnut Street, Philadelphia, PA 19102.

American Society of Women Accountants. Suite 1036, 35 East Wacker Drive, Chicago, IL 60601.

American Women's Society of Certified Public Accountants. Suite 1400, 500 North Michigan Avenue, Chicago, IL 60611.

Federation of Organizations for Professional Women. Suite 309, 2437 15th Street, NW, Washington, DC 20009.

International Organization of Women in Telecommunications. 2308 Oakwood Lane, Arlington, TX 76012.

National Association for Professional Saleswomen. Box 255708, Sacramento, CA 95865.

National Association of Bank Women. Suite 1400, 500 North Michigan Avenue, Chicago, IL 60611.

National Association of Business and Industrial Saleswomen. 2221 West Lake Street, Fort Collins, CO 80521.

National Association of Insurance Women (International). 1847 East 15th Street, Box 4410, Tulsa, OK 74159.

National Council of Administrative Women in Education. 17 Forsyth Road, Pittsburgh, PA 15220.

National Federation of Business and Professional Women's Clubs. 2012 Massachusetts Avenue, NW, Washington, DC 20036.

Professional Women in Construction. 26 Easton Avenue, White Plains, NY 10605.

Women in Communications. Box 9561, Austin, TX 78766.

Women in Energy. c/o Volt Energy Systems, Suite 211, 2500 McCain Place, North Little Rock, AR 72116.

Women Life Underwriters Conference. 1922 F Street, NW, Washington, DC 20006.

Women's Council of Realtors. 430 North Michigan Avenue, Chicago, IL 60611.

Geographical Areas

Books

Adams, Bob. *The Ohio Job Bank.* Boston: Bob Adams Inc., 1987.

Camden, Thomas, and Nancy Bishop. *How to Get a Job in Dallas/Fort Worth: The Insider's Guide.* Chicago: Surrey Books, 1984.

Camden, Thomas, and Susan Fleming Holland. *How to Get a Job in New York: The Insider's Guide.* Chicago: Surrey Books, 1986.

Camden, Thomas M., and Susan Schwartz. *How to Get a Job in Chicago: The Insider's Guide.* Chicago: Surrey Books, 1986.

Grayson, Carl T. Jr., and Susan Lukowski. *Washington V: A Comprehensive Directory of the Nation's Capital.* Washington: Potomac Books, 1979.

Levine, Renbee. *How to Get a Job in Boston or Anywhere Else.* Chester, Conn.: The Globe Pequot Press, 1983.

Washington 87: A Comprehensive Directory. Washington: Columbia Books, 1987.

Directories

Atlanta Manufacturing—Atlanta Chambers of Commerce. Atlanta: Georgia Manufacturing Association and Georgia Department of Industry and Trade, 1985.

Directory of Washington Internships. Washington: National Center for Public Service Internship Programs, 1983.

Industrial Directory of the Commonwealth of Pennsylvania. Harrisburg: Bureau of Statistical Research and Planning of Pennsylvania, 1989.

Johnson's World Wide Chamber of Commerce Directory. Loveland, Colo.: Johnson Publishing Co., 1983.

Lorber, Charlotte. *Directory of Florida Industries 1985–86.* Coral Gables, Fla.: Florida Chamber of Commerce, 1986.

McRae's State Industrial Directory: Maryland, D.C., Delaware '87. New York: McRae Publishing, 1987.

The Metropolitan New York Job Bank. Boston: Bob Adams Inc., 1985.

Minority Owned Businesses. Richmond: Virginia State Office of Minority Business Enterprise, 1985.

North Carolina Directory of Employers and Educational Institutions. Raleigh: North Carolina Placement Association, 1986.

Northeastern Hospital Blue Book. Atlanta: Billian Publishing Inc.

Salmon, Richard D. *The Jobhunter's Guide to the Sunbelt.* Cambridge: Brattle Publications, 1983.

Southern Hospital Blue Book. Atlanta: Billian Publishing Inc.

Stores of the World Directory. London: Newman Books, 1984.

Virginia Industrial Directory. Richmond: Virginia Chamber of Commerce.

Who's Who in the East. Chicago: Marquis Who's Who, 1985.

International

Books

Foreign Policy Association. *Guide to Careers in World Affairs.* New York: Foreign Policy Association, 1987.

International Directory of Executive Recruiters. Fitzwilliam, N.H.: Consultants News.

Looking for Employment in Foreign Countries. 7th ed. New York: World Trade Academy Press, 1986.

Sheehan, Gerald F. *Careers in International Affairs.* Washington: School of Foreign Service, 1982.

Directories

American Export Register. New York: Thomas International Publishing Co., 1986.

Directory of American Firms Operating in Foreign Countries. New York: Uniworld Business Publications, 1984.

Guide to Careers in World Affairs. New York: Foreign Policy Association, 1982.

Kocher, Eric. *International Jobs—Where They Are, How to Get Them.* Reading, Mass.: Addison-Wesley, 1984.

Professional Associations

Academy of International Business. World Trade Education Center, Cleveland State University, Cleveland, OH 44415.

American Association of Exporters and Importers. 30th Floor, 11 West 42nd Street, New York, NY 10036.

International Trade Council. 750 13th Street, SE, Washington, DC 20003.

National Association of Export Companies. Suite 603, 396 Broadway, New York, NY 10013.

National Foreign Trade Council. 100 East 42nd Street, New York, NY 10017.

Life Planning

Books

Best, Fred. *Flexible Life Scheduling.* New York: Praeger Publishers, 1980.

Bolles, Richard. *The Three Boxes of Life (and How to Get out of Them).* Berkeley: Ten Speed Press, 1978.

Crystal, John, and Richard Bolles. *Where Do I Go from Here with My Life?* New York: Seabury Press, 1974.

Irish, Dick. *How to Live Separately Together.* Garden City, N.Y.: Anchor Press, 1981.

Shattuck, Alfred. *The Greener Pastures Relocation Guide: Finding the Best State in the U.S. for You.* Englewood Cliffs, N.J.: Prentice Hall, 1984.

Sheehy, Gail. *Passages.* New York: E. P. Dutton, 1970.

Sheehy, Gail. *Pathfinders.* New York: William Morrow and Co., 1981.

References

The following works were consulted by the author in the preparation of this book.

"Alcohol and Drugs in the Workplace," unpublished paper presented by Smith, Helms, Mulliss, and Moore at the North Carolina Placement Association meeting, May 1987.

Alcohol and Drugs in the Workplace: A BNA Special Report. 1986. Washington: Bureau of National Affairs.

Angarola, Robert T. "Drug Testing in the Workplace: Is It Legal?" *Personnel Administration.* September 1985, 79–89.

Applbaum, Ronald L., and Karl W. E. Anatol. 1982. *Effective Oral Communication for Business and the Professions.* Science Research Associates Inc.

Bolles, Richard N. *The Three Boxes of Life (and How to Get out of Them).* 1978. Berkeley: Ten Speed Press.

Bolles, Richard N. *What Color Is Your Parachute?* 1988. Berkeley: Ten Speed Press.

Bolles, Richard N., and John C. Crystal. 1974. *Where Do I Go from Here with My Life?* Berkeley: Ten Speed Press.

Brown, Duane, and Linda Brooks, eds. *Career Choice and Development.* San Francisco: Jossey-Bass, 1984.

Campbell, David P. *If You Don't Know Where You're Going, You'll Probably End Up Somewhere Else.* 1974. Allen, Tex.: Argus Communications.

College Placement Council Salary Survey. 1989. Bethlehem, Pa.: College Placement Council.

Davis, Stanley M. *Managing Corporate Culture.* 1984. Cambridge: Ballinger Publishing Co.

Demoss, Arthur, and Nancy Demoss, eds. *The Family Album.* 1969. Old Tappon, N.J.: Fleming H. Revell Co.

Digest of Educational Statistics. 1988. Washington: Center for Education Statistics, U.S. Department of Education.

Dogoloff, Lee I., Robert T. Angarola, and Susan C. Price, eds. "Urine Testing in the Workplace," 1985. Rockville, Md.: American Council for Drug Education.

"Drug Testing in Major U.S. Corporations: A Survey of the Fortune 500," unpublished survey conducted by Noel Dunivant & Associates for Compuchem Laboratories Inc., Raleigh, N.C., 1985.

Employment Projections 2000. 1988. Washington: Bureau of Labor Statistics, U.S. Department of Labor.

Fast, Julius. *Body Language.* 1970. New York: Pocket Books.

Gysbers, Norman C., ed. *Designing Careers.* San Francisco: Jossey-Bass, 1984.

Half, Robert. *The Robert Half Way to Get Hired in Today's Job Market.* 1981. New York: Bantam Books.

Henry, Ralph, and Lucile Pannell, eds. *My American Heritage.* 1949. Chicago: Rand McNally & Co.

Holland, John L. *Making Vocational Choices.* Englewood Cliffs, N.J.: Prentice Hall, 1985.

Jackson, Tom. *Guerrilla Tactics in the Job Market.* 1978. New York: Bantam Books.

Jenkins, Roger L., and Richard C. Reizenstein. "Insights into the MBA: Its Contents, Output and Relevance." *Harvard Business Review.* Spring 1984, 19–24.

Jenkins, R. L., R. C. Reizenstein, and F. G. Rodgers. "Report Cards on the MBA." *Harvard Business Review,* September–October 1984, 20–30.

Kaplan, Rochelle K. "Pre-employment Drug Screening: Does It Pass the Test?" *Journal of Career Planning and Employment.* Fall 1986, 28–35.

Kaplan, Rochelle K. "When an Employer Says Yes . . . and Then No." *Journal of Career Planning and Employment.* Winter 1986, 48–54.

Kotter, John P., Victor A. Faux, and Charles McArthur. *Self-Assessment and Career Development: A Systematic Approach to the Selection and Management of a Career.* 1978. Englewood Cliffs, N.J.: Prentice Hall.

Lathrop, Richard. *Who's Hiring Who.* 1977. Berkeley: Ten Speed Press.

Loughary, John W., and M. Theresa Ripley. *Career and Life Planning Guide.* 1976. Chicago: Follett Publishing Co.

Medley, H. Anthony. *Sweaty Palms: The Neglected Art of Being Interviewed.* 1978. Berkeley: Ten Speed Press.

Mentzer, John T., and David J. Schwartz. *Marketing Today.* 4th ed. 1985. New York: Harcourt Brace Jovanovich.

Miller-Tiedeman, Anna. *How to Not Make It . . . and Succeed.* Vista, Calif.: Lifecareer Foundation, 1987.

Molloy, John T. *New Dress for Success.* New York: Warner, 1988.

Muczyk, Jan P., and Brian P. Heshizer. "Managing in an Era of Substance Abuse." *Personnel Administrator.* August 1986, 91–103.

Myers, Isabel Briggs. *Introduction to Type.* 1980. Palo Alto: Consulting Psychologists Press.

Myers, Isabel Briggs, with Peter B. Myers. *Gifts Differing.* 1980. Palo Alto: Consulting Psychologists Press.

The 1984–85 MBA Career and Salary Census. 1985. New York: Association of MBA Executives.

Northwestern Endicott Report 1983. Evanston, Ill.: Northwestern University.

Northwestern Lindquist-Endicott Report 1989. Evanston, Ill.: Northwestern University.

Occupational Projections and Training Data 1988. 1986. Washington: U.S. Department of Labor.

Parker, Yana. *The Damn Good Resume Guide.* 1983. Berkeley: Ten Speed Press.

Powell, C. Randall. *Career Planning Today.* 1981. Dubuque, Iowa: Kendall/Hunt Publishing Co.

Preemployment Drug Screening: A Survey of Practices Among National Employers of College Graduates. 1986. Bethlehem, Pa.: College Placement Council.

Projections of Education Statistics to 1992–93. 1985. Washington: Center for Education Statistics, U.S. Department of Education.

Rogers, Carl R. *On Becoming a Person.* 1961. Boston: Houghton Mifflin.

Scientific and Technical Guidelines for Drug Testing Programs. 1987. Washington: Department of Health and Human Services.

Scott, Gary J. "All Those in Favor of Drug Screening. . . ." *Journal of Career Planning and Employment.* Winter 1987, 37–42.

Simon, Sidney B., Leland W. Howe, and Howard Kirschenbaum. *Values Clarifications.* 1972. Hart Publishing Co.

MORE TOP-FLIGHT CAREER RESOURCES FROM PETERSON'S!

TOP PROFESSIONS
The 100 Most Popular, Dynamic, and Profitable Careers in America Today

by Nicholas Basta

If you are anxious to know what the job market will hold in the final decade of the twentieth century, *Top Professions* is an indispensable handbook.

Top Professions brings together the 100 most promising career opportunities for the 1990s. A product of extensive market research by the author—including exclusive surveys of professional associations and interviews with the key players in selected professions—it provides fresh, realistic guidance on the job market. It not only uncovers promising options that are not widely publicized, but it gives advice on how to capitalize on today's business and economic trends in career decision making.

Describing the top careers—from arts and media to engineering sciences—each entry includes:

- Average starting salary range
- Number of professionals in the field and whether the number is growing or declining
- Forecast of demand for professionals in the field
- Highlights of entry-level positions
- Contact numbers at professional associations

Written in an engaging journalistic style for today's emerging professional, *Top Professions* is a truly "modern" career resource.

"At last, a career book that doesn't hash over the stale government advice provided by the Occupational Outlook Handbook! Basta's book covers—with wit and wisdom—the careers that will engage 99% of all new college grads."

Steven S. Ross
Columbia University

November 1989
350 pages $10.95 paperback

PETERSON'S BUSINESS AND MANAGEMENT JOBS 1990

The newest edition of this classic career guide details hundreds of organizations that are recruiting employees in the areas of business and management this year—information that is crucial to job seekers.

Individual employer profiles cover key facts, such as:

- Products and services provided
- Majors sought
- Doctoral-level opportunities
- Opportunities for experienced personnel
- Starting locations by city *and* state
- Whom to contact for more information

Directories make other information easy to find, including:

- Benefits
- Training programs
- Tuition reimbursement and continuing education
- Summer jobs, co-op jobs, and internships
- International assignments

A career guide, employment directory, and job-hunting manual in one volume, *Peterson's Business and Management Jobs 1990* provides all the information you need to match your academic background to specific job openings in 1990.

"Best source for numerous identifications of employers (recommend students purchase personal copy). Recommend highly for alums entering job market again."

Jackie Coke
Vanderbilt University

September 1989 $18.95 paperback
300 pages $33.95 hardcover

Look for these and other Peterson's publications in your local bookstore

Peterson's
Princeton, New Jersey